Cloud
COMPUTING

SaaS, PaaS, IaaS, Virtualization,
Business Models, Mobile, Security,
and More

Kris Jamsa, PhD, MBA

JONES & BARTLETT
LEARNING

World Headquarters
Jones & Bartlett Learning
5 Wall Street
Burlington, MA 01803
978-443-5000
info@jblearning.com
www.jblearning.com

Jones & Bartlett Learning books and products are available through most bookstores and online booksellers. To contact Jones & Bartlett Learning directly, call 800-832-0034, fax 978-443-8000, or visit our website, www.jblearning.com.

Production Credits

Chief Executive Officer: Ty Field
President: James Homer
SVP, Editor-in-Chief: Michael Johnson
SVP, Chief Technology Officer: Dean Fossella
SVP, Chief Marketing Officer: Alison M. Pendergast
SVP, Curriculum Solutions: Christopher Will
VP, Design and Production: Anne Spencer
Editorial Management: High Stakes Writing, LLC, Editor and Publisher: Lawrence J. Goodrich
Copy Editor, HSW: Ruth Walker
Reprints and Special Projects Manager: Susan Schultz
Production Editor: Keith Henry
Senior Marketing Manager: Andrea DeFronzo

VP, Business Development: Todd Giorza
Marketing Manager: Lindsay White
VP, Manufacturing and Inventory Control: Therese Connell
Manufacturing and Inventory Control Supervisor: Amy Bacus
Composition: Cenveo Publisher Services
Cover Design: Kristin E. Parker
Rights & Photo Research Manager: Katherine Crighton
Rights & Photo Research Assistant: Lian Bruno
Cover Image: © majeczka/ShutterStock, Inc.
Chapter Opener Image: © Risto Viita/ShutterStock, Inc.
Printing and Binding: Edwards Brothers Malloy
Cover Printing: Edwards Brothers Malloy

Library of Congress Cataloging-in-Publication Data
Jamsa, Kris A.
  Cloud computing / Kris Jamsa.—1st ed.
    p. cm.
  Includes index.
  ISBN 978-1-4496-4739-1
1. Cloud computing. I. Title.
  QA76.585.J36 2012
  004.6782—dc23
                        2011051300

6048
Printed in the United States of America
16 15 14 13 12   10 9 8 7 6 5 4 3 2 1

To Ashton,
May all your clouds have a silver lining.

To Michelle,
With Best wishes!

Brief Contents

Contents

Preface

FOR YEARS, SOFTWARE DEVELOPERS and network administrators have used the image of a cloud to represent the myriad of communication details that occur as messages flow across the Internet from one computer network to another. This cloud abstraction has now exploded to include processors, both physical and virtual, data storage, software-as-a-service solutions, and mobile applications. Today, cloud-based applications and new capabilities are emerging daily and bringing with them lower cost of entry, pay-for-use processor and data-storage models, greater scalability, improved performance, ease of redundancy, and improved business continuity. With these advantages come increased security challenges and IT-governance concerns. This book examines these issues. As you will learn, two things are certain: The dynamic nature of the cloud will continue and we have only just begun to scratch the cloud's surface.

Chapter 1: Introducing Cloud Computing introduces the abstract nature of cloud computing and the factors that led to its evolution. The chapter examines software as a service (SaaS), platform as a service (PaaS), and infrastructure as a service (IaaS) and includes real-world examples of each. The chapter discusses the key advantages of cloud computing, including scalability, redundancy, low cost of entry, and virtualization.

Chapter 2: Software as a Service (SaaS) examines browser-based SaaS solutions and their advantages. The chapter features real-world solutions such as SalesForce.com for customer relationship management, Taleo for human resources solutions, ADT for SaaS-based payroll processing, and many others.

Chapter 3: Platform as a Service (PaaS) introduces cloud-based hardware and software platforms which allow companies, large and small, to move their applications to the cloud quickly and cost effectively. The chapter examines PaaS providers such as Amazon, Google, and Microsoft.

Chapter 4: Infrastructure as a Service (IaaS) introduces the concept of a cloud-based data center which reduces or eliminates a company's need for a large in-house data center. Because of the IaaS provider's economies of scale, it can reduce a company's cost of IT operations significantly.

Chapter 5: Identity as a Service (IDaaS) examines cloud-based identity-management solutions that simplify user provisioning and resource access. With more solutions distributed across the cloud, IDaaS facilitates the user's sign-on process across solution providers.

Chapter 6: Data Storage in the Cloud examines the integration of cloud-based data storage and the evolution of network-based storage, which led to its creation. The chapter presents several cloud-based data storage solutions that can be enabled at little or no cost. The chapter also examines several low-cost turnkey based backup solutions.

Chapter 7: Collaboration in the Cloud looks at cloud-based technologies that allow two or more users to work together to accomplish a task. The chapter describes the evolution of collaboration technologies from instant messaging to virtual meetings to shared documents that support simultaneous editing by multiple users.

Chapter 8: Virtualization introduces hardware and software used to create the perception that one or more entities exist, when they may not actually be physically present. The chapter examines solutions for virtual servers, virtual desktops, and virtual networks.

Chapter 9: Securing the Cloud examines the real-world security issues that people (even some sophisticated IT users) are uncomfortable with when placing their personal data, or their company's data, in the cloud. The chapter examines specific security threats and the measures that should be taken to minimize them.

Chapter 10: Disaster Recovery and Business Continuity and the Cloud discusses ways that the cloud and its redundant resources improve a company's ability to recover and continue to operate after a disaster or serious event. The chapter examines common threats to business operations and some cloud-computing solutions that can mitigate them.

Chapter 11: Service-Oriented Architecture looks at how the availability of web-based services is changing how developers create programs and the speed at which they can deploy solutions. The chapter examines a variety of real-world web services that are available to programmers for integration into programs.

Chapter 12: Managing the Cloud examines the tasks a manager must perform after a company migrates its applications to the cloud, including auditing logs, monitoring system performance, and identifying bottlenecks within the data flow.

Chapter 13: Migrating to the Cloud discusses managerial considerations to be evaluated before migrating to the cloud, such as avoiding vendor lock-in, identifying remote data backup operations and security considerations, preparing a budget, and integrating developer and user training.

Chapter 14: Mobile Cloud Computing evaluates whether mobile computing is driving the growth of cloud computing or vice versa. The chapter examines the "ecosystem" that is mobile computing as well as how HTML5 will change computing models.

Chapter 15: Governing the Cloud discusses the role of IT governance and its extensions for cloud-based computing. The chapter examines the need for and ways to implement cloud-based internal controls.

Chapter 16: Evaluating the Cloud's Business Impact and Economics examines how the cloud's economy of scale and pay-for-use model will accelerate the ability for companies, large and small, to release cloud-based solutions. The chapter also evaluates the cloud's impact on operational and capital expenses.

Chapter 17: Designing Cloud-Based Solutions discusses the fact that developers will simply pick up and move many existing applications to the cloud. In the future, however, developers should design cloud-based solutions to utilize scalability and redundancy. The chapter examines many common design considerations and ways the cloud will impact them.

Chapter 18: Coding Cloud-Based Applications looks at two PaaS providers, Google Apps and Windows Azure, and implements cloud-based applications with each. Developers will learn that creating and deploying cloud-based applications is fast, easy, and inexpensive.

Chapter 19: Application Scalability examines how developers can scale applications—vertically, by using faster processors or more powerful servers and horizontally, by supporting the ability to distribute processing better. The chapter looks at design considerations to be evaluated when designing applications for scalability.

Chapter 20: The Future of the Cloud examines ways the cloud will extend its reach into cars, televisions, appliances, and even our clothes. By the end of the chapter, readers will realize that we have just scratched the cloud's surface.

Introducing Cloud Computing

FOR YEARS DEVELOPERS AND network administrators have represented the Internet within design documents as a cloud. By abstracting the Internet's technologies and underlying protocols as simply a cloud, as shown in **FIGURE 1-1**, the developers could temporarily ignore the communication complexity and simply assume that messages would flow successfully from one Internet-connected network to another.

Learning Objectives

This chapter introduces cloud computing. By the time you finish this chapter, you will be able to do the following:

- Understand the abstract nature of cloud computing.
- Describe evolutionary factors of computing that led to the cloud.
- Describe virtualization at both the desktop and the server level.
- Describe and identify common cloud types, which include software as a service, platform as a service, and infrastructure as a service.
- Know how businesses and individuals use the cloud.
- Describe the benefits and disadvantages of cloud computing.
- Understand common security considerations with respect to the cloud.
- Describe ways cloud computing can improve system fault tolerance.
- Describe Web 2.0 and its relationship to cloud computing.

Today the term **cloud computing** describes the abstraction of web-based computers, resources, and services that system developers can utilize to implement complex web-based systems. Often these cloud-based resources are viewed as virtual, meaning that if a system or solution needs more resources, such as processors or disk space, the resources can simply be added on demand and usually

1

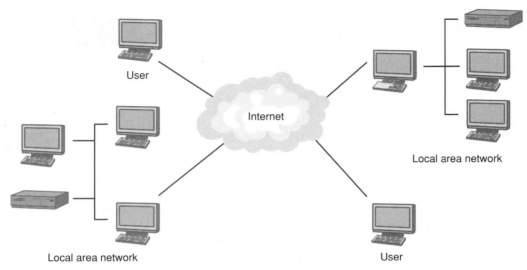

FIGURE 1–1 For years developers and network administrators have represented the Internet as a cloud.

CASE 1-1 THE APPLE ICLOUD

Whether one is a PC user or a Mac evangelist, one must recognize Apple's ability to introduce technology that changes industries and the way people work and communicate. Apple's first entrée into the cloud was the iTunes virtual music store. Today iTunes offers millions of songs for download to PCs and Macs, as well as iPods, iPhones, iPads, and other handheld devices. More than just music on a web-based storage device, iTunes laid a foundation for scalable e-commerce, high-bandwidth download transactions, and user device independence.

Apple's **iCloud** extends the company's existing functionality by providing users with a cloud-based storage facility for their phones, music, videos, books, and other documents. Using iCloud as a centralized virtual storage facility, users can quickly exchange digital content among their various devices. In fact, users can customize the iCloud settings to make the file exchange seamless and automatic. In other words, if a user stores a digital file within iCloud, behind the scenes iCloud software will push the content to each of the user's registered devices, as shown in **FIGURE 1–2**.

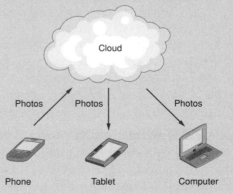

FIGURE 1–2 Using iCloud, users can synchronize their content to a variety of devices.

continues

CASE 1-1 THE APPLE ICLOUD, continued

Exercise What industries might iCloud disrupt? What business services do you anticipate Apple to offer in order to drive revenue through the iCloud?

Web Resources For more information on iCloud, see www.CloudBookContent.com/Chapter01/index.html.

transparently to the application that uses them. Through their virtual nature, cloud-based solutions can be scaled up or down in size, and the companies whose solutions reside in the clouds normally pay only for the resources they consume. Thus, companies that once relied on expensive data centers to house their processing resources can now shift their costs and maintenance efforts to pay-as-you-go, scalable, cloud-based alternatives.

Web 2.0 and the Cloud

For years, when companies wanted to place content on the web, they hired web developers, who created the underlying HTML documents. Through this process, the number of documents on the web exploded to billions worldwide. **Web 2.0** is a term used to describe the set of tools and websites that allow users to publish content to the web without the direct use of HTML. Behind the scenes, the tools and sites build the HTML documents for the user and then upload the documents to a web server. **TABLE 1-1** describes the common Web 2.0 applications.

TABLE 1-1   COMMON WEB 2.0 SITES AND APPLICATIONS

Application/Site	Purpose
Blog	A web log that users can write and use to publish content directly to the web.
Wiki	A software program that allows users to collaborate on shared web-based documents.
Twitter	A microblogging service that allows users to send messages of up to 140 characters to those who *follow* the users' *tweets*.
Facebook	A social networking site to which users can post text, photos, and video-based content.
YouTube	A site to which users can upload video content for sharing with others.

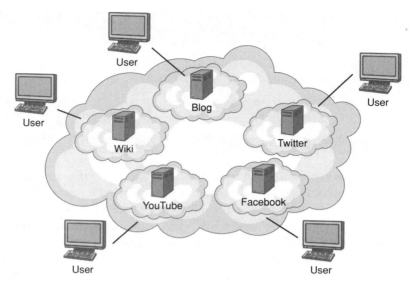

FIGURE 1-3 Web 2.0 tools make it easy for users who do not possess web development skills to easily publish content on the web.

As shown in **FIGURE 1-3**, with Web 2.0 tools and sites, users essentially publish content directly to the cloud for access by other users.

Distinguishing Cloud Types

Cloud-based applications provide a wide range of solutions to a very large number of users. To help us analyze and describe cloud-based systems, many people refer to a cloud solution in terms of its deployment model and services model. These two terms originated within a cloud computing document from the National Institute of Standards and Technology (NIST), as shown in **FIGURE 1-4**.

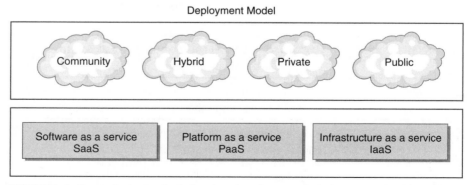

FIGURE 1-4 Users refer to cloud solutions based on the system's deployment and services models.

CASE 1-2 THE MICROSOFT WINDOWS AZURE PLATFORM

When web developers create web pages, they need to host the corresponding HTML files on a web server before other users can access the content from across the web. Developers have two choices when it comes to publishing their content. First, they can host the pages on their own web server, which may require hardware support and maintenance. Second, the developers can host the files at a server that resides at an Internet service provider (ISP), which allows the developer to focus on web page development as opposed to server management. Today developers can host their web pages at an ISP for a few dollars per month.

Windows Azure is a Microsoft platform that developers can use to move their applications to the cloud. Unlike support for a simple HTML page, which requires only the presence of a web server, Windows Azure provides operating-system support for .NET applications and a cloud-based SQL server (SQL Azure). You can think of Windows Azure as a cloud-based data center within which developers can house their applications. The Windows Azure platform, in turn, maintains servers, operating systems, database software, and other supporting applications. As a developer's application grows in terms of users, processor demands, or disk storage, the Windows Azure environment grows to meet the developer's needs. In this way, the Windows Azure platform provides the following:

- **Scalability**: Windows Azure can scale up, or scale down, processor and storage resources on demand.
- **Redundancy**: Windows Azure provides server, disk storage, and network redundancy.
- **Cost benefits from resource pooling**: Windows Azure shares IT resources across a very large number of companies, which provides cost savings to each.
- **Outsourced server management**: Microsoft provides Windows Azure IT staff who maintain operating systems and underlying support software.
- **Low cost of entry**: To release a cloud-based solution, companies do not need to invest in their own IT data center.

Exercise Discuss the pros and cons of hosting an application within one's own data center as opposed to using a service provider such as Windows Azure.

Web Resources For more information on Windows Azure, see www.CloudBookContent.com/Chapter01/index.html.

Cloud Deployment Models

A cloud deployment model specifies how resources within the cloud are shared. As discussed in **TABLE 1-2**, there are four primary cloud deployment models: **private cloud**, **public cloud**, **community cloud**, and **hybrid cloud**. Each model influences the corresponding **scalability**, **reliability**, security, and cost.

TABLE 1-2   CLOUD DEPLOYMENT MODELS

Deployment Model	Characteristics
Private cloud	Owned by a specific entity and normally used only by that entity or one of its customers. The underlying technology may reside on- or off-site. A private cloud offers increased security at a greater cost.
Public cloud	Available for use by the general public. May be owned by a large organization or company offering cloud services. Because of its openness, the cloud may be less secure. A public cloud is usually the least expensive solution.
Community cloud	The cloud is shared by two or more organizations, typically with shared concerns (such as schools within a university).
Hybrid cloud	A cloud that consists of two or more private, public, or community clouds.

Cloud Service Models

A cloud can interact with a client (user or application) in a variety of ways, through capabilities called services. Across the web, three major types, or models, of services have emerged, which are defined in **TABLE 1-3**.

Examining Software as a Service (SaaS)

The **software as a service (SaaS)** model provides a cloud-based foundation for software on demand. In general, an SaaS solution is web-delivered content

TABLE 1-3   COMMON CLOUD SERVICE MODELS

Cloud Service Model	Characteristics
Software as a service (SaaS)	A complete software application with a user interface.
Platform as a service (PaaS)	A platform within which developers can deploy their applications. A PaaS solution includes hardware (servers and disks), operating systems, development tools, and administrative tools.
Infrastructure as a service (IaaS)	Provides machines, storage, and network resources that developers can manage by installing their own operating system, applications, and support resources.

that users access via a web browser. The software can reside within any of the deployment-model clouds. **FIGURE 1-5** illustrates the SaaS model.

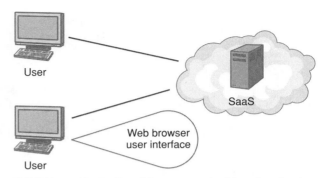

The advantages of SaaS solutions are simplicity of integration (users need only a browser), cost (the data center resides within the cloud), and scalability (customers can add user licenses or seats as needed). The disadvantage of SaaS solutions is the perception of security issues. Users who are new to the cloud may not feel comfortable storing company data in a remote data-storage facility (the cloud).

FIGURE 1-5 The SaaS model presents a cloud-based application with a user interface to users running only a web browser.

Well-known SaaS solution providers include Salesforce.com, Google Apps, TurboTax, and QuickBooks.

Examining Platform as a Service (PaaS)

The **platform as a service (PaaS)** model provides the underlying hardware technology, such as one or more servers (or virtual servers), operating systems, database solutions, developer tools, and network support, for developers to deploy their own solutions. The hardware and software within a PaaS solution is managed by the platform provider. Developers need not worry about performing hardware or operating system upgrades. Instead, developers can focus on their own applications. **FIGURE 1-6** illustrates the PaaS model. Well-known PaaS solution providers include Windows Azure and Google App Engine.

Examining Infrastructure as a Service (IaaS)

The **infrastructure as a service (IaaS)** model provides a virtual data center within the cloud. IaaS provides servers (physical and virtualized), cloud-based data storage, and more. Within an IaaS solution, developers must install their own operating system, database management software, and support software. Then the developers (or the company's system administrators) must manage both the hardware and the software. **FIGURE 1-7** illustrates the IaaS model. The Amazon Elastic Compute Cloud (Amazon EC2) is an IaaS solution.

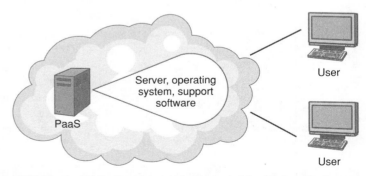

FIGURE 1-6 The PaaS model provides the underlying hardware and operating system a developer needs to launch an application.

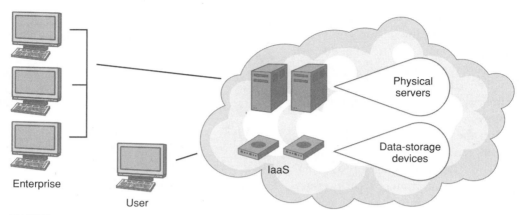

FIGURE 1-7 The IaaS model provides the underlying hardware (servers and storage). Clients must install and then manage their own operating system, database software, and support software.

CASE 1-3 AMAZON WEB SERVICES (AWS)

If you ask people to rank order the top e-commerce companies, Amazon.com will make the top of most lists. Amazon has grown from selling books to selling a virtually endless range of products.

As Amazon evolved its sales plan, the company recognized the value of extending its product base (the things they sell) to other sites. The other sites (Amazon affiliates), in turn, could offer links to products, the sales and fulfillment of which would be handled by Amazon, in a revenue-sharing model. This affiliate program was one of the first cloud-based sales partnerships.

As Amazon continued to grow, its internal developers created a system architecture that was redundant, scalable, and **robust**. With these services fully operational, Amazon recognized that most software companies would need similar capabilities. To meet that demand, Amazon released **Amazon Web Services (AWS)**, which companies can use to host their own systems. Today, AWS process hundreds of thousands of web-based requests for companies every second!

One of Amazon's primary cloud tools is the Amazon Elastic Compute Cloud (Amazon EC2), which lets companies rent cloud-based services for their applications. Using Amazon EC2, companies can pay by the hour for the processing they need and scale processor support up or down to meet user demands.

To complement the processing power of Amazon EC2, Amazon Simple Storage Service (Amazon S3) provides cloud-based data-storage facilities, and companies pay only for the data storage they consume. Behind the scenes, Amazon provides data redundancy.

To further support developers, Amazon offers virtual-network support, database support, and e-commerce capabilities.

continues

CASE 1-3 AMAZON WEB SERVICES (AWS), continued

Exercise Assume your company wants to use Amazon as its disk-backup provider. What pros and cons would you consider? Discuss how you might leverage Amazon Web Services to bring an e-commerce site online.

Web Resources For more information on Amazon Web Services, see www.CloudBookContent .com/Chapter01/index.html.

Exploring Uses of the Cloud

The cloud is now host to a wide range of large-scale and small-scale (custom) applications. The number and type of applications that users can deploy to the cloud is virtually limitless. Many software companies are now moving key applications from expensive internal data centers to cost-effective and resource-redundant cloud solutions.

As a user, you might already use cloud-based personal productivity software, such as TurboTax, bank-specific bill-pay software, or a stock tool such as E*TRADE. Or you may leverage a cloud-based collaboration tool, such as Google Calendar or

CASE 1-4 SALESFORCE.COM

One of the first companies to launch a large-scale SaaS solution was Salesforce.com. The company recognized that as much as three-fourths of a salesperson's day was spent on nonsales tasks (calendar management, contract management, presentation management, and contact management). Salesforce.com recognized that regardless of the items a company sold, the selling process was similar across companies and even industries. Salesforce.com automated these tasks and put the underlying data storage in the cloud—the sales cloud.

In a similar way, Salesforce.com has recognized that after the sale, customer service is key. As a result, the company released a customer service cloud, which integrates common customer service operations. The software manages the process of responding to customer calls, e-mails, Facebook updates, live chats, and more. After customer cases are resolved, managers can monitor the results via cloud-based dashboards.

Exercise Discuss the common sales and customer service tasks supported by Salesforce.com.

Web Resources For more information on Salesforce.com, see www.CloudBookContent.com/ Chapter01/index.html.

Google Docs, to share information and documents with other users. Or you may store files, such as your music, photos, or videos, on cloud-based data storage.

Introducing Scalability

When they launch a new website, many developers have visions of having created the next Google, Amazon, or Facebook. Unfortunately, the developers have no way of knowing what the actual user demand will be. Should the site become widely used, it may require additional servers or disk-storage capacity.

Scalability defines a site or application's ability to use additional resources on demand. The site or application may scale up to utilize additional resources when the system is experiencing high user demand and may later scale down its resource usage when the user demand declines.

Applications that run within the cloud are normally highly scalable. An application administrator can manually add or remove resources, or the application can be configured to scale automatically. As shown in **FIGURE 1–8**, applications scale through the use of additional servers (physical or virtual) or through the addition of disk-storage space.

Introducing Virtualization

Chapter 8, *Virtualization*, examines desktop and server virtualization in detail. For now think of **virtualization** as the use of hardware and/or software to create the perception of something. For example, most servers have a CPU that is capable of running a specific operating system, such as Windows or Linux. Using special software, the server can be made to appear as if it has multiple CPUs running the same or different operating systems, as shown in **FIGURE 1–9**.

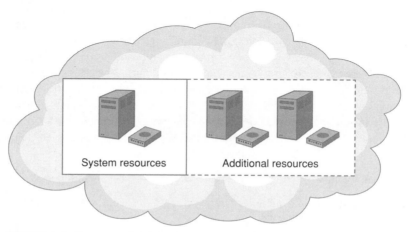

FIGURE 1–8 Sites or applications can scale up or down through the addition or removal of servers or disk-storage capacity.

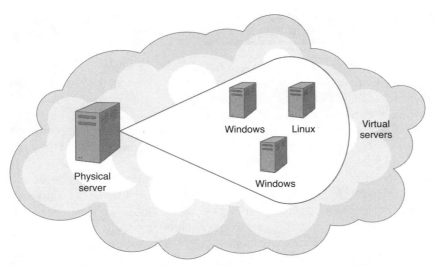

FIGURE 1-9 Server virtualization makes a single server appear as multiple independent servers running the same or different operating systems.

Behind the scenes, the server CPU switches its processing power rapidly among the various operating systems.

In a similar way, most desktop PCs typically run one operating system. Again, using special virtualization software, a desktop PC, as shown in **FIGURE 1-10**, can be made to appear as if the system is simultaneously running different operating systems. Desktop virtualization provides an excellent solution for developers, application testers, and help desk support personnel who must support multiple operating systems. Rather than having multiple desktop systems on their desk, with each system running a specific operating system, the user can instead use a single desktop PC with multiple (virtual) operating systems.

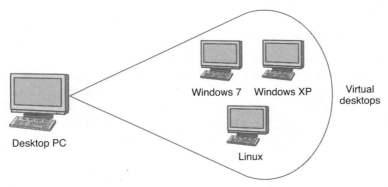

FIGURE 1-10 Desktop virtualization allows a PC to run multiple operating systems simultaneously.

CASE 1-5 GOOGLE CLOUD-BASED SOLUTIONS

Google is one of the world's most successful web-based businesses. Through its high-performing search engine, Google leverages high-margin automated advertising solutions. Beyond this, Google offers a variety of applications that leverage the cloud's ease of access and device independence to a wide range of users.

To start, Gmail, an early cloud-based solution, has become one of the most widely used e-mail services. By storing user e-mails within the cloud, Gmail provides ease of access to e-mail from any computer or handheld device, at any time and from any place.

Google Docs, an online set of collaborative document editing tools, provides many of the common capabilities of Microsoft Office tools, such as Word, Excel, and PowerPoint, from within a web browser, with no software to install and no cost! Not only do the Google Docs tools make it easy for developers to share documents, they provide a preview of how future cloud-based solutions will allow users to perform their daily computing tasks without the need for a computer operating system such as Windows or Mac OS.

As you might expect, Google is not conceding sole custody of the music market to Apple. Google is protective of its web domain and now offers services users can access for common cloud-based solutions.

Exercise Explain how Google makes money. Describe the pros and cons of PCs that do not require an operating system.

Web Resources For more information on Google cloud-based solutions, see www.CloudBook Content.com/Chapter01/index.html.

Collecting Processing Power Through Grid Computing

Through cloud computing, users leverage virtual processing power and data storage via Internet-based computing resources that reside in the cloud. Through CPU (or server) farms and load balancing, cloud-based applications can scale on the fly to meet user demands.

Before the advent of the cloud, developers sought ways to leverage the potential processing power of networked computers. The concept of **grid computing** is based on the fact that throughout the day most PCs have spiked use. This means that when a user is active, the CPU utilization may grow to 30 to 50 percent of the processor's capacity. When the user is not active, the CPU is idle, often using 1 percent or less of its processing capabilities.

By utilizing the fact that most computers are connected to a network, the grid-computing architects look to design applications that could hand off work across the network to idle CPUs. When the CPU completes its task, it simply

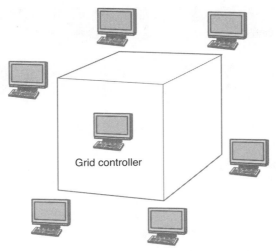

Grid controller

FIGURE 1–11 Grid computing breaks a complex task into smaller pieces that are distributed to CPUs that reside within the network (grid).

returns its result. Shown in **FIGURE 1–11**, a grid-computing application is well suited for scientific and complex mathematical processing.

As you might anticipate, grid computing introduces a wide range of security issues. The applications that move across the grid must bring with them code to execute, data, and other state information. The University of California, Berkeley, is one of the leaders in grid computing. To facilitate computer interaction across grids, the university developed the Berkeley Open Infrastructure for Network Computing (BOINC). For specifics, visit http://boinc.berkeley.edu.

A FEW GOOD CLOUD-CONTENT READS

Across the web—OK, make that across the cloud—there are many sites that provide great information about cloud issues. The following sections describe several items you should review.

DISTRIBUTED MANAGEMENT TASK FORCE INC. (DMTF) CLOUD MANAGEMENT

Distributed Management Task Force Inc. (DMTF) provides information technology standards, which exist to simplify computer system management and reduce related costs. Within DMTF, the Cloud Management Work Group (CMWG) and the Cloud Auditing Data Federation (CADF) provide standards for cloud architecture, environments, and interactions. You should take time, for example, to visit the Cloud Standards Wiki, shown in **FIGURE 1–12**.

continues

A FEW GOOD CLOUD-CONTENT READS, continued

FIGURE 1–12 The Cloud Standards Wiki.

STORAGE NETWORKING INDUSTRY ASSOCIATION (SNIA)

One of the largest uses of the cloud is for remote data storage, perhaps for live data, music, video, or even backups. The Storage Networking Industry Association (SNIA) is a nonprofit organization that provides standards and solutions on matters related to disk storage. As you might expect, SNIA provides content on cloud-based data storage. At the SNIA website, you can find overviews, podcasts, and standards on cloud-based storage issues. For specifics, visit the SNIA cloud site at www.snia.org/cloud.

OBJECT MANAGEMENT GROUP

The Object Management Group (OMG) is a nonprofit organization that provides standards for a wide range of technology, including real-time and embedded software, analysis and design, middleware, and more. Within the OMG, the Cloud Standards Customer Council (CSCC) is currently working on a variety of cloud computing initiatives, which will be consolidated into a user guide. For specifics on their research and publications, visit the CSCC website.

CHAPTER SUMMARY

The concept of a cloud and the Internet is not new. For years developers and network administrators have represented the Internet as a cloud. Using the cloud abstraction, developers could temporarily ignore the underlying communication complexity and simply assume that messages would flow successfully from one Internet-connected network to another.

Cloud computing is an abstraction of web-based computers, resources, and services that system developers can utilize to implement complex web-based systems. Developers often view cloud-based resources as virtual. This means that if a system or solution need more resources, such as servers or disk space, the resources can simply be added on demand and usually transparently to the cloud-based application. Cloud-based solutions can normally scale up or down in size based on user demands. Companies whose solutions reside in the cloud normally pay only for the resources they consume. As a result, companies that once relied on expensive data centers to house their processing resources can now shift their costs and maintenance efforts to pay-as-you-go, scalable, cloud-based alternatives.

KEY TERMS

Amazon Web Services (AWS)
Cloud computing
Community cloud
Grid computing
Hybrid cloud
iCloud
Infrastructure as a service (IaaS)
Platform as a service (PaaS)
Private cloud

Public cloud
Reliability
Robust
Scalability
Software as a service (SaaS)
Virtualization
Web 2.0
Windows Azure

CHAPTER REVIEW

1. Define and discuss cloud computing.
2. Discuss how cloud computing has changed how companies budget for software solutions.
3. Compare and contrast SaaS, PaaS, and IaaS, and provide an example of each.
4. Define scalability and discuss how the cloud impacts it.
5. List three advantages and three disadvantages of cloud computing.
6. Define virtualization and discuss how the cloud impacts it.
7. Describe three cloud-based solutions for individuals and three cloud-based solutions for businesses.
8. Discuss how Web 2.0 has driven the growth of the web.
9. Compare and contrast public, private, community, and hybrid clouds.

Software as a Service (SaaS)

SOFTWARE AS A SERVICE (SaaS) is a solution model in which users use a web browser to access software that resides, along with the programs and user data, in the cloud. Companies that use SaaS solutions eliminate the need for in-house (data-center-based) applications, administrative support for the applications, and data storage. Because SaaS solutions reside within the cloud, the solutions can easily scale to meet customer needs. Further, most companies can pay for the SaaS solutions on demand—meaning that the companies pay only for the resources they consume, normally on a per-user basis. SaaS solutions exist for a wide range of applications and provide customers with a cost-effective way to get started and an affordable long-term solution.

Learning Objectives

This chapter examines SaaS solutions in detail. By the time you finish this chapter, you will be able to do the following:

- Define and describe SaaS.
- List the advantages and disadvantages of SaaS solutions.
- Define and describe OpenSaaS.
- Define and describe mashups.
- Discuss the wide range of SaaS solutions and their providers.

Getting Started with SaaS

SaaS solutions offer the following advantages:

- They reduce or eliminate the need for an on-site data center
- They eliminate the need for application administration
- They allow customers to pay on demand for software use, normally on a per-user basis
- They offer application, processor, and data storage scalability
- They offer device-independent access to key applications
- They increase disaster recovery and business continuity

The biggest concern, or potential disadvantage, is that the data, like the applications, reside in the cloud. Many companies are concerned about letting go of their data. Also, because the company does not own the solution, it can be challenging or expensive to customize the application.

CASE 2-1 SALESFORCE.COM SAAS FOR CUSTOMER RELATIONSHIP MANAGEMENT (CRM)

Salesforce.com was one of the first companies to unlock the power of cloud-based SaaS. The site delivers cloud-based **customer relationship management (CRM)** solutions, which let companies accomplish the following:

- Manage sales contacts and leads
- Centralize contact information, presentations, and project details
- Access sales information and reports from anyplace, at any time, with any device
- Manage project quotes and project work flow
- Sync sales contacts and meetings with existing tools, such as Microsoft Outlook

Salesforce.com offers a variety of solutions that support not only the small business, but also the large enterprise.

Exercise Salesforce.com was one of the companies to leverage the power of the cloud. Discuss the features Salesforce.com provides that are well suited for companies large and small.

Web Resource For more information on Salesforce.com, see www.CloudBookContent.com/Chapter02/index.html.

Understanding the Multitenant Nature of SaaS Solutions

SaaS applications are often **multitenant solutions**; that is, within the cloud, two or more companies may share the same server resources, as shown in **FIGURE 2-1**. Depending on their size and fees, customers may also share database resources. Further, depending on the SaaS provider, customizing a multitenant solution may be difficult, expensive, or impossible.

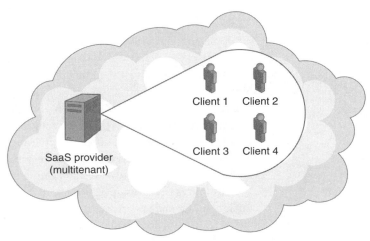

FIGURE 2-1 Many SaaS solutions are multitenant, which means that behind the scenes customers may share computing resources.

CASE 2-2 TALEO SAAS FOR HUMAN RESOURCES MANAGEMENT

To achieve wide-scale use, an SaaS solution must have large market potential. Every business must recruit, hire, train, and compensate employees. The Taleo cloud-based talent management system provides applications and services to meet company human resources demands. Specifically, Taleo SaaS solutions provide the following:

- Recruitment tools companies can use to attract, hire, and integrate talented individuals into the company culture
- Performance-management tools companies can use to evaluate employees and plan their growth and eventual replacement
- Compensation tools appropriate for companies with a global workforce
- Workforce training and professional development tools companies can use to educate and train employees

Exercise For an SaaS solution to be successful, the solution must be disruptive. Discuss whether or not you consider the Taleo cloud-based solutions disruptive.

Web Resource For more information on Taleo cloud-based human resources solutions, see www.CloudBookContent.com/Chapter02/index.html.

Understanding OpenSaaS Solutions

The application programs that run as SaaS solutions in the cloud were developed using a specific programming language and were designed to run on a specific operating system using a specific database management system. An OpenSaaS solution is an SaaS application created using an open source programming language and designed to run on an open source operating system and database.

Many customers believe that if a solution is open source, it will be easier for them to move the data to a different application in the future if the current solution fails to meet their needs. Because customers do not own the SaaS software, they will not be able to move the application itself.

Customers that are concerned about moving their data in the future should consider an OpenSaaS provider. That said, most SaaS solutions, open source or not, provide a way for customers to export their data if the need arises.

CASE 2-3 ADP SAAS FOR PAYROLL PROCESSING AND HUMAN RESOURCES MANAGEMENT

One of the first companies to leverage the power of the cloud was ADP—a payroll processing company. Reaching far beyond payroll today, ADP offers cloud-based solutions for time management, employee benefits processing, workers compensation, human resources issues, and more. Further, ADP has extended many of its services to mobile users, allowing payroll processing to occur any time, from any place.

Exercise Discuss the market potential for ADP products beyond payroll processing.

Web Resource For more information on ADP cloud solutions, see www.CloudBookContent.com/Chapter02/index.html.

CASE 2-4 WEBEX SAAS FOR VIRTUAL MEETINGS

To gain market share, an SaaS solution must be disruptive; it must change its industry. The WebEx solution not only changes how and when people meet, it disrupts the travel industry by reducing business trips, hotel stays, and business meals. Millions of users rely on WebEx to provide a virtual yet face-to-face meeting platform. A side effect of less travel is the greening of business, which means it has less impact on the environment. In fact, as shown in **FIGURE 2-2**, WebEx provides an online calculator that shows the dollars saved and the carbon footprint reduced through WebEx-based meetings, as opposed to corporate travel.

continues

CASE 2-4 WEBEX SAAS FOR VIRTUAL MEETINGS, continued

Beyond holding online meetings, companies use WebEx for the following:

- Training webinars for hundreds or thousands of attendees, within the company and beyond
- Press conferences
- Product sales demonstrations
- Remote technical support
- And more

FIGURE 2-3 shows a WebEx presentation on cloud computing.

Exercise Assume that your company must invite 500 employees into the corporate office from states across the country (an average airline ticket cost of $350). Using the WebEx calculator, determine the potential company savings by hosting the meeting online.

Web Resource For more information on WebEx, see www.CloudBookContent.com/Chapter02/index.html.

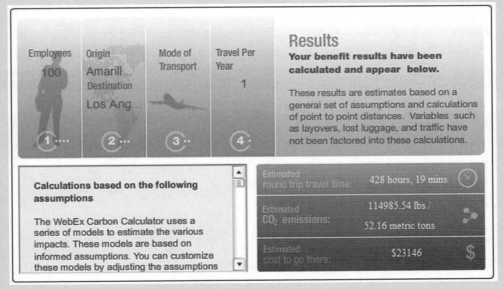

FIGURE 2-2 Calculation of cost savings and carbon footprint reduction resulting from WebEx meetings.

Courtesy of Cisco Systems, Inc. Unauthorized use not permitted. www.webex.com/overview/environment.html. (6/1/11).

continues

CASE 2-4 WEBEX SAAS FOR VIRTUAL MEETINGS, continued

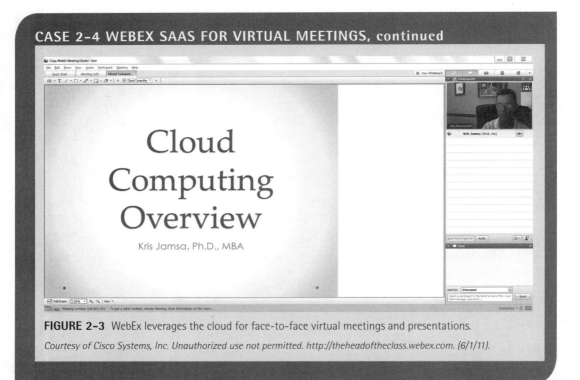

FIGURE 2-3 WebEx leverages the cloud for face-to-face virtual meetings and presentations.

Courtesy of Cisco Systems, Inc. Unauthorized use not permitted. http://theheadoftheclass.webex.com. (6/1/11).

CASE 2-5 CARBONITE SAAS FOR FILE BACKUPS

Businesses often rely on a process known as cloud-based colocation to duplicate their company resources at a remote site. If fire, theft, or some other disaster occurs, the business significantly reduces its risk of data loss.

Most user-based computer books tell users that they, too, should perform regular disk and file backup operations. However, because the process is generally too time consuming, most users fail to back up their files on a regular basis. Worse yet, users who do perform backups often store the copies within the same facility (home or office) as their computer. The backups are at risk to many of the same factors that threaten the original data.

To provide users and companies with a backup solution, many SaaS providers have emerged to back up user data files to redundant storage facilities that reside within the cloud, as shown in **FIGURE 2-4.**

The SaaS cloud-based backup systems provide reliable and secure storage. Users simply select the files or folders they want to back up and then schedule when and how often they want the backups to occur. The actual backup operations then happen behind the scenes, automatically.

continues

CASE 2-5 CARBONITE SAAS FOR FILE BACKUPS, continued

FIGURE 2-5 shows a screen for a Carbonite-based backup operation occurring as a background process while the user performs other tasks.

Exercise Assume your company has 1,000 employees. Calculate the potential cost to integrate cloud-based backup operations through Carbonite. Do you have an alternative backup solution?

Web Resource For more information on Carbonite cloud-based backups, see www.CloudBook Content.com/Chapter02/index.html.

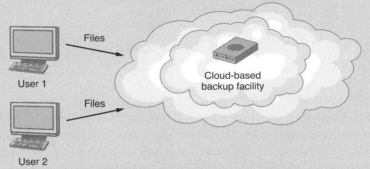

FIGURE 2-4 Cloud-based SaaS backup providers store secure copies of user and company files at data storage facilities that reside in the cloud.

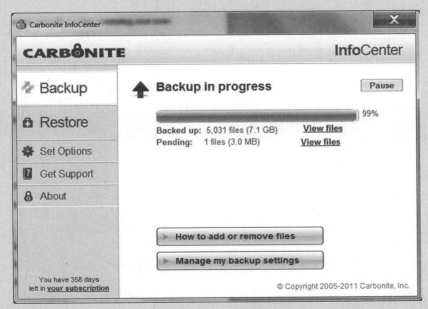

FIGURE 2-5 The Carbonite software running as a background task to back up files to the cloud.

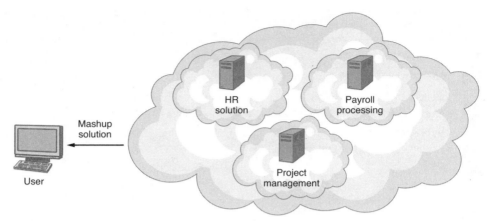

FIGURE 2-6 A mashup is a collection of services joined to create an overall solution.

Understanding Mashups

Many companies need a variety of SaaS solutions. Depending on the various solution providers, the company may create a **mashup**, a collection of services joined to create an overall solution. **FIGURE 2-6** illustrates the concept of a solution mashup.

Developers categorize mashups as web-based or server-based. In a web-based mashup, the user's browser (perhaps via JavaScript) combines the various content sources to create a unified display. In server-based mashups, an application running on a server combines the data.

Not surprisingly, the open philosophy has reached mashups. In fact, organizations are working on the Enterprise Markup Mashup Language (EMML) to simplify the design and implementation of mashup solutions while increasing their portability. For more information, visit www.openmashup.org.

CASE 2-6 ONLINE SCHOOL SAAS SOLUTIONS

Online education has remained one of the fastest growing segments within education markets. Millions of learners now take courses online. Using cloud-based learning management systems, universities offer courses in both synchronous (learners meet at a specific day and time) and asynchronous (learners make their own schedule) formats. By leveraging cloud-based systems, schools can reduce their IT resources and staffing costs, essentially paying for learning services on demand.

Exercise Using the web, search for demographic information on the size of the online learning environment. Discuss how you expect this market to evolve over the next 10 years.

Web Resource For more information on cloud-based online learning, see www.CloudBook Content.com/Chapter02/index.html.

CASE 2–7 MICROSOFT OFFICE 365 SAAS FOR DOCUMENT CREATION, EDITING, AND SHARING

For as long as most of us can remember, computer users have made extensive use of the Microsoft Office suite: Word, PowerPoint, Excel, Outlook, and more. Traditionally users have had to purchase and install Office, a relatively expensive investment. Then users have had to keep installing updates to the software as they became available from Microsoft. Businesses, in turn, would normally license Office for each of their employees.

Over the past few years, to reduce costs many users began to use products such as Open-Office (LibreOffice), an open source, free, Office-compatible solution. Recently users have found Google Docs, which can be used from any computer—a compelling tool.

To meet user demands and to match competitor offerings, Microsoft released Office 365, a pay-by-the-month subscription to the Office applications, which, as shown in **FIGURE 2–7**, resides in the cloud.

Using Office 365, users can access and edit their documents from any computer, as well as many handheld devices. If needed, users can save their documents to local devices. **FIGURE 2–8**, for example, shows a PowerPoint document in Office 365.

Further, because the Office 365 documents are cloud based, users and teams can easily collaborate and share documents.

Exercise Assume your company has 1,000 employees who need access to the Microsoft Office suite of products. Analyze the potential cost savings of using Microsoft Office 365 over purchasing seat licenses for each user.

Web Resource For more information on Microsoft Office 365, see www.CloudBookContent.com/Chapter02/index.html.

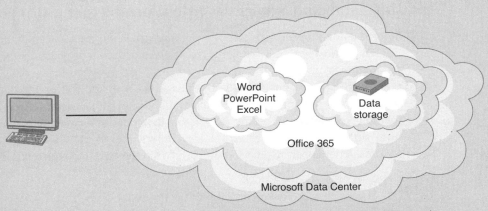

FIGURE 2-7 Office 365 provides cloud-based subscription access to the Office suite of applications.

continues

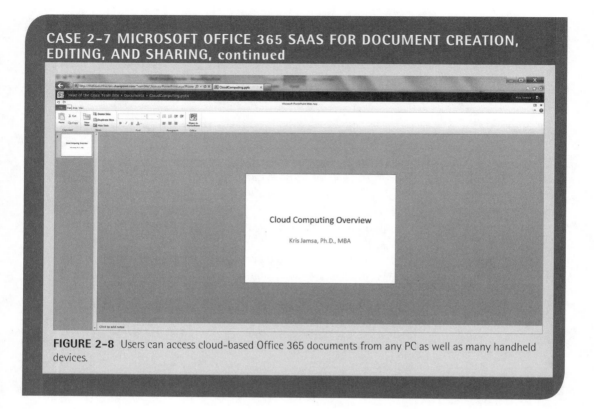

FIGURE 2-8 Users can access cloud-based Office 365 documents from any PC as well as many handheld devices.

Understanding Service-Oriented Architecture (SOA)

Most SaaS solutions provide complete solutions, meaning an application that can be used within a web browser. For example, Salesforce.com provides a web application for customer relationship management, TurboTax provides a web application for filing taxes, and QuickBooks provides a web application for business accounting. Beyond providing a complete application with a user interface, many solution providers offer specific services that developers can access across the web from within programs they create. Developers refer to these services as **web services**. A developer might, for example, use web services to do the following:

- Query the price of a stock
- Check a warehouse for current product inventory levels
- Get real-time road or weather conditions
- Check airline flight departure or arrival information
- Purchase a product or service
- Perform credit card processing

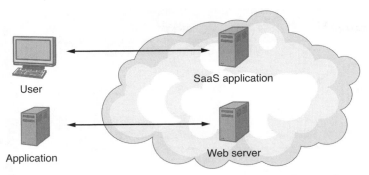

FIGURE 2-9 Web services are solutions that programs can call across the web to perform specific tasks.

As shown in **FIGURE 2-9**, an SaaS application interacts with a user, whereas a web service interacts with a program.

Service-oriented architecture (SOA) is an application development methodology with which developers create solutions by integrating one or more web services. Think of a web service as a function or subroutine a program can call to accomplish a specific task. As shown in **FIGURE 2-10**, when a program running on one computer calls a web service, a message, possibly containing parameter values, is sent across the network (or Internet) to the computer housing the web service. That computer, in turn, performs its processing and normally returns a result to the caller.

Some developers refer to web services as remote-procedure calls. Further, developers refer to a set of web services as an **application program interface (API)**. Amazon and eBay, for example, provide APIs that programmers can use to purchase products from across the web using the programs they create. To gain a better understanding of the processing that web services can perform, visit the XMethods website shown in **FIGURE 2-11**. XMethods provides a variety of web services that perform a wide range of tasks.

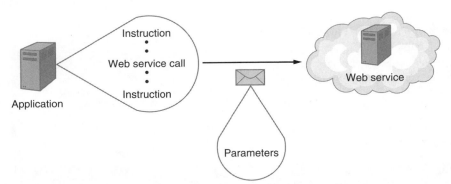

FIGURE 2-10 To call a web service, a program typically sends a message to the web service that resides on a remote computer and then waits for the web service to return a result.

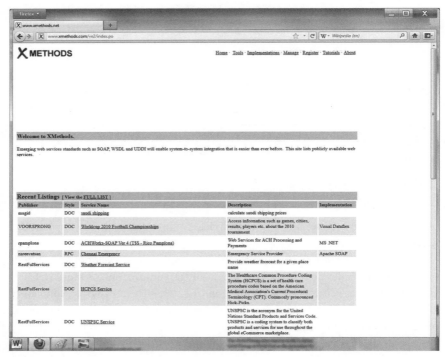

FIGURE 2-11 The XMethods website at www.xmethods.com provides web services that perform a wide range of tasks.

CASE 2-8 FACEBOOK: AN SAAS MEDIA SITE?

If you ask 10 cloud experts if Facebook is an SaaS social media site, you will likely get 10 "maybe" answers. Facebook definitely has a variety of SaaS characteristics:

- Ability to scale with respect to processor demands and data storage needs
- No user software to purchase or install
- Redundant server hardware and data storage
- Accessibility through a myriad of devices

Exercise Justify whether Facebook is an SaaS solution.

Web Resource For more information on Facebook as an SaaS provider, see www.CloudBook Content.com/Chapter02/index.html.

CASE 2–9 IS GOOGLE+ A BETTER, OR JUST ANOTHER, SOCIAL NETWORK?

G oogle+ is a new social networking site that lets users define and manage various groups of people and how they interact with them. With Google+, users can define various circles, which might include people from work, good friends, and family, as well as casual acquaintances. Using such circle definitions, users can better control the posts they allow others to view.

FIGURE 2–12 Shows the Google+ home page.

Exercise Compare and contrast the Google+ features with those of other social networks, such as Facebook.

Web Resource For more information on Google+, see www.CloudBookContent.com/Chapter02/index.html.

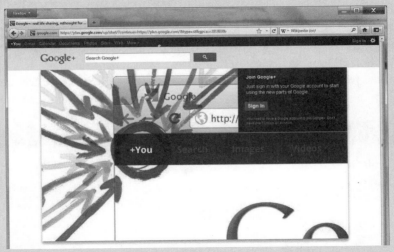

FIGURE 2–12 Google+ is a social network that resides in the cloud.

CHAPTER SUMMARY

SaaS provides a solution model that allows users to use a web browser to access software that resides in the cloud. SaaS solutions allow companies to eliminate or reduce their need for on-site, data-center-based applications. By eliminating in-house applications, companies can also reduce administrative support for the applications, as well as data storage. SaaS solutions reside within the cloud, which lets the solutions easily scale processors or disk storage to meet customer needs. Companies normally pay for SaaS solutions on demand for the resources they consume, usually on a per-user basis. SaaS solutions exist for a wide range of applications. Using SaaS solutions, customers have a cost-effective way to get started and an affordable, long-term solution to their data storage needs. Finally, this chapter examined web services, which are cloud-based services that developers can call from within the programs they create to accomplish specific tasks. Many SaaS solution providers offer their services directly to users via SaaS applications and to developer-created programs using web services.

KEY TERMS

Application program interface (API)   Multitenant solution
Customer relationship management (CRM)   Service-oriented architecture (SOA)
Mashup   Web services

CHAPTER REVIEW

1. Define and describe SaaS.
2. Search the web and list an SaaS provider for each of the following industries:
   - Sales and customer relationship management
   - Accounting
   - Income tax filing
   - Web-based meetings
   - Human resources
   - Payroll processing
   - Backup automation
   - Office document creation
   - Social networking
3. Define and describe mashups.
4. List the advantages and disadvantages of SaaS solutions.
5. Describe the role of OpenSaaS.
6. Compare and contrast a web service and an SaaS solution.
7. Define and describe SOA.

Platform as a Service (PaaS)

PLATFORM AS A SERVICE (PaaS) solutions provide a collection of hardware and software resources that developers can use to build and deploy applications within the cloud. Depending on their needs, developers may use a Windows-based PaaS solution or a Linux-based PaaS.

Using PaaS, developers eliminate the need to buy and maintain hardware, as well as the need to install and manage operating system and database software. Because the computing resources no longer reside in the data center, but rather in the cloud, the resources can scale up or down based on application demand, and the company can pay for only those resources it consumes. Further, because PaaS eliminates the developers' need to worry about servers, they can more quickly deploy their web-based solutions.

Learning Objectives

This chapter examines the PaaS model in detail. By the time you finish this chapter, you will be able to do the following:

- Define and describe the PaaS model.
- Describe the advantages and disadvantages of PaaS solutions.
- List and describe several real-world PaaS solutions.
- List and describe cloud-based database solutions and describe their advantages.
- Discuss the development history that led to PaaS.

CASE 3-1 GOOGLE APP ENGINE AS A PAAS

Google App Engine, sometimes called GAE, is a PaaS solution that lets developers create and host web-based applications that reside and run on services managed by Google, as shown in **FIGURE 3-1**.

Like many Google services and offerings, Google App Engine is a free service (until applications reach a large size and consume significant bandwidth). Google estimates that most developers can use Google App Engine free of charge. Once they have 5 million hits per month the developers must then pay, but only for the resources they use.

Currently, Google App Engine provides platform support for a variety of programming languages, the three most common of which are Java, Python, and Go. The primary Google App Engine features include the following:

- Support for dynamic web pages
- Data storage and query support
- Load balancing for application scalability
- Application program interface (API) support for application-based e-mail through Google services
- A local development, environment that simulates Google App Engine on the developer's computer
- Support for event scheduling and triggering
- An application sandbox that limits access to the underlying operating system
- Software development kits specific to programming languages
- An administrative console for managing applications and databases

For more information on Google App Engine, visit www.appengine.google.com.

Exercise Assume your company must deploy Java and PHP solutions. Discuss how your company might use Google App Engine and the company's potential cost.

Web Resources For additional information on Google App Engine, see www.CloudBook Content.com/Chapter03/index.html.

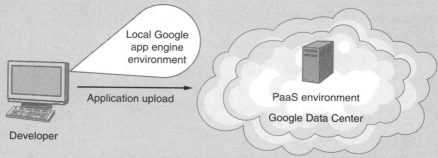

FIGURE 3-1 Google App Engine helps developers create web-based applications and then hosts the applications in the cloud.

IT Evolution Leading to the Cloud

The evolution of information technology solutions has been defined by several distinct hardware and software models. To start, early IT solutions from the 1960s to mid-1980s were characterized by mainframe computers similar to that shown in **FIGURE 3-2**, which had the following characteristics:

FIGURE 3-2 Computing from the 1960s through the mid-1980s was mainframe driven.

- Large capital investment for data-center-based computers
- Large, expensive disk and tape storage systems that often provided only limited storage capacity
- User interface to the system provided through dumb terminals
- Limited computer–network interconnectivity
- System security maintained through physical security (few users had direct access to the computer hardware)

With the advent of the IBM PC in 1981, users shifted to local applications and data storage. Early network solutions provided in-house e-mail communication and limited printer and file sharing. System security was implemented primarily at the individual computer level because network simplicity did not yet provide an environment for sophisticated computer viruses.

As the use of the Internet became more widespread, companies extended their e-mail communication beyond company users to vendors, customers, and others. Things changed drastically with the commercialization of the web in 1995 and the release of company websites. Initially, many companies brought in expensive T1 or T3 Internet connections and housed their own web servers. These initial servers looked like large desktop systems, as shown in **FIGURE 3-3**.

FIGURE 3-3 Early PC-based servers were tower-based systems with a large footprint. They consumed considerable power and generated considerable heat.

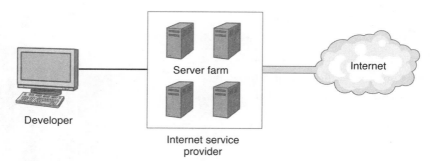

FIGURE 3-4 ISPs were the first to offer cloud-like remote computing services.

For smaller companies, however, the cost to connect to the Internet was prohibitive. As a result, Internet service providers (ISPs), which maintained web servers and high-speed, high-bandwidth connections, began to emerge. As shown in **FIGURE 3-4**, developers would use languages such as HTML, Perl, and active server pages (ASP) to develop content locally and then use a file transfer protocol (FTP) application to transfer the files to the server, which resides within the ISP.

The advantages of hosting solutions at an ISP included the following:

- **Reduced cost**: The ISP provided the high-speed, high-bandwidth Internet connection, which it shared across several companies.
- **Less server administration**: The ISP managed the servers to which developers uploaded their solutions.
- **Less hardware to purchase and maintain**: The ISP purchased and managed the hardware and managed the infrastructure software, such as the operating system.
- **Greater system uptime**: Through the use of redundant hardware resources, the ISP provided high system uptime.
- **Potential scalability**: The ISP had the ability to move a high-demand application to a faster bandwidth connection.

As the use of the Internet and web continued to drive processing requirements, many data centers began to move to blade servers, similar to that shown in **FIGURE 3-5**, which required a smaller footprint, involved less cost, and could easily access shared network devices.

By 2005, many companies used Windows- and Linux-based web servers that were housed at remote ISPs and laid the groundwork for the eventual creation of what we describe today as cloud-based PaaS solutions, as shown in **FIGURE 3-6**.

FIGURE 3-5 Blade computers allowed companies to reduce server footprint, power requirements, and heat within the data center.

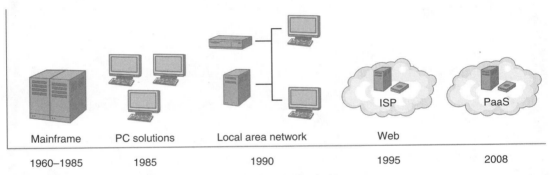

Mainframe	PC solutions	Local area network	Web	
1960–1985	1985	1990	1995	2008

FIGURE 3-6 The evolution of technology leading to cloud PaaS solutions.

CASE 3-2 FORCE.COM AS A PAAS

One of the best known software as a service (SaaS) solutions is Salesforce.com. To extend its cloud capabilities to application developers, Salesforce.com has released the Force.com PaaS. Although it was originally developed to provide a home for business applications, Force.com now runs applications across most sectors.

As shown in **FIGURE 3-7**, Force.com provides four different development environments that sit in a cloud-based data management facility.

continues

CASE 3-2 FORCE.COM AS A PAAS, continued

FIGURE 3-7 Force.com provides four primary development products that leverage a cloud-based database.

The following briefly describes the Force.com application interface:

- **Appforce**: Provides a user interface that lets nonprogrammers create applications to support finance, human resources, project management, and more. Through a drag-and-drop interface, users can develop business solutions without writing code.
- **Siteforce**: Provides the ability for nondevelopers to quickly create a data-rich website using the Salesforce.com customer relationship management (CRM) editor. Users do not need to know HTML or coding to produce powerful web pages.
- **VMforce**: Provides a **platform** for Java-based solutions in which programmers can code locally using the Eclipse **integrated development environment (IDE)** and then drag and drop their solutions to VMforce.com for hosting.
- **ISVforce**: Provides a platform that independent software vendors can use to distribute their applications and updates to users via the cloud. The platform includes access to an application storefront that developers can use to expose their application to potential customers.

The Force.com applications sit on top of a cloud-based database provided by Salesforce.com at Database.com. The **cloud-based database** provides high performance, scalability, backups, and data redundancy. Database.com provides an API that developers can use within their programs to interact with the database.

Exercise Assume your company's vice president of sales wants to produce sales reports from your company's cloud-based sales data. Unfortunately, your company does not have programming resources it can allocate to the project. Discuss how your company might leverage a Force.com solution to meet the requirement.

Web Resources For additional information on Force.com, see www.CloudBookContent.com/Chapter03/index.html.

Benefits of PaaS Solutions

By shifting computing resources from an on-site data center to the cloud, PaaS solutions offer many advantages:

- **Lower total cost of ownership**: Companies no longer need to purchase and maintain expensive hardware for servers, power, and data storage.
- **Lower administrative overhead**: Companies shift the burden of system software administration from in-house administration to employees of the cloud provider.
- **More current system software**: The cloud administrator is responsible for maintaining software versions and patch installations.
- **Increased business and IT alignment**: Company IT personnel can focus on solutions rather than on server-related issues.
- **Scalable solutions**: Cloud-based solutions can scale up or down automatically based on application resource demands. Companies pay only for the resources they consume.

CASE 3-3 LONGJUMP AS A PAAS

LongJump provides a PaaS solution that includes cloud-based database management support. What makes LongJump unique is its focus on the entire software development life cycle. To start an application design, nonprogrammers can capture business requirements, forms, and data relationships without coding. The LongJump application development is Java based and supports key protocols such as SOAP and REST. After the developer hosts the site, LongJump provides release management and software maintenance support. Developers can try LongJump free of charge.

Exercise Discuss the role of web services and specifically the use of the SOAP and REST protocols.

Web Resources For additional information on LongJump, see www.CloudBookContent.com/Chapter03/index.html.

Disadvantages of PaaS Solutions

Potential disadvantages of PaaS solutions include the following:

- **Concerns about data security**: Some companies are hesitant to move their data storage off-site.
- **Challenges to integrating cloud solutions with legacy software**: A company may need to support on-site solutions as well as cloud-based solutions. Communication between the two application types may be difficult to impossible.
- **Risk of breach by the PaaS provider**: If the company providing the PaaS service fails to meet agreed-upon service levels, performance, security, and availability may be at risk, and moving the application may be difficult.

CASE 3-4 NETSUITE AS A PAAS

NetSuite is somewhat of a hybrid in that it is a provider of both SaaS and PaaS. On the SaaS side, NetSuite offers turnkey enterprise resource planning (ERP), customer relationship management (CRM), and accounting solutions. The benefits of using the NetSuite cloud-based solution include the following:

- Reduced total cost of ownership compared with running on-site solutions within an IT data center
- Reduced duplication of data entry through the use of integrated storage solutions
- Enhanced distributed access to computer data
- Simplified application updates because NetSuite maintains and manages software solutions

On the PaaS side, NetSuite provides a development environment that sits on top of the Net-Suite business solutions. Using a drag-and-drop environment, developers can quickly build and deploy enterprise solutions.

Exercise Visit the NetSuite website and then discuss the role and capability of drag-and-drop solutions that do not require a programmer to create and deploy applications.

Web Resources For additional information on NetSuite, see www.CloudBookContent.com/Chapter03/index.html.

CASE 3-5 CLOUD FOUNDRY AS A PAAS

Cloud Foundry is an open source project enabled by VMware. Developers have access to and contribute to the project. Cloud Foundry provides developers with a complete PaaS solution that supports programming languages including Spring for Java applications, Rails and Sinatra for Ruby, and other Java virtual machine (JVM) frameworks. Cloud Foundry supports various open source databases, such as MongoDB and MySQL.

The primary Cloud Foundry is multitenant, but through the use of MicroCloud, developers can use a single instance of Cloud Foundry.

Exercise Research cloud applications on the web. Discuss the programming languages that cloud developers use most often to implement the applications they create.

Web Resources For additional information on Cloud Foundry, see www.CloudBookContent .com/Chapter03/index.html.

CASE 3-6 OPENSHIFT AS A PAAS

Red Hat is well known for providing and supporting open source solutions. Red Hat also distributes Red Hat Linux. OpenShift is the Red Hat PaaS offering, which lets developers quickly deploy browser-based and command-line-based applications. OpenShift has three primary development tools:

- **Express**: A free platform for cloud-based solutions written in PHP, Python, and Ruby.
- **Flex**: Well suited for cloud-based Java, JBoss, and PHP solutions.
- **Power**: Designed for Linux-based solutions written in the C programming language.

Exercise Discuss the pros and cons of using a Linux-based PaaS solution as opposed to a Windows-based environment.

Web Resources For additional information on OpenShift, see www.CloudBookContent.com/ Chapter03/index.html.

CASE 3-7 WINDOWS AZURE AND SQL AZURE AS A PAAS

Microsoft .NET has driven the development of many dynamic web solutions and web services. Windows Azure is a PaaS running within Microsoft data centers. Users pay only for the scalable processor resources that they consume. SQL Azure provides a cloud-based database solution for applications running within Windows Azure. **FIGURE 3-8** illustrates the Windows Azure PaaS environment.

Windows Azure goes beyond .NET and includes support for Java, PHP, and Ruby. Developers can build and deploy their solutions to Azure using an IDE such as Visual Studio or Eclipse. Developers can interface to SQL Azure using much of the same code they would use to access a local database.

Exercise Discuss advantages and disadvantages of using Microsoft as a PaaS solution provider.

Web Resources For additional information on Windows Azure and SQL Azure, see www.Cloud BookContent.com/Chapter03/index.html.

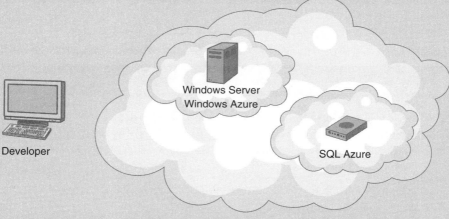

Windows Server
Windows Azure

Developer

SQL Azure

FIGURE 3-8 The Windows Azure PaaS environment.

CHAPTER SUMMARY

A PaaS solution provides a collection of hardware and software resources that developers use to build and deploy cloud-based applications. PaaS solutions run a Windows- or a Linux-based operating system and normally support a specific programming environment, such as .NET or Java.

PaaS solutions eliminate the need for developers to buy and maintain hardware and install and manage operating system and database software. Because the PaaS computing resources reside in the cloud, the resources can scale up or down based on application demand, and the company pays only for the resources it consumes. Finally, because PaaS eliminates the developers' need to worry about servers, they can more quickly deploy their web-based solutions.

KEY TERMS

Cloud-based database   Platform
Integrated development environment (IDE)

CHAPTER REVIEW

1. Define and describe PaaS.

2. List the benefits of PaaS solutions.

3. Describe potential disadvantages of PaaS.

4. Describe how a cloud-based database management system differs from an on-site database.

5. List the computing resources normally provided with a PaaS.

6. Assume your company must deploy a .NET solution to the cloud. Discuss the options available to developers. Research on the web and estimate the costs associated with deploying a PaaS solution.

7. Assume your company must deploy a PHP or Java solution to the cloud. Discuss the options available to developers. Research on the web and estimate the costs associated with deploying a PaaS solution.

Infrastructure as a Service (IaaS)

MANY COMPANIES THAT DEPLOY applications to the cloud will need a specific platform, such as Windows, .NET, and Microsoft SQL Server, or Linux, Perl, and MySQL. Utilizing a platform as a service (PaaS) solution eliminates the company's need to administer the operating system and supporting software. Other companies, because of security needs or a desire to manage all resources, turn to infrastructure as a service (IaaS) providers. An IaaS provider makes all of the computing hardware resources available; the customers, in turn, are responsible for installing and managing the systems, which they can normally do over the Internet.

Learning Objectives

This chapter examines IaaS in detail. By the time you finish this chapter, you will be able to do the following:

- Define and describe IaaS and identify IaaS solution providers.
- Define and describe colocation.
- Define and describe system and storage redundancy.
- Define and describe cloud-based network-attached storage (NAS) devices and identify solution providers.
- Define and describe load balancing and identify cloud-based solution providers.
- Describe the pros and cons of IaaS solutions.

Understanding IaaS

Running a data center is an expensive and staff-intensive process. To start, one must create a facility with the following capabilities:

- Access to high-speed and redundant Internet service
- Sufficient air conditioning to eliminate the heat generated by servers and disk storage devices
- Conditioned power with the potential for uninterrupted power supply in the short term and long term through the use of on-site diesel-powered generators
- Fire suppression systems
- Administrative staffing to support hardware, networks, and operating systems

FIGURE 4-1 illustrates a typical data center facility.

After a company creates an operation data center, it has a second significant problem—the data center is a single point of failure. Should the data center be damaged by fire, flood, weather, or an act of terrorism, the company's entire data processing capabilities will be shut down.

To reduce the risk of a single point of failure, companies often create a duplicate data center at a remote location, as shown in **FIGURE 4-2**. Should one of the data centers fail, the other can immediately take over operations. Unfortunately, the second data center will increase the company's costs—essentially doubling them—because there are duplicate servers, storage devices, network equipment, Internet access, and staffing.

FIGURE 4-1 Racks of servers within a data center.

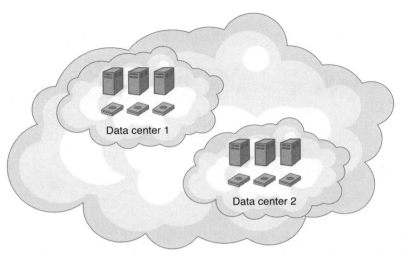

FIGURE 4-2 To eliminate a single point of failure, many companies colocate duplicate data centers.

For many smaller companies with simpler data processing needs, a PaaS may eliminate the need for their own data center. As you will recall, a PaaS solution typically provides one or more virtual servers running a specific operating system, as shown in **FIGURE 4-3**. Most PaaS solutions eliminate the customer's need to manage the operating system and supporting software.

In contrast, larger companies or companies with specific server needs may require their own independent server hardware and data storage devices. For such situations, IaaS is ideal. An IaaS solution provides a customer with its own hardware resources. You can think of IaaS as a mini data center within a large data center facility. Most IaaS providers, as shown in **FIGURE 4-4**, house data centers for multiple companies. Because the IaaS provider spreads the cost of power, air conditioning, fire suppression, and staff across multiple customers, it can normally offer pricing that beats what each individual company would have to pay for its own facility.

Further, just as with software as a service (SaaS) and PaaS solutions, customers pay IaaS providers only for the resources consumed. Simply put, IaaS solutions provide the least expensive (and fastest) way for companies to launch a data center or colocation facility.

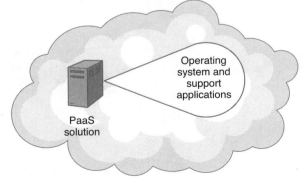

FIGURE 4-3 PaaS solutions allow smaller companies to eliminate the need for their own on-site data center.

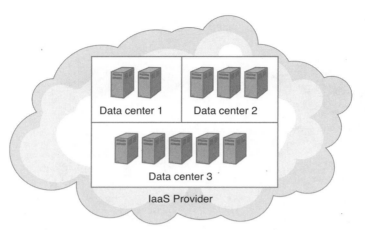

FIGURE 4–4 IaaS providers normally house data centers for many companies.

Improving Performance Through Load Balancing

Across the web, sites experience a wide range of network traffic requirements. Sites such as Google, Yahoo!, Amazon, and Microsoft experience millions of user hits per day. To handle such web requests, the sites use a technique known as **load balancing**, as shown in **FIGURE 4–5**, to share the requests across multiple servers.

For a simple web page, a client's web browser requests an HTML page and then the related graphics, CSS, and JavaScript files from the web server, as shown in **FIGURE 4–6**.

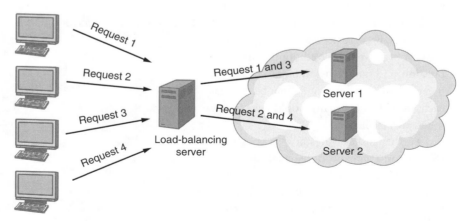

FIGURE 4–5 Load balancing uses a server to route traffic to multiple servers which, in turn, share the workload.

When the demand becomes too great for the server, the company can place a load-balancing server in front of two or more servers to which the load balancer distributes the web requests. Load balancing for simple applications is quite straightforward because either server can handle all requests.

When server-based applications become more complex, such as accessing data within a database, the developers must provide shared access to the database. To eliminate a single point of failure, companies often replicate copies of the database on multiple servers. The database software, in turn, must then synchronize data updates across the systems, as shown in **FIGURE 4-7**.

As an alternative, the company may choose to simplify the solution using a cloud-based database or a cloud-based **network-attached storage (NAS)** device, as shown in **FIGURE 4-8**. In this way, the applications do not need to worry about the data synchronization and replication—that task is handled within the cloud.

Taking a Closer Look at Load Balancing

To better understand load balancing, consider the processing that occurs when a user visits a site such

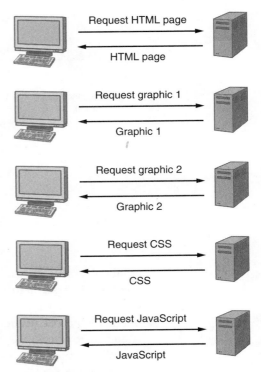

FIGURE 4-6 A client (browser) typically makes multiple requests to a server in order to download the HTML, CSS, JavaScript, and page graphics.

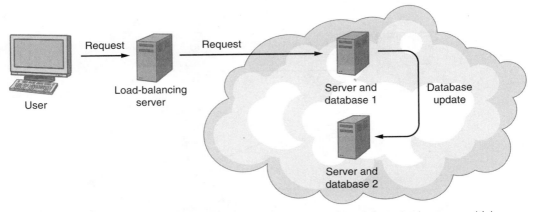

FIGURE 4-7 Load-balanced systems, for data redundancy purposes, often replicate databases on multiple servers. Each database, in turn, will send data updates to the other to maintain data synchronization between the servers.

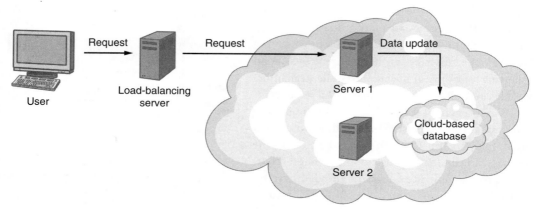

FIGURE 4-8 Using a cloud-based NAS device and a cloud-based database to handle database replication and load balancing.

as Yahoo! To start, the user types in a domain name, such as www.yahoo.com. The user's web browser, in turn, sends the domain name to a special server on the web called a domain name server (DNS), which, in turn, returns the site's (Yahoo!'s) Internet protocol (IP) address. As shown in **FIGURE 4-9**, the browser then uses the IP address to contact the server.

When a site uses load balancing, the IP address returned by the DNS might correspond to the load-balancing server. When the load balancer receives the browser request, it simply sends the request to one of the servers on a round-robin basis. If demand on the site increases, additional servers can be added, to which the load balancer can distribute requests. Using a similar technique, most IaaS solutions provide on-demand scaling and load balancing.

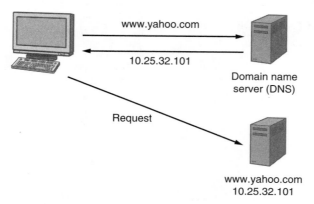

FIGURE 4-9 Web browsers use the IP address they receive from a DNS to access a server on the web.

System and Storage Redundancy

One of the greatest benefits of cloud-based computing is that it does not matter where the physical computing resources and data storage devices are located. As a result, companies often employ duplicate off-site servers or disk storage devices through a process known as **colocation**. As shown in **FIGURE 4-10**, by employing duplicate resources, systems can fail over from one location to another or they can use the duplicate systems for load balancing.

In this way, the colocated resources accomplish the following:

- Makes the company less susceptible to fire, acts of God, and terrorism
- Improves performance through a distributed workload
- Makes the company less susceptible to downtime due to power loss from a blackout or brownout

Over the past few years, the low-cost options offered by IaaS providers have made hardware **redundancy** a must-have item for companies that rely on the availability of key applications and data. Likewise, by leveraging cloud-based NAS devices and cloud-based database systems, companies can also easily replicate their data, as shown in **FIGURE 4-11**.

IaaS providers allow companies to add servers, processors, and RAM to their applications on demand. **FIGURE 4-12** shows an administrator window that allows an application administrator to select the resources the application needs—scaling resources up or down. Further, IaaS providers can also scale resource allocation up or down automatically. Customers, in turn, pay only for the resources they require.

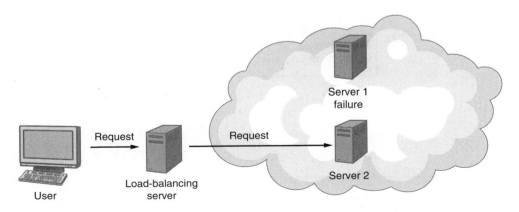

FIGURE 4-10 Companies use colocated computing resources for system failover or load balancing.

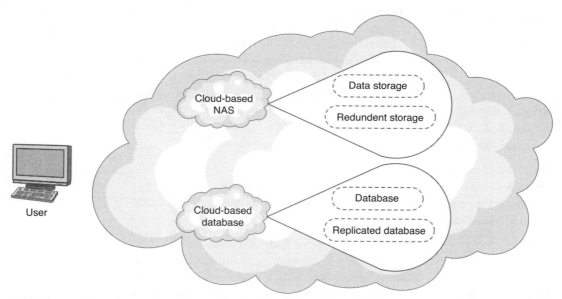

FIGURE 4–11 Using cloud-based NAS devices and cloud-based databases, companies can replicate key data within the cloud.

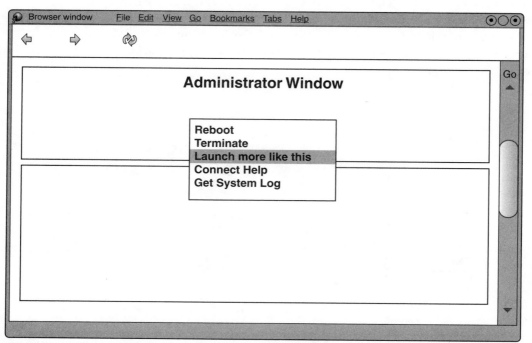

FIGURE 4–12 Using an administrator menu to allocate application resources.

CASE 4-1 RACKSPACE IAAS

Rackspace has emerged as one of the largest players in the IaaS market. Rackspace offers a set of solutions that include cloud hosting, managed hosting (including 24/7 data-center-like management), and hybrid solutions that combine the cloud and managed services.

Within minutes, from the Rackspace website an administrator can select a solution that deploys from 1 to 50 servers. Larger configurations are available. Today Rackspace offers cloud-based solutions to hundreds of thousands of clients. Rackspace houses its data centers at very large facilities located around the world.

With respect to the cloud, Rackspace offers pay-as-you-go scalability, with on-demand storage and load balancing. Beyond cloud hosting, Rackspace provides solutions for cloud-based e-mail, Exchange hosting, file sharing, backups, and collaboration.

Rackspace storage on demand is provided through a service called Cloud Files, a high-performance file system that provides very inexpensive redundant storage. The Cloud Files system was developed using OpenStack, a new open source software initiative for building private and public clouds. The goal of OpenStack is to create a massively scalable cloud operating system to accomplish the following:

- Leverage open standards to produce an environment less susceptible to vendor lock in (a situation in which a customer cannot easily move from an existing vendor)
- Increase industry-wide cloud standards
- Provide a platform that leverages performance and flexibility

Exercise Assume your company is planning to release a new .NET-based website. The company's developers estimate the application will require 10 servers to manage the workload. Visit the Rackspace website and recommend a solution for the company (you can use physical servers, virtual servers, or a combination of both). What start-up and monthly costs should your company expect?

Web Resources For additional information on Rackspace and OpenStack, see www.CloudBook Content.com/Chapter04/index.html.

Utilizing Cloud-Based NAS Devices

Chapter 6, *Data Storage in the Cloud*, examines cloud-based data storage and database systems in detail. The chapter also presents several solution providers. For now, you should understand that companies can move their data storage to the cloud in a number of ways. One of the most innovative disk storage solutions utilizes cloud-based NAS devices, which present devices and applications as

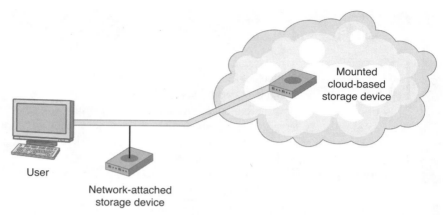

User

Network-attached
storage device

FIGURE 4-13 Cloud-based NAS devices present cloud-based storage as mountable devices, which may be replicated in the cloud to meet a company's data redundancy needs.

mountable drives and file systems. Normally customers can scale their cloud-based storage on demand and pay only for the storage they consume.

As shown in **FIGURE 4-13**, some cloud-based NAS devices provide behind-the-scenes data replication for data redundancy needs.

CASE 4-2 NIRVANIX IAAS

Nirvanix provides a wide range of cloud solutions, from public, private, and hybrid clouds to backup and off-site storage and **CloudNAS**, which is a cloud-based NAS solution. As shown in **FIGURE 4-14**, CloudNAS is a high-performance, scalable, secure, cloud-based file system that supports Linux- and Windows-based applications.

By supporting both the **Common Internet File System (CIFS)** and the **Network File System (NFS)**, CloudNAS seamlessly integrates into existing applications. In general, CloudNAS does not require programming or the development of an application program interface (API).

Exercise Within the cloud, IaaS providers offer a variety of ways for users and applications to access storage. Discuss the importance of having a cloud-based mountable storage device.

Web Resources For additional information on Nirvanix and CloudNAS, see www.CloudBook Content.com/Chapter04/index.html.

continues

CASE 4-2 NIRVANIX IAAS, continued

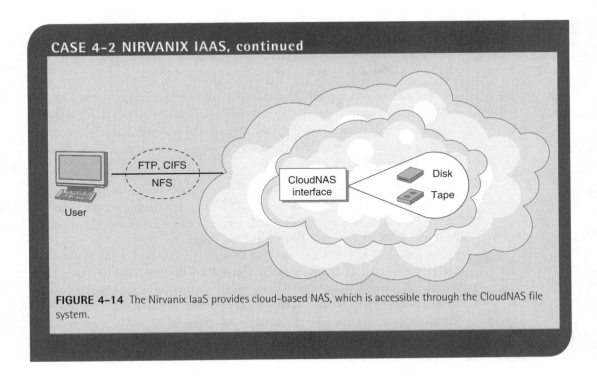

FIGURE 4-14 The Nirvanix IaaS provides cloud-based NAS, which is accessible through the CloudNAS file system.

Advantages of IaaS Solutions

In the simplest sense, IaaS is the process of providing the hardware necessary to run an application. By utilizing IaaS solutions, companies eliminate the need to house and maintain expensive data centers. Unlike PaaS, which also manages and administers the operating system and support software, an IaaS solution requires the customer to manage all software and take responsibility for maintaining system updates. Advantages of using an IaaS solution include the following:

- Elimination of an expensive and staff-intensive data center
- Ease of hardware scalability
- Reduced hardware cost
- On-demand, pay-as-you-go scalability
- Reduction of IT staff
- Ad hoc test environments suitability
- Complete system administration and management

Server Types Within an IaaS Solution

Within an IaaS environment, customers can acquire one or more servers. As shown in **FIGURE 4-15**, these servers fall under one of three types:

- **Physical server**: Actual hardware is allocated for the customer's dedicated use.
- **Dedicated virtual server**: The customer is allocated a virtual server, which runs on a physical server that may or may not have other virtual servers.
- **Shared virtual server**: The customer can access a virtual server on a device that may be shared with other customers.

An IaaS physical server solution allocates one or more physical servers to the customer. The servers will not be shared with other customers. The physical server, because it is not shared by others, will be more expensive. However, the customer will have complete control over the system.

A dedicated virtual server solution allocates to a customer one or more virtual servers, which, as discussed in Chapter 8, *Virtualization*, runs on a server that has special software installed to allow it to run multiple operating systems (which do not have to be the same). Each operating system is protected from others on the server and often can be configured by the customer. The virtual server is used by only one customer, which, again, will result in a slightly higher cost per month.

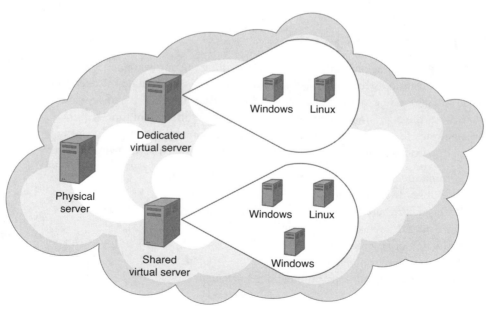

FIGURE 4-15 Within an IaaS environment, customers can allocate various server types.

A shared virtual server solution allocates a shared virtual server to a customer. The server may, for example, provide web server capabilities to multiple users. The customer cannot configure the shared virtual server.

CASE 4-3 LAYERED TECH IAAS

Layered Tech supports grid, virtualization, and cloud computing platforms. With Layered Tech solutions customers can quickly launch cloud-based applications, satisfy backup and remote storage requirements, or utilize high-security, high-availability servers.

Layered Tech provides traditional cloud-based services, such as dedicated servers, virtual servers, and managed server solutions. In addition, Layered Tech provides large-scale enterprise solutions, such as hosting, colocation, and virtualization.

If a client performs e-commerce operations, Layered Tech provides a Payment Card Industry (PCI)-compliant hosting system. By examining the PCI Data Security Standard (DSS), you can gain considerable insight into cloud-based security issues. For more information on the PCI DSS, visit the PCI Security Standards Council website at www.pcisecuritystandards.org.

Exercise Many cloud-based sites implement e-commerce operations. Discuss the purpose of and some of the standards involved in the PCI standards.

Web Resources For additional information on Layer Tech and PCI standards, see www.Cloud BookContent.com/Chapter04/index.html.

CHAPTER SUMMARY

Smaller companies that deploy applications to the cloud typically use a specific platform, such as Windows, .NET, and Microsoft SQL, or Linux, Perl, and MySQL. Companies that use a PaaS solution eliminate the need to administer the operating system and supporting software. Larger companies, because of security needs or a desire to manage all resources, turn to IaaS providers, which make all of the computing hardware resources available but leave the customer responsible for installing and managing the systems. This can normally be done over the Internet. You can think of an IaaS solution as a turnkey remote data center.

KEY TERMS

CloudNAS   Network-attached storage (NAS)
Colocation   Network File System (NFS)
Common Internet File System (CIFS)   Redundancy
Load balancing

CHAPTER REVIEW

1. Define and describe IaaS.

2. Define and describe system redundancy. Discuss how you might use IaaS to implement a redundancy plan.

3. Define and describe load balancing. Discuss how you might use IaaS to implement load balancing.

4. Define and describe NAS. Assume you must implement a shared file system within the cloud. What company would you select? Why? What costs should your client expect to pay for cloud-based data on a gigabyte (GB) basis?

5. Define and describe colocation. Discuss how you might use IaaS to implement colocation.

6. Compare and contrast a cloud-based disk storage device (with a file system) with a cloud-based database.

7. Compare and contrast physical, dedicated virtual, and shared virtual servers. Search the web for companies that provide each. What cost should a customer expect to pay for each?

Identity as a Service (IDaaS)

TODAY, WITHIN MOST COMPANIES, users must log in to a variety of different systems in order to perform various tasks. Some of the systems may be cloud based, some may be based on local servers, and some may be accessible through different devices. The challenge of having multiple servers to access is that users must remember and manage multiple username and password combinations. Further, if an employee leaves the company, the IT staff must coordinate with the human resources department to ensure that each of the user's accounts has been disabled. User identity management (ID management) is difficult, time consuming, and expensive. Over the past few years, companies have begun to emerge to provide **identity (or identification) as a service (IDaaS),** or cloud-based ID management.

Learning Objectives

This chapter examines cloud-based ID management in detail. By the time you finish this chapter, you will be able to do the following:

- Describe challenges related to ID management.
- Describe and discuss single sign-on (SSO) capabilities.
- List the advantages of IDaaS solutions.
- Discuss IDaaS solutions offered by various companies.

Understanding Single Sign-On (SSO)

As discussed, business users today must log in to a variety of applications, which may reside on many different servers. The users, therefore, must manage numerous username and password combinations. To simplify user access to multiple systems, many companies now use **single sign-on (SSO)** software, which, as shown in **FIGURE 5-1**, requires the user to sign on only one time. Behind the scenes, the SSO software manages the user's access to other systems.

The advantages of SSO software include the following:

- Fewer username and password combinations for users to remember and manage
- Less password fatigue caused by the stress of managing multiple passwords
- Less user time consumed by having to log in to individual systems
- Fewer calls to help desks for forgotten passwords
- A centralized location for IT staff to manage password compliance and reporting

The primary disadvantage of SSO systems is the potential for a single source of failure. If the authentication server fails, users will not be able to log in to other servers. Thus, having a cloud-based authentication server with system redundancy reduces the risk of system unavailability.

Understanding How SSO Works

Although different implementations of SSO exist, many solutions employ a secure ticket. When a user logs in to the authentication server, he or she is given a secure ticket. Later, when the user accesses a server, that server, in turn, validates the

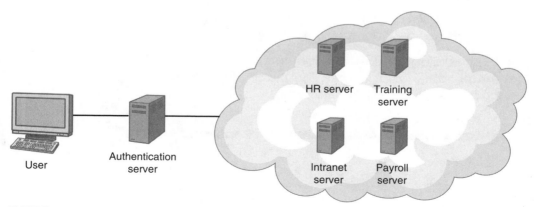

FIGURE 5-1 An SSO system lets a user log in to a system one time and then move freely among related servers and applications without having to authenticate him- or herself each time.

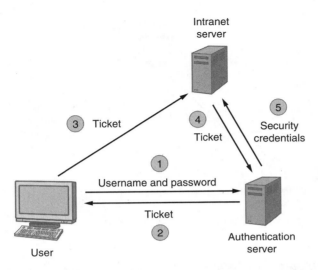

Step 1: User logs into the authentication server using a username and password

Step 2: The authentication server returns the user's ticket

Step 3: User sends the ticket to the intranet server

Step 4: Intranet server sends the ticket to the authentication server

Step 5: Authentication server sends the user's security credentials for that server
         back to the intranet server

FIGURE 5-2 SSO systems often assign authenticated users a ticket, which the software presents behind the scenes to the servers that the user accesses. Each server can use the ticket to determine the user's access rights on that particular server.

ticket with the authentication server. The authentication server, as shown in **FIGURE 5-2**, not only confirms that the user is authorized to use the server, but may also provide the user's access rights that are specific to that server.

If an employee leaves the company, the IT staff need only disable the user at the authentication server in order to disable the user's access to all systems.

Understanding Federated Identity Management

As you examine SSO solutions, you may encounter the term **federated identity management (FIDM)**. In short, FIDM describes the technologies and protocols that combine to enable a user to bring security credentials across different security domains (different servers running potentially different operating systems). Behind the scenes, many FIDM systems use the **Security Assertion Markup Language (SAML)** to package a user's security credentials, as shown in **FIGURE 5-3**. For specifics on SAML, visit the SAML website at www.saml.xml.org.

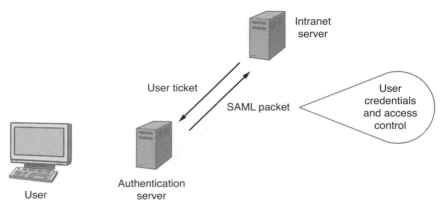

FIGURE 5-3 SAML allows software to package user security credentials.

Understanding Account Provisioning

In many companies, when an employee is hired the human resources department sends an e-mail to the IT staff, who creates a user account for the employee. Sometime during the employee's first week, his or her manager will decide that the employee needs to access other systems. The manager will send additional e-mails to the IT staff requesting various account access. The process of creating a user account on a system is called account **provisioning**. As you might guess, because different employees may need different capabilities on each system, the provisioning process can be complex.

When an employee leaves the company, a deprovisioning process must occur to remove the user's accounts. Unfortunately, the IT staff is not always immediately informed that an employee no longer works for the company, or the IT staff misses a server account and the user may still have access to one or more systems.

CASE 5-1 PING IDENTITY IDAAS

Ping Identity provides cloud-based ID management software that supports FIDM and user account provisioning. The company's website provides an excellent article called "The 4 A's of Cloud Identity," which are as follows:

- **Authentication**: The process of determining and validating a user for on-site as well as cloud-based solutions.
- **Authorization**: The process of determining and specifying what the user is allowed to do on each server.

continues

CASE 5-1 PING IDENTITY IDAAS, continued

- **Account management**: The process of synchronizing user accounts by provisioning and deprovisioning access.
- **Audit logging**: The process of tracking which applications users access and when. To perform its ID management, Ping Identity makes extensive use of SAML.

Exercise Discuss the importance of the audit logging process within an IDaaS solution.

Web Resources For additional information on Ping Identity and SAML, see www.CloudBook Content.com/Chapter05/index.html.

CASE 5-2 PASSWORDBANK IDAAS

PasswordBank provides an IDaaS solution that supports on-site and cloud-based system access. Its FIDM service supports enterprise-wide SSO (E-SSO) and SSO for web-based applications (WebSSO). The PasswordBank solutions perform the FIDM without the use of SAML. PasswordBank solutions support a myriad of devices, including the iPhone.

Exercise Within the cloud, some IDaaS providers use SAML to package a user's security credentials, and some do not. Discuss the arguments for and against using SAML.

Web Resources For additional information on PasswordBank, see www.CloudBookContent .com/Chapter05/index.html.

Understanding OpenID

For companies to support FIDM across autonomous systems, the security policies and protocols must be open. OpenID allows users to use an existing account to log in to multiple websites. Today, more than 1 billion OpenID accounts exist and are accepted by thousands of websites. Companies that support OpenID include Google, Yahoo!, Flickr, Myspace, WordPress.com, and more. For companies, the advantages of using OpenID include the following:

- Increased site conversion rates (rates at which customers choose to join websites) because users do not need to register
- Access to greater user profile content
- Fewer problems with lost passwords
- Ease of content integration into social networking sites

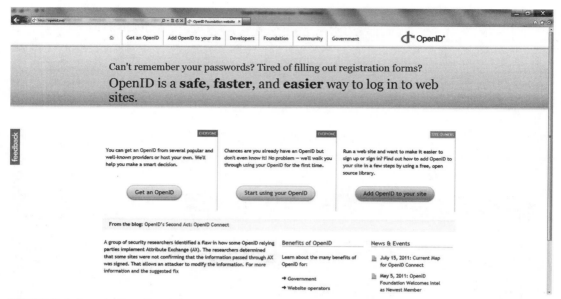

FIGURE 5-4 From the OpenID website, you can create your own OpenID username and password, which you can then use to access thousands of websites.

For more information on OpenID, or to get your own OpenID username and password, visit the OpenID website at www.openid.net, as shown in **FIGURE 5-4**.

Mobile ID Management

Every day employees access e-mail and other business applications through hand-held devices. More and more business applications support mobile device

CASE 5-3 SYMPLIFIED IDAAS

Symplified provides ID management solutions for on-site and cloud-based applications. The solutions support a variety of device types, such as mobile devices. Symplified solutions support SAML and non-SAML-based applications, which significantly extends the company's product reach. Symplified's key products include:

- **Symplified Access Manager**: This compliance tool provides on-demand web access management for access control and audit of software as a service (SaaS), private cloud, and public cloud applications.

continues

CASE 5-3 SYMPLIFIED IDAAS, continued

- **Symplified Identity Manager**: This account management tool provides user account support for on-site and SaaS solutions.
- **SinglePoint**: This platform as a service (PaaS) solution provides a cloud-based platform for deploying ID management, with the following capabilities:
  - Access control
  - Authentication
  - Auditing
  - Federation
  - Provisioning and user management
  - Support for portals

Exercise Symplified provides IDaaS solutions for on-site and cloud operations. Discuss the additional requirements and challenges of implementing a solution for cloud-based applications over on-ground applications.

Web Resources For additional information on Symplified and the company's IDaaS solutions, see www.CloudBookContent.com/Chapter05/index.html.

interfaces. The challenge for developers today is not only getting content to the mobile device, but also securing the device. Threats to mobile devices include the following:

- Identity theft if a device is lost or stolen
- Eavesdropping on data communications
- Surveillance of confidential screen content
- Phishing of content from rogue sites
- Man-in-the-middle attacks through intercepted signals
- Inadequate device resources to provide a strong security implementation
- Social attacks on unaware users that yield identity information

CHAPTER SUMMARY

To accomplish a wide range of tasks, users must often log in to a variety of different systems. Today some of the systems may be cloud based and some may reside on local servers. Further, users often access servers (and their services) through different devices. Requiring users to access multiple servers means that users must often remember and manage multiple username and password combinations. To reduce this burden on users as well as the IT staff who must help retrieve forgotten passwords, many companies now use a technique called SSO. Users log in to a central authorization server that, in turn, uses a ticket that grants users access to other specific servers without requiring them to log in again. In this way, users must remember only one username and password.

If an employee leaves the company, the IT staff need only disable the user's account on the centralized authorization server in order to shut down the user's access to all other servers.

User ID management is difficult, time consuming, and expensive. To address the challenges and cost of user management, many companies are turning to IDaaS solutions that reside in the cloud.

KEY TERMS

Federated identity management (FIDM)
Identity (or identification) as
   a service (IDaaS)
Provisioning

Security Assertion Markup
   Language (SAML)
Single sign-on (SSO)

CHAPTER REVIEW

1. Define and describe SSO.
2. Define and describe IDaaS.
3. Define SAML and describe its purpose.
4. Define and describe provisioning.
5. Define and describe FIDM.
6. List factors that make mobile ID management difficult.

Data Storage in the Cloud

CHAPTER 4, "INFRASTRUCTURE AS a Service (IaaS)," examined the process of using a service provider's servers and data storage equipment. Within the IaaS model, the customer is responsible for installing and maintaining the software that runs on the platform. Chapter 4 introduced the use of cloud-based data storage and databases.

Learning Objectives

This chapter will examine cloud-based storage in detail. By the time you finish this chapter, you will be able to do the following:

- Discuss the role of storage-area networks.
- Discuss the role of network-attached storage.
- Describe cloud-based storage solutions.
- List the pros and cons of cloud-based storage.
- Describe cloud-based database solutions.
- List the pros and cons of cloud-based databases.
- Describe specific cloud-based data storage solutions such as backups and encrypted file storage.
- Provide an example of an industry-specific cloud-based storage solution.

Examining the Evolution of Network Storage

Years ago, local-area networks used special servers, called file servers, to support file sharing, file replication, and storage for large files. As shown in **FIGURE 6-1**,

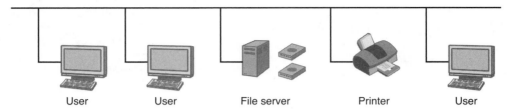

FIGURE 6-1 Local-area networks had one or more file servers that users could access across the network to store and retrieve files.

the file server was a server on the network with large disk capacity that users could use to store and retrieve files. Over time, operating systems, specifically the **file system** within the operating system, evolved to allow users and applications to open files directly on the file server.

As computer networks evolved, the file server was extended through the use of **storage-area networks (SANs)**, which, as shown in **FIGURE 6-2**, could make one or more storage devices appear to be directly connected to the network. Behind the scenes, the devices were actually connected to SAN hardware through the use of network cables. Software running within the SAN device made the devices appear directly accessible to the rest of the network.

As storage demands continued to increase—as did disk storage capacities—network-attached storage (NAS) devices emerged, which, as shown in **FIGURE 6-3**, plug directly into the network.

The advantages of SANs include the following:

- **Reliability**: A NAS device typically provides advanced data striping across multiple volumes within the device. If one (or more) volumes fail, the data striping would maintain the data and allow reconstruction of the file contents.
- **Performance**: Because a NAS device does not run a complete operating system, the hardware has less system overhead, which allows it to outperform a file server.

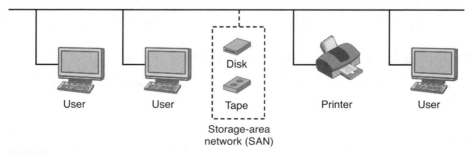

FIGURE 6-2 SANs allowed administrators to connect various storage devices to a computer network.

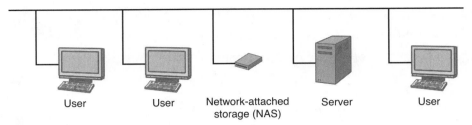

FIGURE 6-3 NAS devices are disk volumes that plug directly into the network.

- **Compatibility:** NAS devices normally support common file systems, which, in turn, make them fully compatible with common operating systems.
- **Ease of performing backups:** NAS devices are commonly used for backup devices. Within a home, for example, all devices can easily access and back up files to a NAS device.

Understanding Cloud-Based Data Storage

Cloud-based data storage is the next step in the evolution of NAS devices. Across the web (the cloud), many providers offer data storage that resides in the cloud. Depending on your access needs, the data may be accessible as follows:

- Through a web browser interface that lets you move files to and from the storage area using a variety of devices

CASE 6-1 HOMEPIPE REMOTE FILE ACCESS

Many users now rely on cloud-based storage to provide them with access to files from anywhere at any time, often with any device. Despite that, users still encounter situations when the file they need resides on a computer at their home or office—often because they made a last-minute change and forgot to upload the file to the cloud. That's where HomePipe comes to rescue. HomePipe is a program that lets users access files on their own system from anywhere on the web. Further, HomePipe supports file access from a variety of devices. And beyond that, HomePipe makes it easy for you to share specific files with other users. **FIGURE 6-4** illustrates the use of HomePipe to access files on a remote system using a web browser.

Exercise Compare and contrast the use of HomePipe with that of a tool such as GoToMyPC.

Web Resources For more information on HomePipe, see www.CloudBookContent.com/Chapter06/index.html.

continues

CASE 6-1 HOMEPIPE REMOTE FILE ACCESS, continued

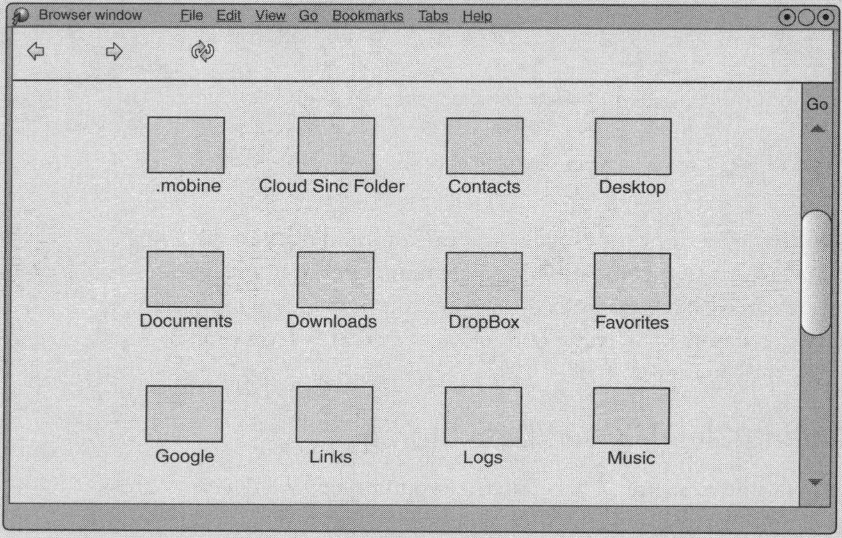

FIGURE 6-4 Using HomePipe to access files from a system across the Internet.

- Through a mounted disk drive that appears locally to your computer as a disk drive letter or mounted file system
- For application developers, the storage area may present itself through a set of application program interface (API) calls

CASE 6-2 ZUMODRIVE CLOUD-BASED STORAGE

ZumoDrive provides cloud-based storage that is scalable to meet customer needs. The company lets a customer get started at no charge and provides sufficient space to store a considerable number of documents. The files that are stored on ZumoDrive are accessible from a variety of devices. From their own PC, customers can use the web interface shown in **FIGURE 6-5** to move files to or from ZumoDrive.

In addition, you can map a drive letter to your ZumoDrive storage and the access your cloud-based files as you would files from your local system. **FIGURE 6-6** shows ZumoDrive as drive Z within Windows Internet Explorer.

continues

CASE 6-2 ZUMODRIVE CLOUD-BASED STORAGE, continued

Exercise Discuss why a user may need access to cloud-based storage from a variety of device types.

Web Resources For more information on ZumoDrive, see www.CloudBookContent.com/Chapter06/index.html.

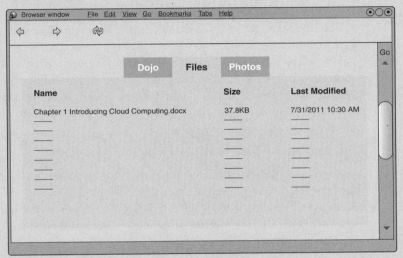

FIGURE 6-5 ZumoDrive provides a web interface that lets users easily move files to or from their ZumoDrive storage from any device.

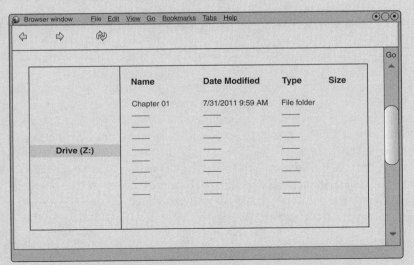

FIGURE 6-6 ZumoDrive lets users map a logical drive letter to their cloud-based storage area.

Advantages and Disadvantages of Cloud-Based Data Storage

Cloud-based data storage provides the following advantages:

- **Scalability**: Most cloud-based data storage providers let you scale your storage capacity (up or down) to align with your storage needs.
- **Pay for use**: With most cloud-based data storage facilities, users pay only for the storage (within a range) that they need.
- **Reliability**: Many cloud-based data storage facilities provide transparent data replication.
- **Ease of access**: Most cloud-based data storage facilities support web-based access to files from any place, at any time, using a variety of devices.
- **Ease of use**: Many cloud-based data storage solutions let users map a drive letter to the remote file storage area and then access the files through the use of a logical drive.

Disadvantages of cloud-based storage include the following:

- **Performance**: Because the cloud-based disk storage devices are accessed over the Internet, they will never be as fast as local drives.
- **Security**: Some users will never feel comfortable with their data in the cloud.
- **Data orphans**: Users may abandon data in cloud storage facilities, leaving confidential private or company data at risk.

CASE 6-3 DROPBOX CLOUD-BASED FILE SHARING AND SYNCHRONIZATION

Most users today manage their content on a variety of devices. Dropbox is a cloud-based storage facility for photos, documents, and other digital content. After you download and install Dropbox, your system will have a user-level Dropbox folder, as shown in **FIGURE 6-7**.

When you place a file into the Dropbox folder (either by cutting and pasting, dragging and dropping, or saving), a copy of the file is automatically saved to the Dropbox cloud storage facility. If you later need to access the file from another computer, you can simply log in to your Dropbox account on the web, and, as shown in **FIGURE 6-8**, your files will be accessible through your browser.

Dropbox also makes it very easy for users to share files. If, for example, you place a file within the Dropbox Public folder, you can then send a link to other users, which they can use to access the file. Dropbox supports a variety of devices. Also, Dropbox lets users try the software free of charge and provides them with ample storage space to get started.

Exercise Discuss the benefits of having web-based access to a cloud storage area.

Web Resources For more information on Dropbox, see www.CloudBookContent.com/Chapter06/index.html.

continues

CASE 6-3 DROPBOX CLOUD–BASED FILE SHARING AND SYNCHRONIZATION, continued

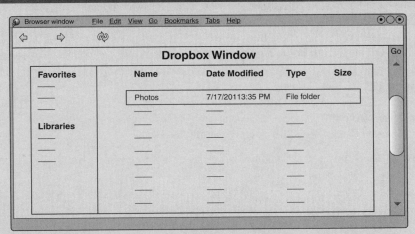

FIGURE 6–7 Users can easily drag and drop files to the Dropbox file folder structure.

FIGURE 6–8 Dropbox users can access their files through the web, from any device.

CASE 6-4 MICROSOFT SKYDRIVE

Cloud-based data storage systems allow users to access their documents from any place at any time. Given Microsoft's presence within software as a service (SaaS) and platform as a service (PaaS) solutions, you might expect them to have a significant presence within cloud-based storage—and you would be right. Microsoft SkyDrive provides cloud-based data storage. Through the SkyDrive web interface, you can drag and drop files to and from the cloud, as shown in **FIGURE 6–9**.

What makes SkyDrive special is that if the PC from which you are accessing the files does not have Microsoft Office installed, SkyDrive lets you launch Word, Excel, and PowerPoint documents within Microsoft Office Web Apps, as shown **FIGURE 6–10**.

Exercise Discuss the need for a company to have a policy covering the types of documents employees can store within the cloud.

Web Resources For more information on SkyDrive, see www.CloudBookContent.com/Chapter06/index.html.

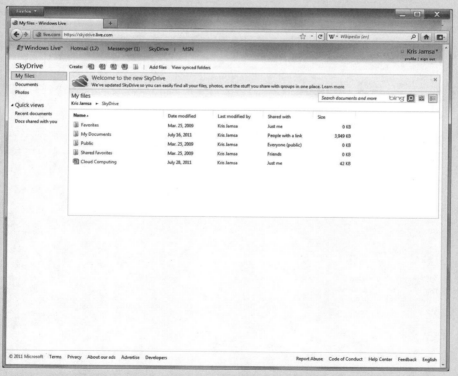

FIGURE 6–9 Using the SkyDrive web interface to access cloud-based files.

continues

CASE 6-4 MICROSOFT SKYDRIVE, continued

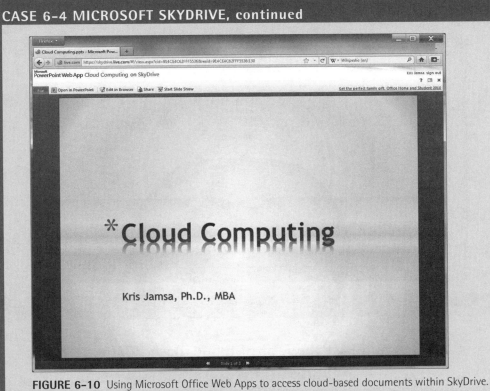

FIGURE 6-10 Using Microsoft Office Web Apps to access cloud-based documents within SkyDrive.

CASE 6-5 MOUNTING CLOUD DEVICES USING GLADINET

As you have learned, most cloud-based data storage facilities provide a drag-and-drop user interface that you can use to move files to and from the cloud. Some cloud storage systems also let you access your files using a logical disk drive letter, treating the cloud-based files as if they reside on a disk drive that is local to your system.

Gladinet provides software you can use to mount many cloud-based data storage services as a drive letter. **FIGURE 6-11**, for example, shows Microsoft SkyDrive mounted using a drive letter. In this way, you can access the SkyDrive-based files just as you would any files on your system.

Exercise Discuss what it means to mount a storage device and the importance of being able to do so.

Web Resources For more information on Gladinet, see www.CloudBookContent.com/Chapter06/index.html.

continues

CASE 6-5 MOUNTING CLOUD DEVICES USING GLADINET, continued

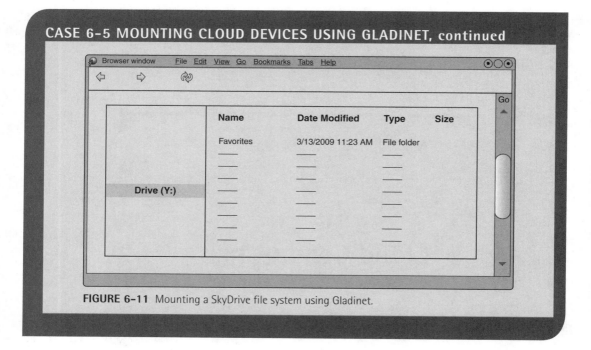

	Name	Date Modified	Type	Size
Drive (Y:)	Favorites	3/13/2009 11:23 AM	File folder	

FIGURE 6-11 Mounting a SkyDrive file system using Gladinet.

Getting Past the Fear of Cloud-Based Data

As discussed, one of the disadvantages of cloud-based data storage is that some users simply do not feel comfortable placing their data within the cloud. One approach to such user apprehension is to encrypt the files that you place on the

CASE 6-6 BOXCRYPTOR CLOUD-BASED FILE ENCRYPTION

BoxCryptor is a software tool that encrypts and decrypts cloud-based files on a file-by-file basis. When you install BoxCryptor, the installation process will create a folder within your cloud-based folder on your system and will map a drive letter to that folder. When you use the drive letter to store a file, BoxCryptor will encrypt the file and place the encrypted contents on the cloud. When you later retrieve the file, BoxCryptor will decrypt the file on the fly. If a hacker gains access to your cloud storage, the encrypted file's contents will be unusable, as shown in **FIGURE 6-12**.

Exercise Discuss your level of confidence that files residing in the cloud are secure.

Web Resources For more information on BoxCryptor, see www.CloudBookContent.com/Chapter06/index.html.

continues

CASE 6-6 BOXCRYPTOR CLOUD-BASED FILE ENCRYPTION, continued

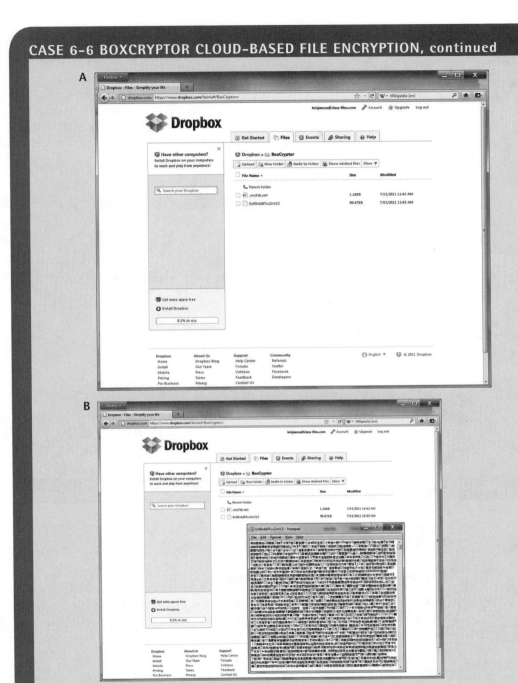

FIGURE 6-12 Encrypted BoxCryptor files within the cloud.

CASE 6-7 MOZY CLOUD-BASED BACKUPS

Mozy provides cloud-based backups for personal and business users. Mozy provides an encrypted backup and runs without the need for user intervention on Windows- and Mac-based systems. Mozy has existed as a company since 2005 and has millions of customers worldwide. **FIGURE 6-13** shows a Mozy screen with which you select files for your backup set.

Exercise Discuss the pros and cons of cloud-based file backups.

Web Resources For more information on Mozy, see www.CloudBookContent.com/Chapter06/index.html.

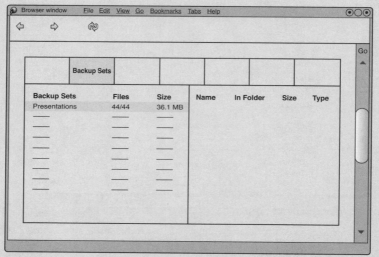

FIGURE 6-13 Selecting files for backup within Mozy.

cloud. Several companies offer software that will encrypt and decrypt files on the fly, as they are sent to and retrieved from the cloud.

Cloud-Based Backup Systems

In Chapter 2, *Software as a Service (SaaS)*, you examined the Carbonite cloud-based backup software. Several companies provide cloud-based backup capabilities. The features that most companies provide are similar:

- Files are backed up in an encrypted format.
- Users can schedule when backup operations are to occur.
- Users can easily retrieve backup files from the cloud.
- Most systems support Windows, Linux, and Mac OS.

Understanding File Systems

Operating systems exist to allow users to run programs and to store and retrieve data (files) from one user session to the next. Within the operating system, special software, called the file system, oversees the storage and retrieval of files to and from a disk. When you copy a file, delete a file, or create and move files between folders, the file system is performing the work.

Initially, file systems allowed users to manipulate only local files that reside on one of the PC's disk drives. As networks became more prevalent, so too did network operating systems, which allow users and programs to manipulate files

CASE 6-8 ORACLE CLOUD FILE SYSTEM

Oracle is one of the world's leading database solution providers. Oracle has on-site and cloud-based database solutions. In addition, Oracle offers a cloud-based file system that users can use to store and retrieve files that will reside outside of the database. As shown in **FIGURE 6-14**, the Oracle Cloud File System resides above cloud-based storage devices and supports Windows- and Linux-based applications.

The advantages of Oracle's Cloud File System include the following:

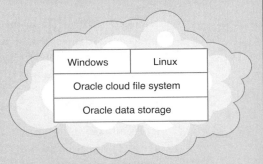

FIGURE 6-14 Oracle provides a cloud-based file system that is accessible by Windows and Linux.

- **Snapshot-based file recovery:** Files can be recovered to a specific data snapshot that allows simpler fallback.
- **File group by tagging:** Users can associate one or more files via a tag name grouping for subsequent group-based file operations, such as replication.
- **File replication:** Key files can be replicated across multiple volumes.
- **Access-control-based security:** Administrators can finely control access to specific files via access control lists.
- **Encryption:** The Oracle Cloud File System supports file-by-file, directory, or file system encryption.

Exercise Explain the process of snapshots and how it may be important to an application developer.

Web Resources For more information on the Oracle Cloud File System, see www.CloudBook Content.com/Chapter06/index.html.

CASE 6-9 APACHE HADOOP DISTRIBUTED FILE SYSTEM

Apache Hadoop is an open source project, the goal of which is to support reliable, scalable distributed computing. Part of the project includes the Hadoop Distributed File System (HDFS), a Java-based file system that is well suited for cloud-based storage. HDFS is designed to be highly fault tolerant and robust to maintain operation in the event of a device failure. For specifics on HDFS, visit http://hadoop.apache.org/hdfs.

Exercise Discuss the features of Hadoop that make it well suited for a cloud-based file system.

Web Resources For more information on the Hadoop system, see www.CloudBookContent.com/Chapter06/index.html.

residing on a device across the network. A **cloud file system (CFS)** allows users or applications to directly manipulate files that reside on the cloud.

Today several cloud file systems are emerging that allow users and programs to manipulate files residing in the cloud.

Industry-Specific Cloud-Based Data Storage

Across different industries, groups have different data storage and access requirements. The healthcare industry, for example, is working to standardize secure electronic medical records, which, as shown in **FIGURE 6-15**, will be accessible from the cloud by a variety of medical facilities.

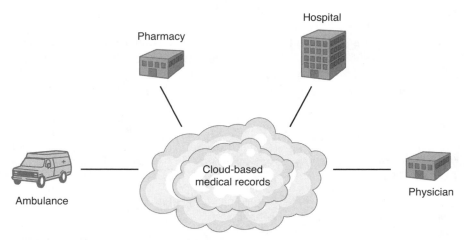

FIGURE 6-15 In the future, healthcare data will be accessible in real time to a wide range of medical facilities, some on-ground and some mobile.

CASE 6-10 MICROSOFT HEALTHVAULT

Microsoft HealthVault provides a secure storage facility within which people can store their medical records, prescriptions, and even measurements from a variety of medical devices. People can use Microsoft HealthVault to track their own medical records or those of family members for whom they assist with medical care. After you store records within Microsoft HealthVault, you can e-mail a link to a physician, other healthcare personnel, or a family member to grant access to all or specific records. You can also set an expiration date that removes an individual's access. **FIGURE 6-16** shows the Microsoft HealthVault home page.

Exercise Discuss potential risks of placing your health data within the cloud.

Web Resources For more information on HealthVault, see www.CloudBookContent.com/ Chapter06/index.html.

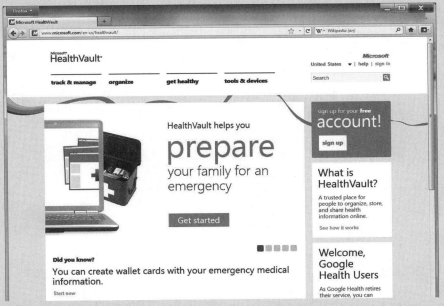

FIGURE 6-16 Microsoft HealthVault lets users store medical records within the cloud.

Cloud-Based Database Solutions

Many PaaS solutions include support for a database, such as Microsoft SQL Server or MySQL. Often these database solutions connect to a cloud-based server, as shown in **FIGURE 6-17**, and, as such, can be considered a cloud-based database.

A better definition of a cloud-based database, however, is a database that can be used not only by applications that reside (are hosted) in the cloud, but also by

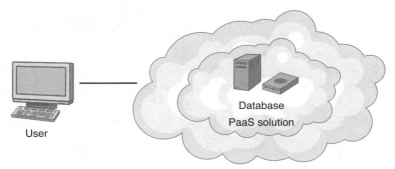

FIGURE 6–17 A cloud-based database provided with a PaaS solution.

applications that reside within the customer's on-site data center, as shown in **FIGURE 6–18**.

Advantages of cloud-based database solutions include the following:

* **Cost-effective database scalability**: Cloud-based databases can scale dynamically to meet customer needs on a pay-as-you-go basis.
* **High availability**: Cloud-based database systems normally reside on redundant hardware, which results in high system uptime.

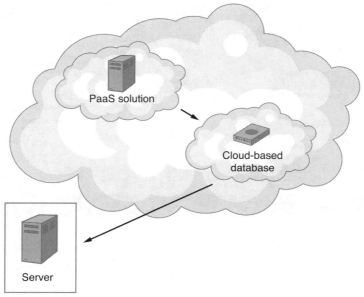

FIGURE 6–18 A cloud-based database should be accessible by systems across the web.

- **High data redundancy**: Cloud-based databases are normally replicated behind the scenes to increase data availability.
- **Reduced administration**: The cloud-based database provider maintains the database version updates and patches.

The disadvantages of cloud-based databases include the following:

- **Data security concerns**: Some users still do not feel comfortable storing a database system in the cloud.
- **Performance**: Because data queries may travel the Internet, the cloud-based database access will not be as fast as a local database solution.

CASE 6-11 MICROSOFT SQL AZURE

Microsoft SQL Azure is a cloud-based database solution that supports not only Windows Azure PaaS, but, as shown in **FIGURE 6-19**, on-site applications as well.

As you would expect, SQL Azure provides scalability, database replication, load balancing, and automatic server failover.

Exercise Discuss the steps a developer must perform to connect to an SQL Azure database.

Web Resources For more information on SQL Azure, see www.CloudBookContent.com/Chapter06/index.html.

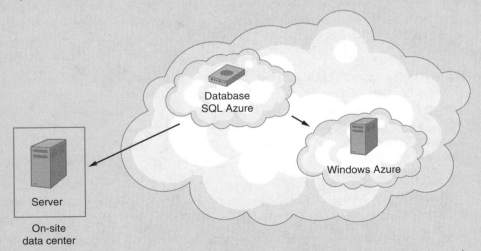

FIGURE 6-19 SQL Azure is a cloud-based database that supports local (PaaS server-based access) and remote application access.

CASE 6-12 AMAZON CLOUD-BASED DATABASE SOLUTIONS

As discussed in Chapter 1, *Introducing Cloud Computing*, Amazon is one of the leading providers of cloud-based hosting solutions. To meet developer demands for cloud-based database storage solutions, Amazon provides two key solutions:

- **Amazon Relational Database Service (Amazon RDS):** A web service that makes available the capabilities of MySQL and Oracle through API web service calls
- **Amazon SimpleDB:** A scalable, nonrelational data store in which developers can quickly store and query data items using API-driven web service calls

Exercise Discuss reasons why Amazon chose to support MySQL and Oracle databases.

Web Resources For more information on the Amazon database solutions, see www.CloudBook Content.com/Chapter06/index.html.

DATABASE.COM CLOUD-BASED DATABASE

Database.com provides applications with access to a cloud-based database through a library of API calls. All access to the underlying database is via developer-written code. Database .com does not provide a user interface to the database—instead, its focus is on the database itself:

- **Administration:** Database.com administers all aspects of the database.
- **Performance tuning:** Database.com monitors and manages the overall database performance.
- **Scalability:** Database.com can scale a solution up or down dynamically to meet user demands.
- **Backups:** Database.com manages data backups and redundancy.
- **Disaster recovery:** Database.com provides redundant hardware and storage to reduce the risk of a disaster.

Developers create applications that call the Database.com API using a variety of programming languages, including C#, Java, Perl, PHP, Ruby, and more.

Exercise Discuss the pros and cons of restricting database access to developers using an API.

Web Resources For more information on Database.com, see www.CloudBookContent.com/Chapter06/index.html.

Cloud-Based Block Storage

In the simplest sense, a block of data storage is a fixed-sized sequence of bits. The size of the block normally corresponds to an underlying unit of storage on the **cloud-based block storage device**. Some applications work with very large blocks of data, the format of which has meaning only to the application itself—meaning that the data may not map well to storage within a file system or database. To support applications with large data block needs, Amazon provides the Amazon Elastic Block Store (EBS), a highly reliable, scalable, and available block storage solution. EBS supports block sizes up to a terabyte.

The data within the EBS is simply a collection of bits. To manage the block data in a meaningful way, developers may need to create their own file system. In this way, the applications that use the cloud-based block storage are in complete control of the data contents.

CLOUD DATA MANAGEMENT INTERFACE (CDMI)

The Storage Networking Industry Association (SNIA) is a not-for-profit association consisting of members from hundreds of companies that share the goal of standardizing data storage solutions. SNIA is working on the **Cloud Data Management Interface (CDMI)**, which defines the behind-the-scenes functional interface that applications will use to create, retrieve, update, and delete cloud-based data items.

A goal of CDMI is that cloud-based storage facilities be discoverable to applications. This means that applications can query the facility for the data services it provides. In addition, CDMI is setting the stage for metadata assignment to data items that will be key to the development of Web 3.0 semantic capabilities.

Exercise Discuss the role of metadata within cloud-based data storage.

Web Resources For more information on the CDMI, see www.CloudBookContent.com/Chapter06/index.html.

Chapter Summary

Within PaaS and IaaS solutions, customers often take advantage of provider-based disk storage solutions. In some cases, users don't need cloud-based processing capabilities, but rather scalable and replicated data storage solutions. In such cases, users and applications can access cloud-based data storage and cloud-based database systems. In some cases local (on-site) applications may access the cloud-based storage, and in other cases the applications may also reside in the cloud. This chapter examined a variety of cloud-based data storage solutions. As you learned, many of the data storage providers include a web-based user interface that lets users access files anywhere at any time, often with any device. Further, some systems allow users to mount the remote storage area using a logical disk drive to which they can refer as they would any local disk drive letter.

Key Terms

Cloud-based block storage device   File system
Cloud Data Management Interface (CDMI)   Storage-area network (SAN)
Cloud file system (CFS)

Chapter Review

1. Define and describe a SAN.
2. Define and describe NAS.
3. Describe how cloud-based data storage works.
4. Assume that you must select a cloud-based data storage solution for your company. List the factors you would consider when selecting a vendor.
5. Many users do not yet feel comfortable storing data within the cloud. Discuss some steps you can take to reduce their concerns.
6. Assume that you must select a cloud-based data storage solution for your company. List the factors you would consider when selecting a vendor.
7. List the pros and cons of cloud-based data storage.
8. List the pros and cons of a cloud-based database.

Collaboration in the Cloud

IT WASN'T ALWAYS A good thing when people at a meeting were said to have their heads in the clouds. Today, however, cloud-based meetings and cloud-based collaboration tools are some of the information technology industry's hottest items. What began as web-based e-mail has exploded to include cloud-based conference meetings, face-to-face voice over Internet protocol phone calls on virtually any device, document sharing, and streaming media content.

Learning Objectives

This chapter examines cloud-based collaboration in detail. By the time you finish this chapter, you will be able to do the following:

- Define and describe collaboration.
- Define and describe cloud-based collaboration.
- List the benefits of cloud-based collaboration.
- List and describe cloud-based tools for document sharing.
- List questions that one should consider with respect to cloud-based collaboration tools.
- Discuss the potential uses of cloud-based streaming media, from presentations to TV.

Collaborating in the Clouds

In the simplest sense, **collaboration** is the process of two or more people working together to achieve a result (a goal). For years, teams would meet in conference

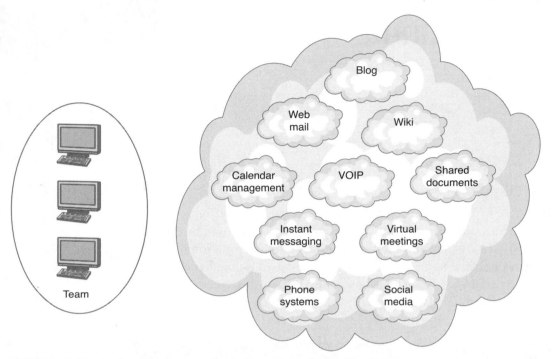

FIGURE 7-1 The cloud provides team members with a variety of tools with which they can collaborate.

rooms to collaborate. Depending on the scope and importance of the project, some team members would fly in for face-to-face meetings. Those team members who could not attend would call in to the speakerphone, which was strategically placed at the center of the conference table.

With the advent of the cloud has come a vast collection of distributed or remote collaboration tools, as shown in **FIGURE 7-1**.

Questions to Ask About Collaborative Tools

Regardless of the collaborative technology you are considering, there is a common set of questions you should consider:

- Can the solution scale to meet the organization's future needs?
- Is the solution secure?
- What are the solution's start-up and operational costs?
- How will the solution impact the company's IT staffing and resource requirements?
- What are the solution's learning curve and training requirements?

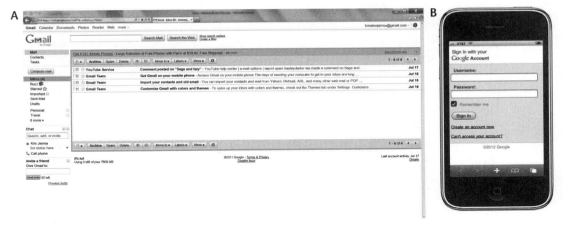

FIGURE 7-2 Most web-based applications today, such as Google Gmail, support computer-based and handheld devices.

Web-Based Collaboration Began with Web Mail

One of the first tools for collaboration on the web (it wasn't always known as the cloud) was web mail. Using only a web browser, users could access their e-mail from any computer at any time. Today web mail has evolved to support access from a wide range of devices. **FIGURE 7-2a** and **FIGURE 7-2b**, for example, show Google Gmail from within a computer and an iPhone.

CASE 7-1 MICROSOFT EXCHANGE ONLINE

Many companies today use Microsoft Exchange to meet their e-mail and calendar-management needs. Microsoft Exchange Online moves Exchange from the data center into the cloud. The advantages of Microsoft Exchange Online include the following:

- Users can access their e-mail and calendar-management tools from any place, at any time, with any device.
- Microsoft manages the Exchange Online software, keeping software versions and patches up to date.
- Companies maintain full control over user e-mail settings.
- Users have virtually unlimited e-mail storage, eliminating the need to move messages to an archive folder.

Exercise Discuss pros and cons of a company hosting its Exchange server within the cloud.

Web Resources For more information on Microsoft Exchange Online, see www.CloudBook Content.com/Chapter07/index.html.

Instant Messaging Isn't What It Used to Be

For years, users took advantage of **instant messaging (IM)** to send a short message to another user outside of e-mail or to have a text-based real-time chat. There is no cost for IM, and the user with whom one was chatting could reside in the next cubicle or across the globe. Today many companies still rely on IM to provide text-based technical support. **FIGURE 7–3** shows a text-based chat within Windows Live Messenger.

Over time, IM tools have expanded to support file sharing and even face-to-face video. **FIGURE 7–4** shows a video-based IM session.

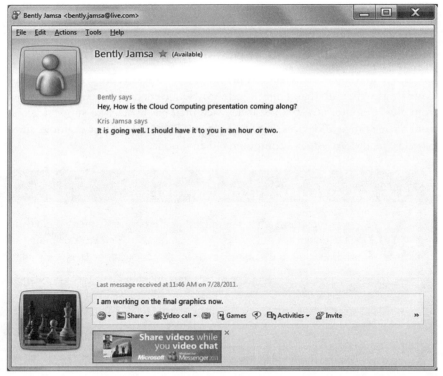

FIGURE 7–3 The IM text-based interaction provided one of the web's early forms of collaboration.

FIGURE 7–4 IM tools have grown from a text-based medium for message exchange to support audio and video streaming.

CASE 7–2 SKYPE VOICE OVER INTERNET PROTOCOL (VOIP) MESSAGING

I t used to be that users around the globe could have text-based chats in real time using IM. Skype changed the computer communications playing field when it used **voice over Internet protocol (VoIP)** to let users place phone calls over the web. Using Skype, computer users can make face-to-face calls, as shown in **FIGURE 7–5**.

Skype then enhanced its services to allow users to make calls from a computer to a traditional phone or mobile phone. In fact, using Skype, mobile users can call each other to talk face to face. Further, as shown in **FIGURE 7–6**, Skype has expanded its services to support group-based conference calling.

Exercise Discuss advantages and disadvantages to using VoIP to drive a company's phone system.

Web Resources For more information on Skype, see www.CloudBookContent.com/Chapter07/index.html.

continues

CASE 7-2 SKYPE VOICE OVER INTERNET PROTOCOL (VOIP) MESSAGING, continued

FIGURE 7-5 Skype leverages VoIP to allow users to place face-to-face or audio-only calls over the Internet.

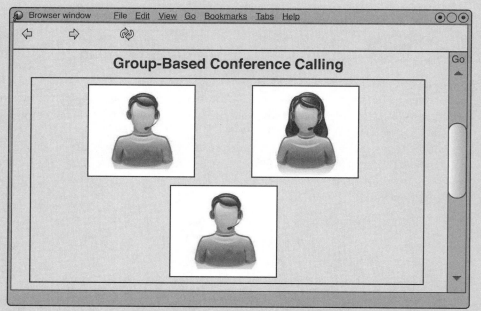

FIGURE 7-6 Using Skype to place VoIP-based conference calls.

Cloud-Based Phone and Fax Systems

Although faxing is becoming (or has become) an ancient technology, businesses still must be able to send and receive a fax. Fortunately, cloud-based companies have made the process of sending and receiving a fax as easy as sending and receiving an e-mail message. In this way, no matter where you are, or which device you have, you can easily send and receive a fax.

CASE 7-3 MYFAX FAXES ANYWHERE, ANYTIME

MyFax is one of several companies that have made the faxing process very easy for those without a fax machine or a land-based phone line. After you sign up for MyFax, you will receive a phone number that corresponds to your virtual fax machine. When, as shown in **FIGURE 7-7**, someone sends a fax to you, MyFax sends the fax contents to your e-mail as a PDF file. In this way, you can receive your faxes any time, any place, with any device.

To send a fax, you simply e-mail the document to your MyFax account. Software at MyFax, in turn, will send the document's contents to the recipient's fax machine (or virtual fax account).

Exercise Discuss the potential cost savings to a company for using cloud-based faxing.

Web Resources For more information on MyFax, see www.CloudBookContent.com/Chapter07/index.html.

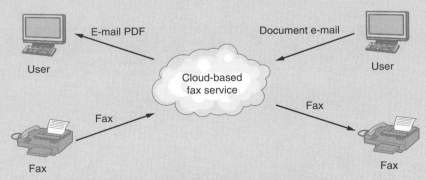

FIGURE 7-7 Cloud-based fax services deliver faxes as PDF documents to a user's e-mail.

For years companies have relied on expensive phone systems to manage employee calls and group-based conference calls. Today, with most employees in possession of a cell phone, most phone operations can be controlled by software. In fact, several companies now provide cloud-based phone systems that will record and optionally transcribe voice messages and send the corresponding text to a user's e-mail as a PDF document.

CASE 7–4 GOOGLE VOICE PHONE SYSTEM

Many people don't like to give out their cell phone numbers to businesses or to strangers. A great solution is to create a Google Voice account, which provides a cloud-based answering system and voice mail. You can also direct Google Voice to forward calls to your cell phone, and if a caller leaves a voice mail, Google Voice will transcribe the voice content into text. Later, from any device, you can retrieve your recorded voice message or view the message transcript, as shown in **FIGURE 7–8**. Also, Google Voice is free!

Exercise Discuss the advantages of using a cloud-based phone system for personal or company use.

Web Resources For more information on Google Voice, see www.CloudBookContent.com/Chapter07/index.html.

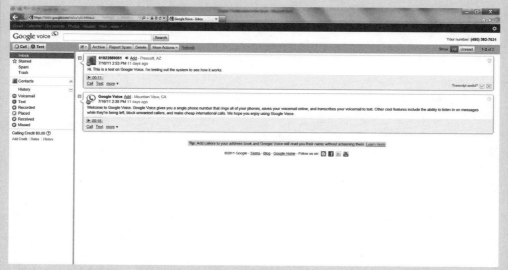

FIGURE 7–8 Google Voice provides you with a virtual phone account that you can forward to your phone. You can receive voice messages or direct Google Voice to transcribe the voice messages as text.

Revisiting File Sharing

In Chapter 6, *Data Storage in the Clouds*, you learned that most cloud-based data storage providers allow you to share folders with other users. Using the shared folder, you can easily exchange photos, documents, and other digital content. In this way, users do not have to track and later manage a myriad of e-mail attachments.

Within collaborative environments, however, users often need to edit the same document, sometimes at the same time. Fortunately, many cloud-based disk storage providers now facilitate simultaneous editing capabilities.

Editing Shared Files Within the Cloud

Depending on a document's size, complexity, and project guidelines, there are times when users will need to edit the contents of the same document at the same time. As you might guess, depending how (and how many) users are editing the document, managing changes to the text can be challenging for collaborative editing software. In other words, if two users edit the same section of text, it becomes tricky to determine which user's edits to apply.

One of the most popular Web 2.0 tools for document sharing is the **wiki**, which lets users collaborate on web-based content. The best-known wiki is Wikipedia, the online user-content-driven encyclopedia, shown in **FIGURE 7-9**.

Using wiki software, users can edit shared content. After the edits are saved, the document's new contents are displayed on the web. Depending on the wiki software, changes to text may have to first be approved by a page moderator; or the wiki software may track edited versions of the content to make it easy to fall back to previous content if users choose to discard a change or content addition.

Many wikis are public and accessible to all users on the web. Some wiki software, however, supports private content, which is well suited for company-based internal messaging and documents.

The advantages of using a wiki for shared content include the following:

- Any member of the team can add or edit content.
- Most users quickly learn how to edit content within the wiki.
- Team members who edit the wiki content can reside anywhere.
- The edits to wiki content are immediate.

The disadvantages of using a wiki for shared content include the following:

- Because any member can edit the content, wikis sometimes contain errors.
- Public wikis are often targets of hacking and spam.
- The wiki's free-flowing format may lead to disorganized content.
- Users are often suspicious of wiki content validity and accuracy.

A

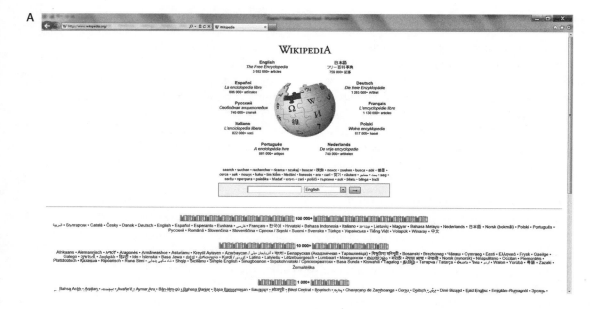

B

FIGURE 7-9 Wikipedia provides the largest collection of web-based, user-contributed, and user-edited content.

CASE 7-5 WIKIA FREE WIKI HOSTING

Getting started with a wiki is very easy. To begin, you select the cloud-based host at which your wiki will reside. Your selection of a wiki site may include such factors as content versioning, content moderator approval, support for private content, and so on. FIGURE 7-10 illustrates a wiki focused on cloud computing, which I created in a matter of minutes using the Wikia editor.

Exercise Discuss the pros and cons of using a wiki for online editing of cloud-based documents.

Web Resources For more information on Wikia, see www.CloudBookContent.com/Chapter07/index.html.

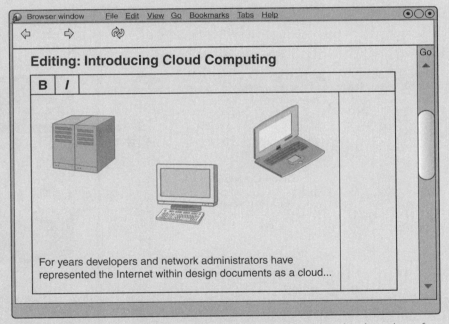

FIGURE 7-10 Creating a cloud-based wiki, which discusses cloud-based topics and uses free software at Wikia.

CASE 7-6 GOOGLE DOCS FOR DOCUMENT SHARING

Google Docs provides users with web-based, free access to a word processor, spreadsheet, and presentation program—yes, Google Docs are meant to compete directly with the Microsoft Office tools.

By default, the documents that you create using Google Docs reside in the cloud. That said, you can easily save your documents to a local file on your computer's disk, print your documents, or share the document's contents with other Google Docs users. To share a Google Docs document, you simply e-mail a link to the document to other users.

FIGURE 7-11, for example, illustrates a presentation on cloud computing that was created using Google Docs. The user can access the document using various devices.

Exercise Discuss the pros and cons of using Google Docs for business-based documents.

Web Resources For more information on Google Docs, see www.CloudBookContent.com/Chapter07/index.html.

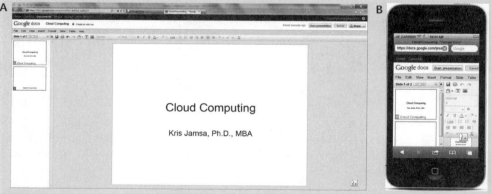

FIGURE 7-11 Accessing a cloud-based Google Docs presentation from different devices.

CASE 7-7 MICROSOFT OFFICE WEB APPS

In Chapter 2, *Software as a Service (SaaS)*, you learned about Microsoft Office 365, which provides cloud-based implementations of Word, PowerPoint, and Excel to users for a monthly fee. Given the popularity of the cloud-based Google Docs, Microsoft responded with Microsoft Office Web Apps—a scaled-down version of its office productivity tools. Using Office Web Apps, you can, free of charge, create a Word, PowerPoint, or Excel document; upload and edit your existing documents; or share your documents with other users for viewing or editing. **FIGURE 7-12** shows a PowerPoint presentation created with Microsoft Office Web Apps.

To share an Office Web Apps document, you simply e-mail a link to the document to another user. Depending on the permissions you have set, the user can view or edit the document's contents.

Exercise Discuss the pros and cons of a business using Microsoft Office Web Apps in lieu of licensing the complete Office suite for each employee.

Web Resources For more information on Microsoft Office Web Apps, see www.CloudBook Content.com/Chapter07/index.html.

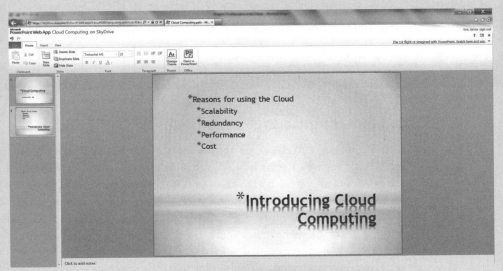

FIGURE 7-12 Microsoft Office Web Apps lets users create and share (for simultaneous editing) cloud-based Word, Excel, and PowerPoint documents.

CASE 7-8 MICROSOFT SHAREPOINT ONLINE

For years, many companies have used Microsoft SharePoint to provide a centralized document repository. Because the SharePoint user interface is similar to that of other Microsoft applications, users quickly come up to speed, and employees who move from a different company that uses SharePoint have only a small learning curve.

In Chapter 2, *Software as a Service (SaaS)*, you learned that Microsoft now makes its Office suite of products available to the cloud through Office 365. Within Office 365, Microsoft includes SharePoint Online, the cloud-based version of the software.

The advantages of Microsoft SharePoint Online include the following:

- Ease of sharing documents
- Centralized storage for key team documents
- Ease of document searching and referencing
- Support for internal and external company sites
- Centralized storage for company reports and data

Exercise Discuss how Microsoft SharePoint Online differs from other web-based document-sharing utilities.

Web Resources For more information on Microsoft SharePoint Online, see www.CloudBook Content.com/Chapter07/index.html.

Collaborating via Web Logs (Blogs)

With the advent of Web 2.0, one of the most widely used communication tools has become the web log, or **blog**. Blogs allow virtually anyone, with little or no web development experience, to easily publish content on the web. Blogs can provide one-way or two-way communication—that is, some users post read-only content to blogs, while others allow readers to comment on the content. Over the past few years, blogs have become so successful that many newspapers have replaced printed content with digital blogs.

The primary advantages of blogs include the following:

- Blogs provide a device-independent way for content consumers to access digital content using only a web browser.
- Users can create and publish content to a blog with little or no web development experience.
- Within an organization, intranet-based blogs provide a convenient way to disseminate information.
- Blogs provide an effective way to collect feedback from readers.

The disadvantages of blogs include the following:

- Maintaining a blog takes time.
- Blogs can become opinion posts as opposed to fact posts.
- User feedback may not always be positive and may require moderation.

Collaborative Meetings in the Cloud

One of the biggest cost savings to businesses due to the cloud is the advent of the **virtual meeting**. Using sites such as WebEx and GoToMeeting, businesses can now reduce travel costs through cloud-based meetings. Additional benefits of cloud-based meetings include the following:

- Streaming video that allows face-to-face interaction
- Shared whiteboards that presenters can use to easily control the presentation of PowerPoint, Word, Excel, or related documents
- Accessibility to users, in most cases, through a myriad of devices
- Shared applications that let presenters easily demonstrate software live within a controlled environment
- The ability to hold company training online instead of on-site
- The ability to record meetings for playback at a later time

CASE 7-9 WORDPRESS, A LEADING BLOG SITE

Creating a blog is very easy. To start, you locate a free blog hosting provider within the cloud, such as WordPress. After you sign up, you will have access to a text editor, which you can use to create your blog.

Most blog providers offer a free user account, which is often advertising based. For a monthly fee, providers may eliminate advertisements, allow greater storage capacity, support **streaming media** such as video, and allow a user domain name. **FIGURE 7-13** shows a blog in edit mode and the same content within presentation mode at WordPress.

Exercise Discuss the pros and cons of using a blog to present content on behalf of a company. Discuss the type of content for which a blog may be most appropriate.

Web Resources For more information on WordPress, see www.CloudBookContent.com/Chapter07/index.html.

continues

CASE 7-9 WORDPRESS, A LEADING BLOG SITE, continued

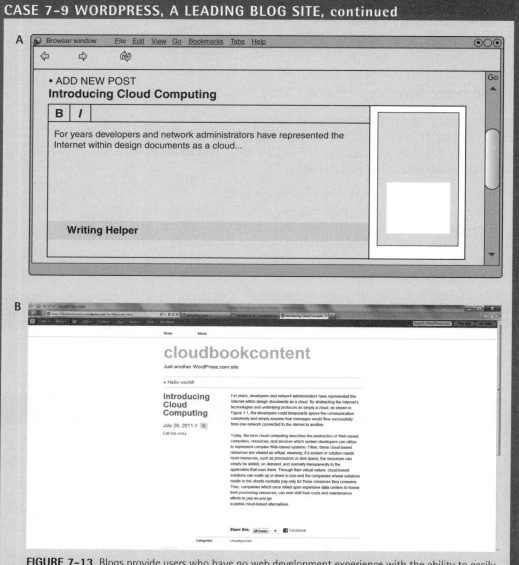

FIGURE 7-13 Blogs provide users who have no web development experience with the ability to easily publish content on the web.

CASE 7-10 GOTOMEETING VIRTUAL MEETINGS

GoToMeeting is one of the leading providers of virtual meetings. The site offers a variety of scalable solutions that should meet most organizations' needs. Using GoToMeeting, companies can host face-to-face meetings with two users or webinars that include 1,000 or more attendees. **FIGURE 7-14** illustrates a virtual presentation within the GoToMeeting environment.

Exercise Discuss the pros and cons of virtual meetings in lieu of face-to-face on-site meetings.

Web Resources For more information on GoToMeeting, see www.CloudBookContent.com/Chapter07/index.html.

Cloud Computing Overview

Kris Jamsa, Ph.D., MBA

FIGURE 7-14 Virtual meetings allow companies to reduce expensive travel while maintaining the benefits of face-to-face interaction.

Virtual Presentations and Lectures

Using cloud-based tools such as WebEx and GoToMeeting, companies can easily host virtual meetings. Often companies will also want to place within the cloud multimedia content that users can access asynchronously at a time that best meets the users' schedules. Using products such as Articulate or iSpring Presenter, companies can record and post cloud-based **virtual presentations** that may be used for marketing, virtual training, and more. The advantages of virtual presentations include the following:

- The costs of production and hosting for multimedia content are low.
- Users can play back content at a time that best meets their needs and as often as they desire.
- Companies can create a library of virtual marketing or training presentations.
- Virtual presentation software is migrating to handheld devices.

Using Social Media for Collaboration

Facebook is obviously the most successful Web 2.0 site. Using Facebook, users communicate with friends to share photos, videos, and text messages. Further, using Facebook groups, teams can share project information in a secure way. Because Facebook resides within the cloud, it must be considered a cloud-based collaborative tool. The advantages to using a social media tool for collaboration include the following:

- Users can exchange project information from anywhere, at anytime, with any device.
- Groups can keep team content secure.
- Most users are already familiar with the social media user interface.

CASE 7-11 ZENTATION VIRTUAL PRESENTATION SOFTWARE

Zentation provides a PowerPoint to streaming-media converter, which allows users to easily deploy multimedia presentations from the cloud. What makes Zentation unique is that it supports the integration of streaming video, as shown in **FIGURE 7-15**. Zentation not only provides software that will combine a video and PowerPoint, but it also offers cloud-based hosting.

Exercise Discuss potential ways a company might leverage virtual presentations.

Web Resources For more information on Zentation, see www.CloudBookContent.com/Chapter07/index.html.

continues

CASE 7-11 ZENTATION VIRTUAL PRESENTATION SOFTWARE, continued

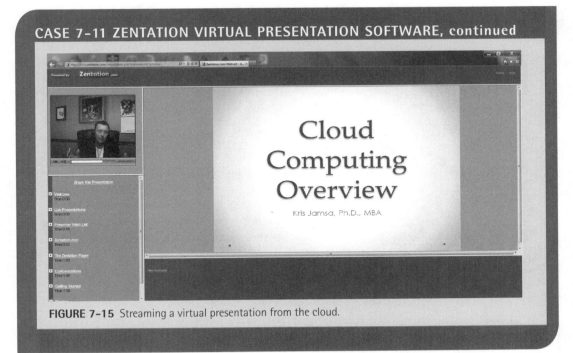

FIGURE 7-15 Streaming a virtual presentation from the cloud.

CASE 7-12 SALESFORCE.COM CHATTER

Salesforce.com was one of the first companies to fully exploit the power of the cloud. Salesforce.com Chatter is a tool, like social media, that integrates with other Salesforce.com tools to improve communication, coordination, and data sharing. Using Chatter, employees can do the following:

- Collaborate privately and securely
- Share project documents and presentations
- Exchange thoughts, ideas, and status information with other group members
- Integrate Salesforce.com reporting data for improved communication and information sharing

Rather than having employees log into a traditional social media site, companies may prefer that team interaction occur within a more professional setting.

Exercise Discuss ways that companies might leverage social networking tools beyond sales management and customer relationship management.

Web Resources For more information on Salesforce.com Chatter, see www.CloudBookContent .com/Chapter07/index.html.

CASE 7-13 GOOGLE CALENDAR

Because it is free, cloud accessible, and easy to use, many users turn to Google Calendar. Users can easily share their schedule with others they choose. Further, users can delegate others as schedule administrators with the right to schedule or cancel meetings on the user's behalf. **FIGURE 7-16** shows the cloud-based Google Calendar user interface.

Exercise Discuss tools beyond schedule management that would make sense for companies such as Google to support in the cloud.

Web Resources For more information on Google Calendar, see www.CloudBookContent.com/Chapter07/index.html.

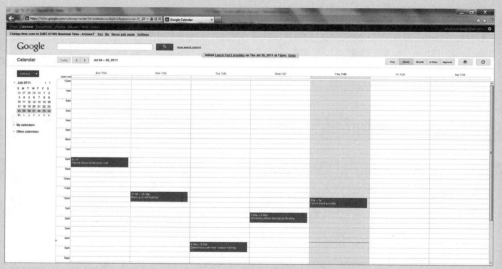

FIGURE 7-16 Using the cloud-based Google Calendar to manage meetings and appointments.

Using Cloud-Based Calendar Management

Within a busy organization, it can be difficult to schedule meetings, reserve meeting space, and track one's own appointments and meetings. Many companies use a calendar, such as that built into Microsoft Outlook, to manage employee appointments and meetings. Smaller companies, which may not have an Exchange server, may turn to cloud-based calendars, the advantages of which include the following:

- No software other than a web browser is required
- Calendars are accessible through most devices
- Many cloud-based calendars will sync with other applications

Using Streaming Video Content to Collaborate

YouTube is one of the Web 2.0 success stories. Each year users upload hundreds of millions of videos, containing a wide variety of content, to YouTube. Many companies use YouTube to market their products and services and even to deploy corporate training. YouTube supports video access from all web browsers and most handheld devices. Users are free to determine when and from where they retrieve the video content. More important, users can easily update their own videos to the YouTube cloud-based storage and then share the videos with other users. **FIGURE 7–17** illustrates an overview of cloud-based video processing at YouTube.

Cloud-Based TV Content

Over the past few years, many households have gotten rid of their land-based phone lines in lieu of cellular phones. Recently, a similar phenomenon is taking

FIGURE 7–17 YouTube makes it very easy for users to upload and later stream video content to and from the cloud.

place that has people getting rid of television sets and instead using cloud-based movie downloads and streaming content. In the near future, companies may also leverage streaming content to provide their own messaging, marketing, and training.

CASE 7-14 HULU STREAMING CONTENT

Hulu is a website that offers on-demand streaming of TV shows, movies, film clips, webisodes (episodes created specifically for the web), and more. Hulu supports media streaming to a variety of devices. **FIGURE 7-18**, for example, presents a TV show streaming from the cloud-based Hulu website.

Exercise Discuss how companies such as Netflix and Hulu are changing how users view television and movies.

Web Resources For more information on Hulu, see www.CloudBookContent.com/Chapter07/index.html.

FIGURE 7-18 Hulu is one company that is deploying streaming media content from the cloud, on demand.

Chapter Summary

Collaboration is the process of two or more people working together to achieve a result (a goal). It used to be that teams would meet in conference rooms to collaborate. Depending on the scope and importance of the project, some team members would fly in for face-to-face meetings. Those team members who could not attend would call in to a speakerphone. The cloud, however, has changed the ways in which teams collaborate. Today, using cloud-based tools, team members can do the following:

- Use cloud-based conferencing software to present documents, share desktops, and benefit from face-to-face video.
- Collaborate in real time and edit the same documents.
- Share calendars to simplify appointment scheduling.
- Use VoIP-based audio or video chats from anywhere with any device.
- Take advantage of virtual faxing services to send and receive faxes, without using a fax machine.
- Forward transcripts of voice mail messages to their e-mail.
- Communicate with team members using wikis and blogs.
- Leverage familiar tools that are like social media for group interaction.
- Stream media for marketing, training, or messaging purposes.

Key Terms

Blog
Collaboration
Instant messaging (IM)
Streaming media

Virtual meeting
Virtual presentation
Voice over Internet protocol (VoIP)
Wiki

Chapter Review

1. Define collaboration.
2. Define and describe cloud-based collaboration.
3. The CIO of Ace Accounting Services suggests that the company can save considerable money using VoIP for phone calls. Define and describe VoIP. Then present three companies that provide VoIP offerings. Compare and contrast each company's offering. Also, discuss whether or not you agree with the CIO and justify your opinion.
4. List the questions one should consider when evaluating a cloud-based collaborative solution.

5. Jan, a project manager at Smith Electronics, wants her team to be able to easily share and edit documents. Most of the documents are Word files—letters and memos—along with many presentations. Discuss the solution that you would recommend to Jan.

6. Mary, the human resources vice president for Baker Equipment, needs to train 500 remote employees on the company's new sexual-harassment policy. Describe the cloud-based solution you would recommend to Mary and why. Within your discussion, include the costs that Mary should expect for the cloud-based training.

7. Describe the pros and cons of using the following collaboration tools:
   - Wiki
   - Blog
   - IM
   - Shared documents

Virtualization

VIRTUALIZATION IS THE USE of hardware and software to create the perception that one or more entities exist, although the entities, in actuality, are not physically present. Using virtualization, we can make one server appear to be many, a desktop computer appear to be running multiple operating systems simultaneously, a network connection appear to exist, or a vast amount of disk space or a vast number of drives to be available.

Learning Objectives

This chapter examines virtualization in detail. By the time you finish this chapter, you will be able to do the following:

- Define and describe virtualization.
- Discuss the history of virtualization.
- Describe various types of virtualization.
- List the pros and cons of virtualization.
- Identify applications that are well suited, as well as those that are not suited, for virtualization.
- Describe why companies should employ virtualization.

Understanding Virtualization

Virtualization uses hardware and software to create the illusion that two or more entities are present, when there is only one physical entity in existence. The most common forms of virtualization include the following:

- **Server virtualization**: Making one server appear as many. Each **virtual server** may run the same or different operating systems. Server virtualization provides greater CPU utilization, a smaller equipment footprint, less power consumption, and support for multiple operating systems.
- **Desktop virtualization**: This allows a user to switch between multiple operating systems on the same computer. (An operating system that resides within a virtualized environment is known as a **guest operating system**.) Some desktop virtualization techniques can provide an operating system environment on demand. Desktop virtualization provides support for multiple operating systems, which is very convenient for software developers, testers, and help desk support staff. In addition, desktop virtualization leads to ease of computer maintenance and reduces desktop IT staff administration.
- **Virtual networks**: These create the illusion that a user is connected directly to a company network and resources, although no such physical connection may exist. Virtual networks are sometimes called virtual private networks or VPNs. Using a virtual private network, users can connect to a network and access the network resources from any Internet-connected computer. Virtual networks also allow network administrators to segment a network, making different departments such as management, development, and sales appear to have their own separate networks.
- **Virtual storage**: This provides users (and applications) with access to scalable and redundant physical storage through the use of abstract, or logical, disk drives or file systems, or a database interface.

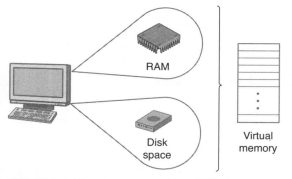

FIGURE 8-1 Virtual memory combines RAM with a page file on disk to create the illusion, to running programs, of the existence of a vast amount of RAM.

The History of Virtualization

Although virtualization has, over the past few years, become one of the hottest topics in computing, it's not a new idea. IBM, more than 30 years ago, had a virtual operating system that allowed a mainframe computer to run multiple copies of the same or different operating systems. Further, most operating systems support virtual memory, which, as shown in **FIGURE 8-1**, combines random access memory (RAM) and a page file on disk to create the illusion that a process (a running program) has much more

CASE 8-1 VIRTUAL MEMORY

Virtual memory is not physical memory (RAM). Instead, virtual memory combines RAM and space on a connected disk, called a page file, to create the illusion, to running programs, that a vast amount of RAM exists.

Before the CPU can execute a program, the program's instructions and data must reside within RAM. Virtual memory takes advantage of the fact that not all of the program's instructions or data must be in RAM at the same time. Rather, the CPU needs only the instructions and data with which it is currently working to reside in RAM.

A virtual memory operating system breaks a program's instruction and data into fixed-size chunks called pages. When the CPU needs specific instructions or data, the operating system loads the corresponding page from disk into RAM. When the CPU no longer needs a set of instructions or data, the operating system can move the pages from RAM back to disk. This process of moving pages between RAM and the page file on disk is called paging.

The advantages of virtual memory include the following:

- A running program (process) appears to have unlimited memory.
- The operating system can easily manage several different programs, running at the same time, and keep each program's data and instructions secure.
- The operating system can take advantage of disk storage, which is considerably less expensive than RAM.

The disadvantage of virtual memory is that the paging process (the process of moving instructions and data between RAM and disk) adds overhead, mostly because disk drives are much slower than RAM.

Exercise With computers supporting larger amounts of physical memory, some users argue that there are applications for which users should turn off virtual memory to improve performance. Discuss whether you agree.

Web Resources For additional information on virtual memory, see www.CloudBookContent .com/Chapter08/index.html.

physical RAM than is present in the computer. Windows, Linux, Mac OS, and other operating systems all support virtual memory.

Leveraging Blade Servers

For years, when user demands required additional servers, the IT department would add a physical server box within the data center, as shown in **FIGURE 8-2**.

Although the server box met user demands, each box consumed space within the data center and required considerable power.

FIGURE 8–2 Server computers originally required their own chassis, disk, power supply, and fan. Servers consumed considerable power, took up considerable space, and generated considerable heat within the data center.

CASE 8-2 GREEN COMPUTING INITIATIVE

Years ago many people made the claim that computers, e-mail, and computer networks would reduce the vast number of printed pages and that many forests would be spared. Unfortunately, the "less paper" thing never happened. Worse yet, with desktops, laptops, and hand-held devices now touching all aspects of our lives 24/7, most devices never get powered off!

The result is that computer and device power usage is growing at exponential rates. Because of the impact that computers now play with respect to our environment, many green computing initiatives have emerged. Some general guidelines for green computing include the following:

- Power off devices when they are not in use.
- Power up energy-intensive devices, such as laser printers, only when needed.
- Use notebooks when possible instead of desktop computers.
- Use the computer's built-in power management features.
- Minimize unnecessary printing.
- Dispose of e-waste (devices, ink cartridges, monitors, and so on) in compliance with government regulations.

For more specifics on green computing, visit the Green Computing Initiative website hosted by the University of California, Berkeley, shown in **FIGURE 8–3**.

Exercise Discuss potential cost savings for a company supporting green computing initiatives.

Web Resources For additional information on green computing, see www.CloudBookContent .com/Chapter08/index.html.

continues

CASE 8-2 GREEN COMPUTING INITIATIVE, continued

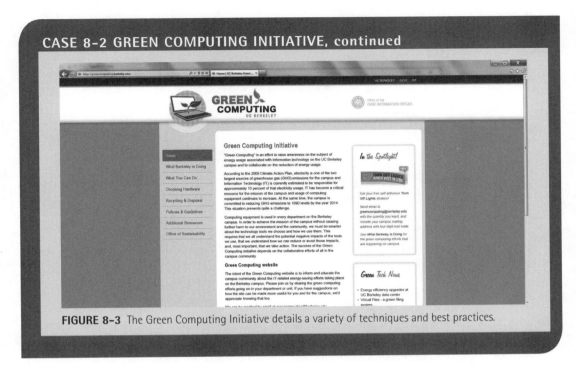

FIGURE 8-3 The Green Computing Initiative details a variety of techniques and best practices.

As the server boxes were outgrowing many data centers, the blade server was born. In short, the blade server, as shown in **FIGURE 8-4**, is a scaled-down server designed to consume less power and to fit within a rack with other blade servers, while still matching or exceeding the processing potential of chassis-based servers.

To share disk space, blade servers support network-attached storage (NAS) devices. Additional advantages of blade servers include the following:

- Consume less physical space (footprint)
- Consume less power
- Generate less heat and are easier to cool
- Easy to install and configure

Server Virtualization

Most servers today are either very busy, running at a high level of CPU utilization, or are idle a significant portion of the time, waiting for something to do. As you have learned, when a server becomes very busy, the IT staff may, as shown in **FIGURE 8-5**, introduce a load-balancing server and then add additional servers, as necessary, to handle the workload.

FIGURE 8-4 The blade server is designed to fit within a rack with other blade servers. This reduces the server's physical footprint, makes the server easier to cool, and reduces the server's power consumption.

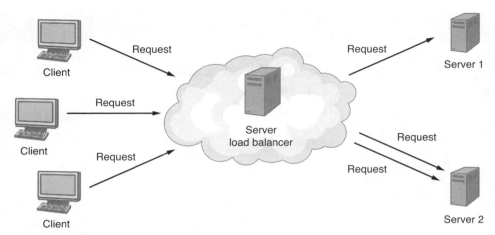

FIGURE 8-5 Using load balancing, the IT staff can supply the number of servers necessary to meet the server workload at a given time.

In contrast, when a server is idle, the server's potential processing power is being wasted. For a cloud-based platform as a service (PaaS) provider, such wasted processing time is a wasted revenue opportunity.

To reduce server idle time and to protect one client's server from another, PaaS providers use special software to divide the single physical server into multiple virtual servers. As shown in **FIGURE 8-6**, each virtual server may run a different operating system.

Improving CPU utilization is one reason to virtualize servers. Second, some companies (including PaaS providers) need to support multiple server operating systems. Fortunately, several tools exist to make it easy to virtualize most server operating systems.

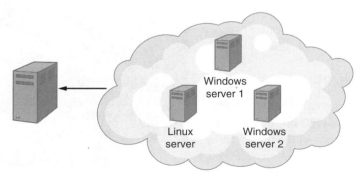

FIGURE 8-6 Through virtualization, a single physical server can be made to look like multiple separate servers, potentially running different operating systems.

CASE 8-3 MICROSOFT WINDOWS SERVER VIRTUALIZATION

Given Microsoft's aggressive approach to cloud computing, it makes sense that Microsoft would also aggressively pursue client and server virtualization. Microsoft servers now utilize an underlying technology the company refers to as Hyper-V to allow administrators to create virtual servers.

The advantages of Microsoft Hyper-V technology include the following:

- The ability to consolidate servers and increase CPU utilization
- Enhanced business continuity and disaster recovery
- Ease of deploying testing and support environments
- Enhanced support for Windows-based client virtualization
- Improved load balancing
- Ability to move live virtual machines from one physical server to another on the fly for load balancing and scalability

Exercise Assume your company primarily deploys .NET-based solutions. Periodically, however, your company releases a PHP or Perl solution running under Linux. Discuss the pros and cons of using Microsoft-based virtual servers.

Web Resources For additional information on Microsoft server virtualization, see www.Cloud BookContent.com/Chapter08/index.html.

Within a virtual server, to support the execution of multiple operating systems, each operating system is actually installed on top of special software called the **hypervisor**. The hypervisor, in turn, essentially manages each operating system's execution and resource use.

CASE 8-4 VMWARE ESXI

VMware is one of the best-known providers of virtualization solutions. For companies that need to support multiple operating systems within a virtual-server environment, VMware ESXi provides the solution. That said, ESXi is more than a simple server-virtualization tool. ESXi provides the following:

- Support for multiple operating systems
- Server consolidation
- Automated resource management to drive disaster recovery and service-level agreements
- Detail cost-reporting services

continues

CASE 8-4 VMWARE ESXI, continued

- Automated load balancing
- Centralized management and administration of virtual servers and the underlying machines

Exercise Assume your company must deploy virtual-server solutions for Windows and Linux. You anticipate that you will require only one physical server running the two virtual operating systems. Research and discuss the pros and cons as well as the costs of using VMware server virtualization.

Web Resources For additional information on VMware server virtualization, see www .CloudBookContent.com/Chapter08/index.html.

Desktop Virtualization

If you continue thinking in terms of the server-virtualization model, virtualizing the desktop means allowing the system to run multiple operating systems at the same time, as shown in **FIGURE 8-7**. The term for a desktop computer that runs two or more operating systems is a **virtual desktop**.

If you consider a software tester who must test multiple operating system platforms, or a help desk staff member who must answer calls from users running a variety of operating systems, you can understand how the ability to quickly switch between operating systems is very convenient and powerful.

The advantages of desktop virtualization of operating systems include the following:

- A single desktop computer can simultaneously run multiple operating systems.
- There is reduced need for duplicate hardware.
- Less power is consumed.

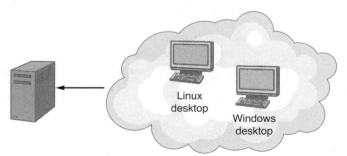

FIGURE 8-7 Desktop virtualization allows a desktop computer to run two or more operating systems at the same time and allows a user to quickly switch between the systems.

CASE 8-5 PARALLELS DESKTOP 4 WINDOWS AND LINUX

Parallels Desktop 4 for Windows and Linux lets users easily integrate and install multiple Windows- and Linux-based operating systems on the same desktop computer. Users can then quickly switch between operating systems as easily as clicking the mouse on the target operating system window. **FIGURE 8-8** shows Windows and Linux running on the same desktop computer using Parallels Desktop 4 for Windows and Linux.

Exercise Assume that your company has 10 programmers who write and test code for applications running on Windows and Linux, and they must also support applications running on these operating systems. Discuss the pros and cons as well as the costs of using Parallels Desktop 4 for Windows and Linux.

Web Resources For additional information on Parallels Desktop 4 for Windows and Linux, see www.CloudBookContent.com/Chapter08/index.html.

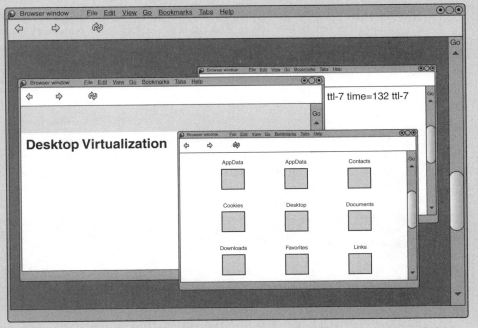

FIGURE 8-8 Using Parallels Desktop 4 for Windows and Linux to allow users to quickly switch between operating system environments.

The primary disadvantage of the virtual desktop is that the system incurs overhead due to the virtualization and will not be as fast as an identical stand-alone system running a single operating system.

Desktop Solutions on Demand

For years, desktop computer management went something like this:

- A new employee joins the company. The IT staff, in turn, prepares a computer with the needed software and delivers it to the new employee's desk.
- When it comes time to upgrade software, an IT support member carrying a CD-ROM disk would visit each desktop computer and take as long as needed to install the software. A high-tech data center, would then have a desktop administrator push the upgrade across the network either at night or early in the morning.
- When users encountered problems, the IT staff member would again show up at the user's desk to troubleshoot the problem, or the high-tech data center would have a help desk support team member remotely log in to the user's computer from across the network.
- Users who were frustrated with the IT staff and its processes would simply install software on their own systems, which the company may or may not own.

In any case, managing user desktop computers took time, money, and labor.

With faster computer networks, along with the migration to cloud-based solutions, the approach to desktop management is changing. Today many data centers are moving to on-demand delivery of desktop operating system environments. In this way, when a user logs in to a system, he or she receives access to his or her system customizations, assigned operating system, and needed applications.

CASE 8-6 MICROSOFT DESKTOP VIRTUALIZATION

Most desktop computers today run a Windows operating system and a Microsoft suite of applications (normally Office). To simplify the management of such desktop systems, Microsoft provides a suite of desktop virtualization tools:

- Microsoft Virtual Desktop Infrastructure (VDI) suite
- Microsoft Application Virtualization (App-V)
- Microsoft Enterprise Desktop Virtualization (MED-V)
- Microsoft Remote Desktop Services (RDS)
- Microsoft User State Virtualization (USV)
- Windows Thin computer

continues

CASE 8-6 MICROSOFT DESKTOP VIRTUALIZATION, continued

The advantages of the Microsoft desktop virtualization include the following:

- Simplified desktop management across the enterprise
- Access to user profiles and data from any computer
- Improved business continuity
- Improved management of software licenses
- Improved security and business compliance

Exercise Assume that your company has 1,000 desktops, for which your CIO wants to deliver an operating system and environment on demand. Discuss which Microsoft desktop virtualization tools you would require and the corresponding cost.

Web Resources For additional information on Microsoft desktop virtualization, see www .CloudBookContent.com/Chapter08/index.html.

As shown in **FIGURE 8-9**, in an on-demand operating system, software and user settings are pushed to a desktop across the network.

Because the operating system and applications reside within a centralized location within an on-demand environment, administrators can easily apply patches and software upgrades, which are transparently downloaded to the user's computer the next time he or she logs in. Further, the on-demand environment frees the user from ties to any one specific computer. A user can log in to the system from any network computer and receive his or her work environment.

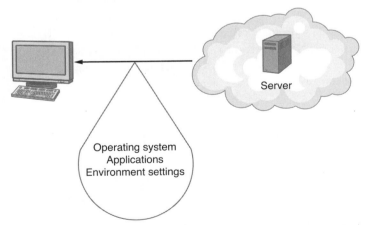

FIGURE 8-9 On-demand operating system environments deliver a user's operating system, environment customizations, and needed applications to any computer the user logs in to.

CASE 8-7 VMWARE VIEW

As one of the top leaders within the virtualization space, VMware offers View, a tool for providing virtual desktops on demand. Using View, system administrators can centralize the on-demand delivery of an operating system and user-assigned applications. The advantages of VMware View include the following:

- Simplified desktop operating system and application management
- Automated desktop provisioning (account generation)
- Virtual-desktop image management
- Support for a variety of client platforms

Exercise Discuss the pros and cons of using VMware, as opposed to Microsoft, to implement a company's desktop virtualization.

Web Resources For additional information on VMware View desktop virtualization, see www .CloudBookContent.com/Chapter08/index.html.

Virtual Networks

Networks allow users to share resources such as printers, storage devices, and applications. Most businesses utilize a local-area network (LAN) to connect users. Typically, LANs are just that—the cables or wireless devices that connect users are local to a specific office, building, or campus, as shown in **FIGURE 8-10**.

Often users who travel and users who work from remote locations must connect to the company's LAN in order to accomplish specific tasks. In such cases, the users can use special software to create a **virtual private network (VPN)** connection to the LAN. VPN software, as shown in **FIGURE 8-11**, uses a secure Internet connection to give the user the illusion that he or she is physically connected to the remote network from his or her current location.

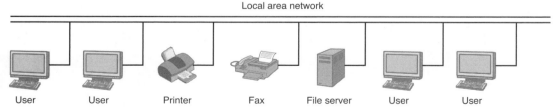

Local area network

| User | User | Printer | Fax | File server | User | User |

FIGURE 8-10 LANs are designed to allow users to share resources within a localized environment such as a home, business, office building, or small campus.

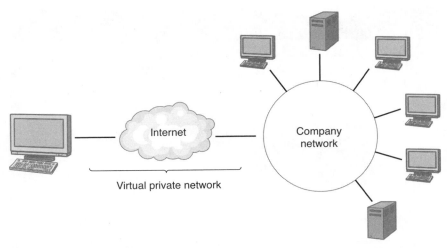

FIGURE 8-11 A VPN creates the illusion of a secure physical connection to a LAN using software and/or hardware to connect the user across the Internet.

When multiple employees work remotely, there may be times when the group needs to establish its own network in order collaborate securely and effectively. Rather than establish a physical network for the group, companies will configure a virtual local-area network (VLAN), which uses special routers to segment part of the physical network in such a way that the group appears to have its own private network.

CASE 8-8 WINDOWS VPN SUPPORT

Across the web, several companies, including Cisco, provide advanced VPN support. Should you need to get a VPN connection up and running quickly, however, Windows provides both client and server support. **FIGURE 8-12**, for example, shows the Windows Create VPN Connection dialog box that lets a client establish a VPN connection across the Internet. To create the connection, the user needs only to know the IP address or domain name of the remote VPN server.

Exercise Discuss the pros and cons of using VPN software provided with Windows as opposed to licensing or buying a solution from a network company such as Cisco.

Web Resources For additional information on Windows VPNs, see www.CloudBookContent .com/Chapter08/index.html.

continues

CASE 8-8 WINDOWS VPN SUPPORT, continued

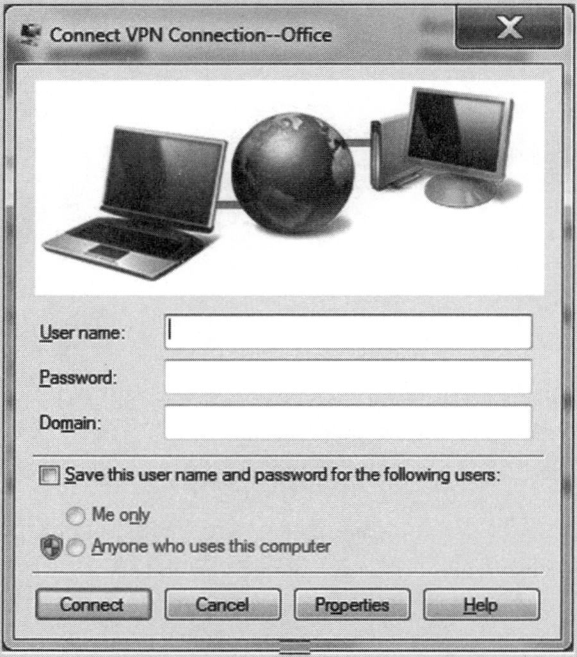

FIGURE 8-12 Windows provides client and server support tools that users can use to establish a VPN connection.

In a similar way, for internal security purposes, companies may use virtual networks to create separate networking environments for sales, management, development, and support, as shown in **FIGURE 8-13**.

Again, many companies such as VMware and Cisco provide support for the creation, management, and security of VLANs.

Data Storage Virtualization

Chapter 6, *Data Storage in the Cloud*, discussed cloud-based data storage in detail. You learned that the advantages of cloud-based data storage include the following:

- Scalable disk storage space on demand
- The ability to pay as you go for the needed storage

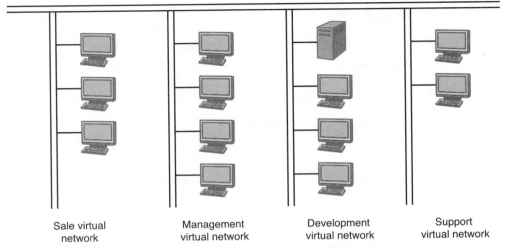

FIGURE 8-13 Virtual networks create the illusion of two or more stand-alone networks.

- Behind-the-scenes backup and data replication
- Support for common operating systems
- Access from anywhere, anytime, and essentially any device
- Ease of document sharing

The primary disadvantages of cloud-based storage include the following:

- Some users are not comfortable with their data residing in the cloud.
- Cloud-based file access is slower than local file access due to network overhead.

Data storage virtualization essentially separates the physical data storage from the logical presentation that users (and applications) use to access the device. For example, computer users will often partition a large (physical) hard drive into two more logical drives (often drives C and D).

The process of making a device available to a user or application is called mounting the device. As you learned in Chapter 6, several cloud-based data storage providers allow users to mount the virtual storage so that the user can refer to the storage area using a familiar disk drive letter.

Again, as shown in **FIGURE 8-14**, the data storage virtualization hides the physical details of the actual storage device, which makes it very easy for administrators to scale the available storage space.

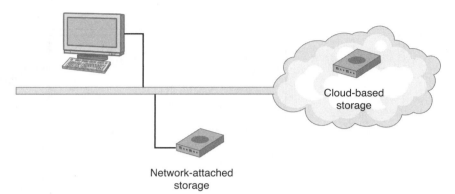

FIGURE 8-14 Data storage virtualization hides the physical storage device or devices from the logical presentation that users or applications use to access the space.

CASE 8-9 VMWARE STORAGE VMOTION

Despite the virtual nature of cloud-based storage, at some point, an administrator, somewhere, must manage the physical data-storage devices. The administrator may want to upgrade a device to a larger or faster drive, or, simply move data for load balancing. Unfortunately, to perform such upgrades, an administrator simply can't call "time out" and take the device off line.

VMware's Storage vMotion allows an administrator to move files from one virtual data store to another while the virtual disk is active for use! If a user updates a file on the source disk while the move is in progress, the Storage vMotion software simply takes note and then later updates the file on the target disk.

Exercise Discuss application types for which a data storage device cannot be taken offline in order to perform system updates.

Web Resources For additional information on VMware Storage vMotion, see www.CloudBook Content.com/Chapter08/index.html.

Not All Applications Are Well Suited for Virtualization

Despite the performance utilization gains that most applications will experience within a virtual environment, some applications are not well suited for virtualization:

- **Applications with unique hardware requirements**: If an application requires a unique device or hardware device driver, the virtualization software may be unable to support the device.
- **Graphics-intensive applications**: If an application is graphics intensive, such as a 3-D modeling program, the virtual device drivers may slow down the I/O processing to an unacceptable level.

Why Virtualize?

Throughout this chapter, you have examined a variety of virtualization techniques. The following list summarizes a company's motivation to virtualize:

- Increased device utilization (particularly CPU utilization)
- Decreased device footprint
- Decreased power consumption
- Simplified operating system and application administration
- Ease of software provisioning and patch releases
- Device and storage scalability
- Increased user access to key resources
- Increased flexibility in supporting multiple operating system environments
- Improved use and management of software licenses
- Improved utilization reporting, which leads to improved capacity planning
- Improved disaster recovery and business continuity

The primary disadvantages of virtualization include the following:

- New staff or staff training may be required to understand the virtualization process.
- Not all applications are well suited for virtualization.
- The virtualization process adds slight overhead, which will make some applications run more slowly.

CHAPTER SUMMARY

Virtualization is the use of hardware and software to create the perception that one or more entities exist, although the entities, in actuality, are not physically present. Using virtualization, we can make one server appear to be many, a desktop computer appear to being running multiple operating systems simultaneously, a network connection appear to exist, or a vast amount of disk space or a vast number of drives to be available.

Through the use of server virtualization, companies reduce their server footprint and power consumption, allow servers to support multiple operating systems, and drive server CPU utilization. Further, through the use of desktop virtualization, companies simplify operating system and application administration. If needed, a virtual desktop can also run two or more operating systems at the same time.

Virtualizing drives increases device utilization, simplifies device administration, and improves business continuity and disaster recovery.

KEY TERMS

Guest operating system
Hypervisor
Virtual desktop

Virtual private network (VPN)
Virtual server

CHAPTER REVIEW

1. Define and describe virtualization.
2. Defend the following statement: Virtualization is not a new concept within computer science.
3. Describe the various types of virtualization.
4. List the pros and cons of virtualization.
5. Discuss the attributes of applications that are *not* well suited for virtualization.
6. List reasons why companies should virtualize.
7. List the benefits of blade servers.
8. Define and describe the hypervisor.
9. Define and describe green computing.
10. Describe the concept of the desktop on demand, and include the benefits of such a system.

Securing the Cloud

FOR YEARS, IT DATA centers have been secured physically to prevent users who do not have a need to physically touch computers, servers, and storage devices from doing so. A general security rule is that if an individual can physically touch a device, the individual can more easily break into the device. As you might imagine, for many IT personnel the thought of hosting applications in the cloud is very concerning. When you consider cloud security issues, you should think in terms of two types of threats. Your first list of threats should correspond to the threats common to both cloud-based and on-site solutions. Your second list should focus on those concerns specific to the cloud.

Learning Objectives

This chapter examines cloud-based security. By the time you finish this chapter, you will be able to do the following:

- List the security advantages of using a cloud-based provider.
- List the security disadvantages of using a cloud-based provider.
- Describe common security threats to cloud-based environments.

General Security Advantages of Cloud-Based Solutions

As you have learned, because cloud-based solution providers spread their costs across multiple customers, the providers benefit from their economies of scale—meaning that most have more money available to invest in different solutions, such as security issues. The following list specifies several advantages cloud-based providers may have with respect to security:

- **Immediate deployment of software patches**: Many software patches address specific security concerns and requirements. Most cloud-based solution providers have a team of patch installation specialists who immediately deploy system patches. In this way, the cloud-based systems may have a shorter period of vulnerability after a software patch is released.

- **Extended human-relations reach**: Because of their financial strength, cloud-based solution providers may be able to better vet potential employees who will administer system software. Such vetting may include increased reference checking, security and background checking, and periodic screening (such as by polygraph).

- **Hardware and software redundancy**: Most cloud-based solution providers have redundant hardware and software resources they can quickly deploy in an emergency.

- **Timeliness of incident response**: Within a data center, key personnel often perform multiple tasks. A company's security specialist may also be the company's patch administrator. As a result, there are often delays between the start of a security incident and its identification—which may have a catastrophic result. A cloud-based solution provider, in contrast, likely has experts monitoring systems for intrusion, system utilization, and more. In this way, should a security incident occur, the cloud-based solution provider is likely to be more responsive.

- **Specialists instead of personnel**: Again, because of their financial advantage, cloud-based solution providers may be better positioned to recruit and hire trained system specialists. A small company that tries to handle its own IT, on the other hand, may have a one-person IT staff—and that employee may have a steep learning curve.

There are also security disadvantages to hosting applications and their data within the cloud:

- **Country or jurisdiction**: It is not always clear where cloud-based resources reside. If a cloud hosts its resources within a remote country, for example, one must be concerned with the laws and the government stability of the country. If the cloud resources reside in multiple states, questions of jurisdiction may arise in the event of a legal matter. If a cloud-based provider, for example, receives a subpoena or a request for an e-discovery process, a customer's data may become part of, and exposed to, an unwanted legal discovery.

- **Multitenant risks:** Many cloud-based solution providers use multitenant solutions, which means that two or more customers may use the same resources, such as a database. As a result, an application error might expose one company's data to another company. Likewise, if a data storage device is shared, data remnants from one company may be exposed to another company.
- **Malicious insiders:** Despite a cloud solution provider's best human-relations efforts, there can sometimes be problems with malicious employees. Depending on the employee's role, a company's cloud-based data may be at risk.
- **Vendor lock in:** Depending on how a cloud-based solution provider stores a company's data, it may become difficult for the company to change providers later in the event of a service-level agreement breach or other problem.
- **Risk of the cloud-based provider failing:** Companies who rely on cloud-based providers are at risk that the provider could fail. Some companies ask for a source code escrow agreement, which places a copy of the provider's source code with a third-party company. If the provider fails, the company can gain access to the source code, with which they may be able to rehost the solution.

CASE 9-1 MCAFEE SECURITY AS A SERVICE

To stay current with virus and spyware threats, most antivirus solutions perform constant updates to their virus signature dictionary/database. When you license an antivirus solution, you normally receive at least one year of automatic security system updates. As you work, the antivirus software updates your system against new threats behind the scenes. In general, the antivirus software, as shown in **FIGURE 9–1**, pulls in the threat signatures from across the cloud.

McAfee now offers a range of security solutions that deploy from the cloud. The solutions protect e-mail (spam, phishing, redirection, and virus elimination), websites, desktop computers, mobile devices, and more. **FIGURE 9–2** shows the McAfee security as a service web page.

Exercise Assume that you must provide desktop antivirus and antispam support for 1,000 desktop computers. Visit the McAfee website and create a proposal that includes your solution features and cost.

Web Resources For additional information on McAfee security as a service, see www.CloudBookContent.com/Chapter09/index.html.

continues

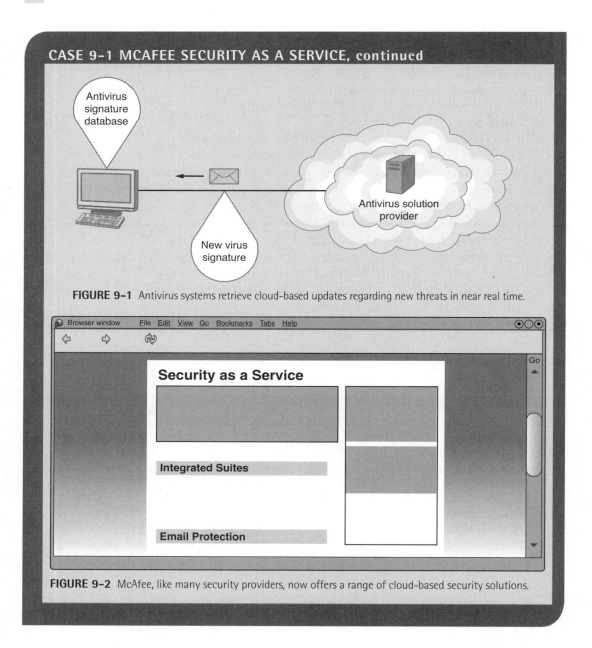

CASE 9-1 MCAFEE SECURITY AS A SERVICE, continued

Antivirus signature database

Antivirus solution provider

New virus signature

FIGURE 9-1 Antivirus systems retrieve cloud-based updates regarding new threats in near real time.

Browser window   File Edit View Go Bookmarks Tabs Help

Go

Security as a Service

Integrated Suites

Email Protection

FIGURE 9-2 McAfee, like many security providers, now offers a range of cloud-based security solutions.

Introducing Business Continuity and Disaster Recovery

Chapter 10, *Disaster Recovery and Business Continuity and the Cloud*, examines business continuity and disaster recovery in detail. Within Chapter 10, you will learn that companies always face a variety of risks. Each company's goal is to evaluate the risks and to determine ways to mitigate (reduce) them. When you work with security issues, the same technique applies. To start, you must determine where your system is vulnerable and then you must take steps to reduce the vulnerability. The following sections examine common security threats.

Understanding Data Storage Wiping

In Chapter 6, *Data Storage in the Cloud*, you learned that many facilities offer cloud-based storage. Often a cloud-based data storage provider may share a storage device across multiple customers. Assume, for example, that you store a confidential company document within the cloud. Later you delete that document. Normally, when the file system deletes a file on disk, the file system simply marks the locations within which the file resided as available for use to store other files. Assume that another customer comes along and allocates space on the disk for storage but does not write any information to the space. If the customer examines the allocated space, the customer may have access to your previously deleted confidential document!

To prevent such inadvertent data access, many cloud-based data storage facilities will *wipe* a file's contents upon deletion. **Data wiping** is the term used when a cloud-based storage device overwrites (wipes) a file's contents when a file is deleted. Wiping involves overwriting the previous file space with a series of values. In this way, as shown in **FIGURE 9-3**, if a customer allocates space within a cloud-based disk, that customer cannot read the disk's previous content.

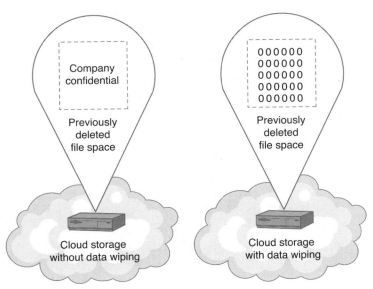

FIGURE 9-3 Within a cloud-based disk storage facility, file wiping overwrites a file's previous contents when the file is deleted.

Understanding Distributed Denial-of-Service (DDoS) Attacks

A **denial–of–service attack** is a hacker attack on a site, the goal of which is to consume system resources so that the resources cannot be used by the site's users. The motivation for and the implementation of denial-of-service attacks differ. The following batch file, for example, repeatedly sends ping requests to a specified website. Because the site must respond to the requests, it may need to deny or delay service to other users:

```
:Loop
ping SomeSite.com
GOTO Loop
```

A distributed denial-of-service (DDoS) attack uses multiple computers distributed across the Internet to attack a target site, as shown in **FIGURE 9-4**.

It can be challenging for a server to defend itself against a denial-of-service attack. Often a server slows down considerably before the attack can be detected and defended. The advantage of a cloud-based host with respect to a denial-of-service attack is that the cloud server may scale its resources quickly to respond to the attack messages in such a way that the site's users are not impacted. The increased scaling will notify the administrators that the site is under attack so they can initiate defensive actions.

Packet Sniffing

Across the Internet and cloud, applications communicate by exchanging packets of data. As shown in **FIGURE 9-5**, within a wired network each computer examines packets to determine which ones are addressed to it.

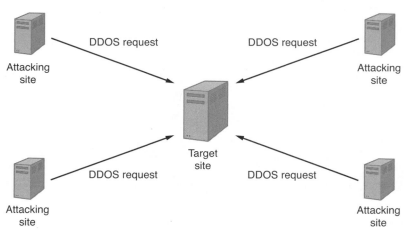

FIGURE 9-4 A DDoS attack employs multiple computers to attack a target site.

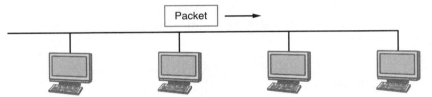

FIGURE 9-5 Network applications communicate by exchanging network packets. Each computer within a wired network examines the message address to determine if the message is for an application it is running.

A hacker can write code that lets his or her system examine the content of each packet that travels past it. Such programs, called packet sniffers, allow the hacker to view, and in some cases change, a packet's contents. Within a wireless network, hackers can simply monitor the airways to intercept packets.

The best defense against a **packet sniffing** attack is to use secure (encrypted) connections. The cloud, because it allows users to connect to applications from anywhere, increases potential risks. Users may connect from an insecure network or a network in which the wireless traffic is being monitored. To reduce the threat of such attacks, more cloud-based applications will require secure connections in the future.

Man-in-the-Middle Attack

A **man-in-the-middle attack** is much as it sounds. In general, the attack occurs when a hacker, as shown in **FIGURE 9-6**, is able to interrupt network messages and essentially place himself or herself between the user and the remote system. When the hacker is positioned in this way, he or she can then then send messages that appear to come from either the user or the system, as needed.

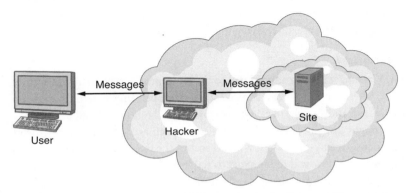

FIGURE 9-6 Within a man-in-the-middle attack, a hacker intercepts the messages a user and system are exchanging. The hacker can view and/or change the message contents.

Because cloud-based solutions rely on user communications across the Internet, the solutions are at risk for man-in-the-middle attacks. A good defense against such attacks is to establish a secure (encrypted) connection with the remote server.

Monitoring Device Screens

Years ago, when employees accessed sensitive or confidential data only from within their office, the physical data were better protected from prying eyes. The cloud, however, extends the delivery of such data to users who are any place, at any time, and often to any device. The net result is that within a busy coffee shop or an airport, strangers can see data ranging from human-relations information or customer sales data to student grades, and more.

Unfortunately, the problems caused by remote data access will only get worse. The best defense against screen monitoring is user training. Users who access sensitive data must be aware of their surroundings.

Malicious Employees

Companies spend considerable amounts of money trying to protect their data and communications from hackers. IT staffs deploy firewalls, use encryption, monitor network traffic for intrusion, and much more. With all of these security features in place, the most difficult challenge for a company to defend itself against is a malicious employee. Developers, for example, have access to databases, and IT staff members have access to various system passwords, which means that each may have access to human-relations data, payroll data, e-mail content, and so on.

By shifting data to the cloud, you move sensitive data away from your own employees. However, the data are now accessible to a staff of IT personnel that you do not know. For many data items, such as payroll data, the cloud-based staff is likely less interested and curious about the data. That said, companies must feel confident that the data they store within the cloud are secure. To meet these concerns, cloud-based solution providers are intensifying their recruitment and hiring processes.

Hypervisor Attack

Chapter 8, *Virtualization*, introduced you to the concept of server virtualization. As you learned, when you virtualize a server, each server operating system runs on top of special virtualization software called the hypervisor, as shown in **FIGURE 9-7**.

As you might imagine, hypervisor developers such as VMware and Microsoft constantly focus on ways to lock down and secure the hypervisor to reduce risks. That said, the hypervisor will remain an attractive hacker target as companies continue to virtualize solutions. Hackers refer to the process of taking over the hypervisor as a **hyperjacking attack**. In the future, to reduce the chance of a hypervisor being taken over by malicious code, the underlying hardware may assign a state

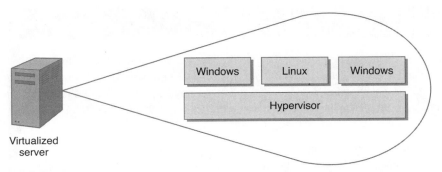

FIGURE 9-7 The hypervisor is special software that allows virtualization of system resources.

value, like a cyclic redundancy check (CRC), to the hypervisor. If this value changes, the hardware can detect that the hypervisor has been attacked or replaced.

Guest-Hopping Attack

Within a virtualized server, the operating systems that execute are called guest operating systems. Assume, as shown in **FIGURE 9-8**, that a virtual server is running three operating systems and a hacker is trying to attack operating system A.

If the hacker is unable to directly attack operating system A, the hacker may then try to attack operating system B. If the hacker is successful, the hacker may then initiate a peer-level attack on operating system A, as shown in **FIGURE 9-9**. Hackers refer to an attack from one guest operating system to another as a **guest-hopping attack**.

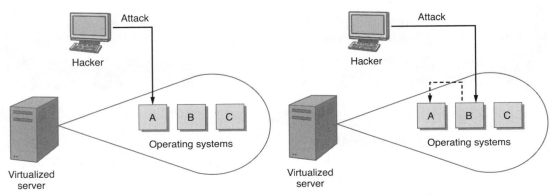

FIGURE 9-8 A virtualized server running three guest operating systems with a hacker trying to attack operating system A.

FIGURE 9-9 A guest-hopping attack occurs when a hacker tries to attack one guest operating system from another.

CASE 9-2 CLOUD SECURITY ALLIANCE

The Cloud Security Alliance is a not-for-profit organization, the goal of which is to promote education of cloud security issues. The Cloud Security Alliance consists of a large coalition of cloud practitioners, companies, associations, and other cloud stakeholders. As shown in **FIGURE 9–10**, the Cloud Security Alliance offers training that can lead to a Certificate of Cloud Security Knowledge.

Exercise Visit the Cloud Security Alliance website. Produce a list of cloud security topics one should understand in preparation for taking the cloud knowledge certification exam.

Web Resources For additional information on the Cloud Security Alliance, see www .CloudBookContent.com/Chapter09/index.html.

FIGURE 9–10 The Cloud Security Alliance offers training and certification in cloud security knowledge.

SQL-Injection Attack

Many web applications present forms that users must complete by filling in fields and then submitting the form contents for processing. The application that receives the form data often stores the data within an SQL database. An **SQL-injection attack** occurs when a malicious user inserts one or more SQL queries within one or more of the fields. For example, rather than simply typing in his or her last name, the hacker might type the following:

```
Smith; DROP DATABASE EMPLOYEES;
```

Depending on how the database uses the user input, the processing may result in the execution of the injected SQL, which in this case would delete the database of the company's employees. When developers prompt users to enter data within forms, the developers must be aware of and test for such injections.

CASE 9-3 EUROPEAN NETWORK AND INFORMATION SECURITY AGENCY (ENISA)

The European Network and Information Security Agency (ENISA), based in Greece, promotes cybersecurity best practices. Within the ENISA website, you will find a broad range of papers and reports on a variety of security topics. **FIGURE 9-11**, for example, illustrates the ENISA Cloud Computing Risk Assessment page which you should read.

Exercise Visit the ENISA website and review the Cloud Computing Risk Assessment page and document. Create a two- to three-page executive summary that describes the risk assessment overview.

Web Resources For additional information on ENISA security recommendations, see www .CloudBookContent.com/Chapter09/index.html.

FIGURE 9-11 The ENISA website provides a wide range of cybersecurity best practices, including recommendations for secure cloud computing.

Many cloud-based SaaS solutions are multitenant applications, which means different customers may share underlying resources such as a database. If the SaaS application falls victim to SQL injection, it might be possible for a user in one company to view, change, or destroy the data of another company.

Physical Security

In Chapter 10, *Disaster Recovery and Business Continuity and the Cloud*, you will examine a variety of system threats, including fire, flood, theft, earthquakes, tornadoes, hurricanes, and power outages. A cloud-based solution provider, like all data center facilities, is subject to each of these threats. Most, however, reduce the risk of such threats by replicating (colocating) identical systems at geographically dispersed locations, as shown in **FIGURE 9–12**.

If one system fails, the service provider can immediately fail over to the other system. Further, because most cloud service providers have state-of-the-art data centers, they normally have fire suppression systems, backup power generators, and strong physical security measures in place.

Servers   Disks

Colocated resources

FIGURE 9–12 By using colocated, replicated hardware and software, cloud solution providers reduce many threats to IT resources.

CHAPTER SUMMARY

For years, IT data centers physically secured resources to prevent users who do not have a need to physically touch computers, servers, and storage devices from doing so. IT security professionals know that anyone who can physically touch a device can more easily break into it, and so much of IT security is based on preventing access. The cloud, however, changes the security model significantly by making data available to users anywhere, anytime, with virtually any device. Securing cloud-based applications takes planning and resources. As you examine cloud security issues, think in terms of two types of threats: those that are common to both cloud-based and on-site solutions, and threats that are specific to the cloud.

KEY TERMS

Data wiping
Denial-of-service attack
Guest-hopping attack
Hyperjacking attack

Man-in-the-middle attack
Packet sniffing
SQL-injection attack

CHAPTER REVIEW

1. List the security advantages of cloud-based solutions.
2. List the security disadvantages of cloud-based solutions.
3. Define and discuss the data wiping process.
4. Discuss how a cloud-based solution provider may reduce the risk of a DDoS attack.
5. Define and discuss hyperjacking attacks.
6. Define and discuss guest-hopping attacks.

Disaster Recovery and Business Continuity and the Cloud

FOR YEARS, A PRIMARY job of the IT staff of an organization was to ensure availability of computing resources (applications, files, and even phone systems) not only on a day-to-day basis, but also in the event of a crisis or natural disaster. Business continuity describes the policies, procedures, and actions taken by an organization to ensure the availability of critical business functions to employees, customers, and other key stakeholders. Disaster recovery describes the steps a business will take to restore operations in the event of a disaster (fire, flood, hurricane, tornado, or other event). Following 9/11, business continuity and disaster recovery became a very real and essential IT function.

Learning Objectives

This chapter examines ways companies can leverage the cloud to increase business continuity and to simplify disaster recovery. By the time you finish this chapter, you will be able to do the following:

- Define and describe business continuity.
- Define and describe disaster recovery.
- Describe the benefits of cloud-based or off-site backups.
- Evaluate the risk of various threats and discuss steps to mitigate each.
- Discuss the role of colocation as a business continuity and disaster recovery solution.
- Identify and discuss a variety of system threats.
- Describe the benefits of a cloud-based phone system.
- Describe the benefit of cloud-based data storage to business continuity.
- Describe the importance of testing/auditing the business continuity and disaster recovery plan.
- Create a business continuity and disaster recovery plan.

Understanding the Threats

An IT staff must anticipate and prepare for a wide range of system threats. The following sections examine common threats, how IT teams traditionally tried to mitigate threat risks, and how cloud-based solutions may further mitigate risks.

Threat: Disk Failure

Disk drives are mechanical devices, and as such they will eventually wear out and fail. Further, other threats, such as fire, flood, theft, or power surges, can result in the loss of disk-based data.

All mechanical devices have an associated **mean time between failure (MTBF)** rating. For a disk drive, the MTBF may be 500,000 hours of use (about 8 years). That said, it is important that you understand how manufacturers calculate the MTBF. To start, the manufacturer may begin running 1,000 disk drives. When the first disk drive fails, the manufacturer will note the time—let's say after 500 hours (less than a month). The manufacturers then multiply that time by the number of devices that they tested to determine the MTBF:

```
MTBF = (500) x (1000)
     = 500,000 hours
```

It's important to note that no device in the group ran near the 500,000 hours!

Traditional Risk Mitigation for Disk Failure

The first and foremost risk mitigation for disk failure is to have up-to-date disk backups. If a disk fails, the company can simply replace the disk and restore the backup. That implies, of course, that the cause of the disk failure (fire, smoke, flood, or theft) did not also damage the disk backup. To reduce such risk, most companies store their disk backups at an off-site storage facility.

CASE 10-1 IRON MOUNTAIN OFF-SITE TAPE VAULTING

Because of their ease of use, inexpensive cost, and high storage capacity, many companies continue to use tape backups for their disk storage. A lot of companies use Iron Mountain to store the tape backups securely. If the company ever needs to restore a disk or retrieve an archived letter, e-mail, or other data for legal or compliance reasons, the company can simply retrieve and restore the magnetic tape. The question then becomes, why use Iron Mountain? The answer is simple: they have been storing key company data since 1951!

continues

CASE 10-1 IRON MOUNTAIN OFF-SITE TAPE VAULTING, continued

Today Iron Mountain provides a variety of services beyond digital tape storage:

- Document management
- Cloud-based automatic backups
- Records management and storage (including health records)
- Secure document shredding
- And more

Exercise Assume your company must back up 500 users' desktops and 20 physical servers. Visit the Iron Mountain website and create two backup plan options.

Web Resources For additional information on Iron Mountain and the company's backup solutions, see www.CloudBookContent.com/Chapter10/index.html.

The problem with the remote tape backup system is that it takes time. To start, the company may need to purchase a replacement disk. Then the company must install and format the disk for use. Finally the company's tape storage facility must locate and return the tape that contains the data.

To reduce the potential need to retrieve and store a tape backup, companies turned to multiple disk storage solutions.

RAID-Protected Storage Today, many data centers use a **redundant array of independent (or inexpensive) disks (RAID)** to reduce the impact of disk failure. A RAID system contains multiple disk drives. Rather than simply store a file on one drive, the RAID system stores the data across several drives. In addition, the RAID system stores data that can be used to reconstruct the file if one of the drives fail. In this way, if a disk drive fails, no file recovery is required from the tape backup. Instead, the IT staff can simply replace the failed disk and the RAID system will rebuild the disk's contents on the fly!

It is important to note that RAID systems do not eliminate the need for disk backups. If fire, flood, or theft occurs, the entire contents of all the RAID drives may be lost. In such a case, the tape backup of the drives becomes the data restoration solution.

Cloud-Based Data Storage and Backup Solutions

Chapter 6 examined cloud-based data storage in detail. As you learned, cloud-based storage not only lets users access their data from any place, at any time, and often with any device, but it also provides enhanced data replication. As shown in

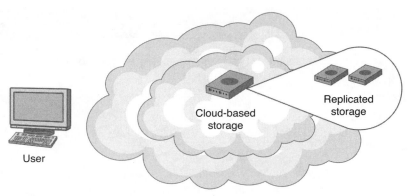

FIGURE 10-1 Most cloud-based data storage facilities provide automatic data replication to another cloud-based data repository.

FIGURE 10-1, many cloud-based data storage systems automatically replicate cloud-based data at a second off-site, cloud-based facility. In this way, if one of the RAID-based cloud devices fail, the cloud-based data provider can immediately fail over to the redundant device.

Further, as discussed in Chapter 6, many cloud-based facilities now use a RAID-like file system, which produces recovery data the facility can use in the event of a device failure.

Cloud-Based Data Backups
Chapter 6 examined the role of cloud-based backups in detail. Because cloud-based backups reside at a remote storage facility, the backups immediately introduce a level of protection. Then, because the backup files are immediately available from any device, anywhere, the backups reduce potential downtime because no time is needed to find, retrieve, and restore a tape backup from a traditional backup storage facility.

Threat: Power Failure or Disruption
Computers are sensitive electronic devices. When a computer loses power, the user's current unsaved data is lost. Further, an electrical spike can permanently damage the computer's electronic components, rendering the device unusable or destroying disk-based data. Although power blackouts can be caused by storms, accidents, or acts of terrorism, the more common power brownout is typically more damaging. And, unfortunately, power brownouts can be quite common, especially in the hot summer months when electrical demands spike.

Traditional Power Loss Risk Mitigation
To reduce the risk of an electrical surge damaging a computer and its peripherals, most users plug their computers and devices into a surge suppressor. Although

A

B

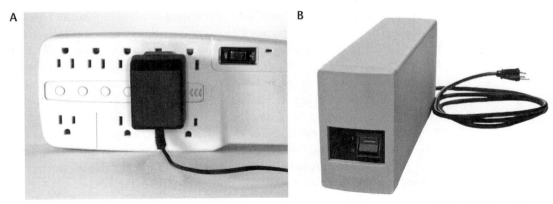

FIGURE 10-2 Users plug devices into surge suppressors to protect the devices from power spikes. A UPS provides users with a few minutes of battery backup power so the users can save their work and shut down their systems in an orderly way.

the surge suppressor can prevent damaging power spikes from reaching the computer's electronic components, the surge suppressor cannot help against power loss. If a power loss occurs, the user's unsaved work will be lost.

To reduce the risk of lost work, many users plug their devices into an **uninterruptible power supply (UPS)**. Most UPS devices provide 10 to 15 minutes of battery backup power, which gives users time to save their work and shut down their systems in a conventional way. **FIGURE 10-2** shows a surge suppressor and a UPS.

Within a data center, as you can imagine, it would be physically impossible to plug every device into its own UPS. Further, within a data center, a loss of power also means a loss of critical air conditioning to cool the computer devices. To mitigate risks from power loss, some data centers use very large UPS-like devices that provide a period of battery power to all of the powered devices. Further, as shown in **FIGURE 10-3**, if the power outage lasts a long time, the data center can switch to a large diesel-powered generator to drive power.

FIGURE 10-3 Many data centers have diesel-powered generators to produce power in the event of a long-term outage.

Colocation of Data Resources Colocation is the process of replicating key data processing, data storage, and possibly telecommunications equipment at a second remote facility. In other words, a company will duplicate its data center at a second facility. The advantage of colocation is that if one data center fails, the system can immediately fail over to the second facility. The disadvantage of colocation is cost. Not only does the company have to replicate its equipment, but it must also pay for the power, air conditioning, and staffing for a second facility.

Colocation is one way to reduce the risk of power failure. It is not enough to simply locate the second facility across the street or even across town. One must place the second facility across the country to eliminate the impact of storms, attacks, or power grid failures.

Cloud-Based Power Loss Risk Mitigation

Chapter 3, *Platform as a Service (PaaS)*, introduced the concept of cloud-based PaaS solutions. Likewise, Chapter 4, *Infrastructure as a Service (IaaS)*, presented the concept of cloud-based IaaS solutions. When you consider the expensive infrastructure needed to reduce the impact of power interruption, that alone should make you consider housing the data center off-site within the cloud. Most PaaS and IaaS solution providers have effectively dealt with power loss issues. Remember, such providers can share the infrastructure costs across many customers. Also, most of the providers have colocated facilities on different power grids.

CASE 10-2 SITE SECURE NET | THE PLANET

Many companies today provide cloud-based PaaS and IaaS solutions with excellent power management facilities. Site Secure Net | The Planet is one such company, featured here because its website, shown in **FIGURE 10-4**, specifically addresses the company's power management infrastructure. Beyond a state-of-the-art power management system, Site Secure Net | The Planet also provides colocation support. If power fails in one facility, the second facility can immediately take over operations.

Exercise Assume that your company has an in-house data center and 500 on-site user computers. Discuss the steps you would recommend that the company pursue to provide power management to the computer resources.

Web Resources For additional information on Site Secure Net | The Planet, see www.Cloud BookContent.com/Chapter10/index.html.

continues

CASE 10-2 SITE SECURE NET | THE PLANET, continued

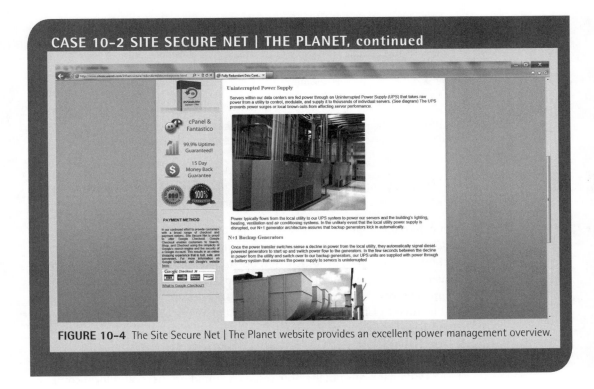

FIGURE 10-4 The Site Secure Net | The Planet website provides an excellent power management overview.

Threat: Computer Viruses

As users surf the web (potentially downloading and installing software) and share drives (such as junk drives), their systems and those in the same network are at risk for a computer **virus** attack or spyware. It is estimated that within the United States alone, lost productivity time due to computer viruses exceeds $10 billion per year!

Traditional Computer Virus Risk Mitigation

The best defense against computer viruses and spyware is to ensure that every system has antivirus software installed. Most antivirus solutions today automatically update themselves across the web, as often as daily, with the most recent virus and spyware signatures.

Second, many organizations prevent users from installing their own software. Not only does this practice reduce the chance of a computer virus infection, it also aids the company in preventing the installation of software that the company does not own.

Third, as shown in **FIGURE 10-5**, home users should enable a firewall on their system, either at their router or on the computer itself. Most companies place a firewall outside the network.

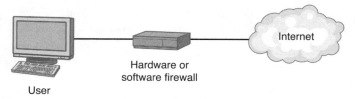

FIGURE 10-5 Home computer users and business users should protect their systems by placing a firewall between the systems and the Internet.

Fourth, companies must train users to not open e-mail attachments in messages they receive from users they do not know.

Cloud-Based Computer Virus Risk Mitigation

In Chapter 8, *Virtualization*, you learned that many companies now virtualize desktop systems and, in some cases, download an operating system image on demand. A side effect of this virtualization process is a reduced opportunity for a computer virus to make its home within a user's desktop environment. Further, as you learned in Chapter 9, *Securing the Cloud*, many companies are moving to cloud-based antivirus solutions.

Threat: Fire

Fire can damage computer resources, data stored on disks, and local copies of system backups. If the fire itself does not damage the equipment, the smoke or the process of putting out the fire will.

Traditional Fire Risk Management

Most offices have sprinkler systems, which, as you can imagine, destroy computers when they deploy. Often there is no good way to protect office hardware other than simply to insure it. The goal, when such damage occurs, is to get the users up and running again as soon as possible—**business continuity**, in other words. That means that system backups must be up to date and must be stored at an off-site location.

Within a data center, you normally won't find sprinkler systems, but rather **halon** systems, based on compounds of carbon and one or more halogens, that stop fire by removing all the oxygen from the room.

Cloud-Based Fire Risk Mitigation

If you house your data center in the cloud, your system will reside in a state-of-the-art data center that provides fire suppression systems and, in most cases, colocated system redundancy. Again, because the PaaS and IaaS solution providers share their costs across many customers, they are able to provide their customers with top-level service at a relatively low cost.

Threat: Floods

During the rainy season, the nightly news often leads with a story about a city or state that is under water due to flooding. Depending on the speed and severity of the flood, companies may have a chance to remove systems from the area before the flood hits. If not, the equipment and the data stored within it is typically lost.

Traditional Flood Risk Mitigation

As with fire, so with flood: the best defense is to have current backups and insured equipment. Within many data centers you will find flood sensors, similar to the one shown in **FIGURE 10-6**, which sound an alarm if water is detected. These sensors do not exist to detect widespread flooding, but rather water leaking from an on-site pipe break.

FIGURE 10-6 Many data centers use water detection systems to sound alarms if a pipe breaks.

Cloud-Based Flood Risk Mitigation

A good rule of thumb is to not place your data center within a flood zone. Historically, most companies had little choice—they had to place their data center near their business offices, often in the same building. Today, however, with cloud-based PaaS and IaaS solutions readily available, the data center can essentially reside anywhere. Thus, the new rule of thumb is to not select a PaaS or IaaS provider located in a flood zone.

Threat: Disgruntled Employees

A disgruntled employee can harm a company by launching a computer virus, changing or deleting files, or exposing system passwords. It is very difficult to defend completely against a disgruntled employee, particularly one who has physical access to systems.

Traditional Disgruntled Employee Risk Mitigation

In the past, businesses protected themselves from disgruntled employees by trying to limit the damage such an employee could cause. First, as previously discussed, companies must ensure that up-to-date backups are in place. Second, the company must use controls to limit the resources that employees can access to only those they need in order to perform their jobs. Then, if an employee is terminated, the company must quickly disable the employee's access to all systems.

Cloud-Based Disgruntled Employee Risk Mitigation

Chapter 5, *Identity as a Service (IDaaS)*, presented the single sign-on process and ways companies are using the cloud to implement IDaaS. In this way, if a company terminates an employee, the company can quickly disable the employee's access to all systems by simply disabling the employee within the authentication server. Chapter 8, *Virtualization*, examined desktop virtualization. If a company provides employees with a desktop on demand, most employees (except for the one in charge of desktop images) can do little to harm the system.

Threat: Lost Equipment

Each year, within airports alone, thousands of notebook computers are lost or stolen. When an employee loses a notebook, not only is the computer lost, but also the user's local data, which may be confidential. Today, with users carrying powerful handheld devices, the opportunity for loss becomes even greater. Given the amount of information a user stores on such a device, identity theft often follows the theft of a device.

Traditional Lost Equipment Risk Mitigation

To reduce the risk of data loss when a device is lost or stolen (or broken), the user must maintain current backups. To reduce access to company sensitive data, many systems require a username and password or biometric sign-on. Although such techniques can be bypassed by an advanced hacker, they will prevent most criminals from accessing data.

Cloud-Based Lost Equipment Risk Mitigation

Typically, the more a company utilizes the cloud, the less risk the company will have with respect to a lost device. If, for example, the user stores (or syncs) key files to a cloud-based data repository, the user is likely to lose only minimal data. Likewise, if the company uses a cloud-based system such as Exchange Online, the user will be without e-mail, calendar, and contact access for only a brief period of time.

Threat: Desktop Failure

Computers, like all devices, may eventually wear out and fail. The cause of failure may be a bad disk drive, motherboard, power supply, and so on. The bottom line is that a user is now without a system.

Traditional Desktop Failure Risk Mitigation

The first step in recovering from a desktop failure is to ensure that current backups of the user's files exist. Many companies have users store key files on a network disk, which the company can easily back up and later restore. In most companies, a user experiencing the desktop failure will be offline until the IT staff can locate a replacement computer, install and configure software, restore backups of any of the user's local files, and then make the system available. A few hours of employee downtime can have a significant cost.

Cloud-Based Desktop Failure Risk Mitigation

Chapter 8, *Virtualization*, examined desktop virtualization. If a company delivers the users' desktops on demand, a user whose system has failed need only stand up, walk to another system, and log in. The employee can then resume work right where he or she left off. Further, if the user stores files in the cloud, he or she can likely access them from any device, and, if necessary, use software such as Office Web Apps to access and edit the files.

Threat: Server Failure

Just as desktop computers can fail, so too can servers. Because most servers today are blade devices, replacing a server is a relatively simple process, as shown in **FIGURE 10-7**, as long as the company has an extra server available. Because most servers boot from a network-attached storage (NAS) device, the process of getting the new server up and running should be easy.

FIGURE 10-7 Blade server replacement is normally fast and simple. Because most servers boot from a NAS device, only minimal software setup is normally required.

Traditional Server Failure Risk Mitigation

If a company has a mission-critical application running on a lone server and does not have a replacement server available, or better yet, online, then shame on that company. Device redundancy is the only way to recover quickly from a server failure.

Cloud-Based Server Failure Risk Mitigation

Given not only the cost factors, but also the advantages discussed throughout this chapter, most server applications should reside in the cloud with a PaaS or IaaS solution provider. Such providers typically provide 99.9 percent uptime through hardware redundancy and automatic failover.

Threat: Network Failure

Although networks consist primarily of cables and simple switching devices, things can break. For simple networks, the network will remain down until the faulty device or cable is identified and replaced.

Traditional Network Failure Risk Mitigation

For home computer users, when a network fails, users are going to be offline until a fix is applied. If the problem resides within the Internet service provider (ISP), the user can do nothing to resolve the issue. As a solution, some users are purchasing 3G and 4G wireless hotspot devices as a backup method of accessing the Internet.

To make sure that the network does not become a single point of failure, some companies bring in a second Internet source from a vendor other than their primary ISP. In this way, if one network provider fails, the company can gain access to the Internet through the backup network. Further, given that the backup network is in place, many companies will use it to load balance their bandwidth demands.

Cloud-Based Network Failure Mitigation

At first consideration, relying on the cloud for application and data storage may make the thought of a network failure quite concerning. However, as you have just read, to reduce the risk of network failure many companies provide redundant network connections to the Internet. The same is true for cloud service providers. Again, most will guarantee 99.9 percent uptime.

Threat: Database System Failure

Most companies today rely on database management systems to store a wide range of data, from customer data, to human resources data, to application-specific data. If a company's database fails, many applications may also fail.

Traditional Database System Failure Risk Mitigation

The first defense in reducing the risk of database failure is to maintain current backups of the database. Most database systems today make the backup process easy and automatic. If the database fails, the IT staff can restore the backup. Unfortunately, the database and the applications that rely on it will be down while the restoration is performed.

To reduce the risk of database downtime as a result of a database failure, companies typically replicate data across two database systems in real time. When an operation updates data within the database, the database replication software will immediately update both database systems, as shown in **FIGURE 10–8**.

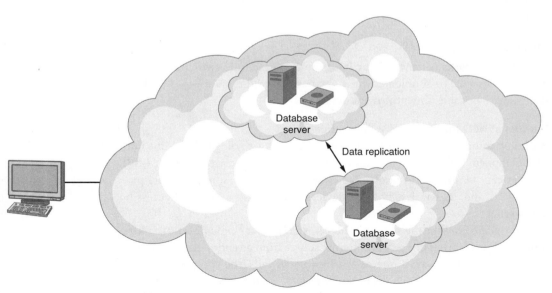

Database
server

Data replication

Database
server

FIGURE 10–8 Database replication creates two live copies of databases on separate servers. If one database fails, the other can immediately take over operations.

Cloud-Based Database System Failure Risk Mitigation

As you just learned, to reduce potential system downtime in the event of a database system failure, many companies replicate the database contents in real time. The disadvantage of database replication is that it requires two servers (ideally in different locations) and may be complicated for developers to initially configure.

Chapter 6, *Data Storage in the Cloud*, discussed cloud-based database management systems in detail. As you learned, most cloud-based database storage providers use transparent database replication. If a database in the cloud fails, the system will fail over to the backup database automatically. Further, because replication can occur in both directions, the system can use the second database for load balancing. If data is updated in either system, the change will be replicated to the other system.

Threat: Phone System Failure

Despite the fact that virtually all employees carry a cell phone today, most organizations still maintain phone systems that provide voice mail, conference calling, and call forwarding. If the phone system fails, the company can resort to cell phones. Unfortunately, customers calling in to the company would not know which numbers to call.

Traditional Phone System Failure Risk Mitigation

Historically, there have been few ways outside of redundancy to reduce the impact of a phone system failure. That was the case until the advent of cloud-based phone systems.

Cloud-Based Phone System Failure Risk Mitigation

To avoid a single point of failure for phone systems, cloud-based phone systems have now emerged. The cloud-based systems provide the functionality of a traditional phone system and, behind the scenes, provide system replication.

CASE 10-3 RINGCENTRAL CLOUD-BASED PHONE SYSTEM

RingCentral is a cloud-based phone system provider. It offers a cost-effective phone system solution. Features of RingCentral include the following:

- Free nationwide calling and faxing
- Support for existing phones and faxes as well as RingCentral IP phones
- Lets users place calls from any phone, anywhere, while appearing to be made from the usual office number
- Caller greetings customized by the time of day

continues

CASE 10-3 RINGCENTRAL CLOUD-BASED PHONE SYSTEM, continued

- Fully customizable call forwarding
- Forwarding of voice mail and faxes to e-mail
- A phone directory system that helps callers locate personnel
- Ability to let companies deliver music or corporate messaging to callers who are on hold

FIGURE 10-9 presents the RingCentral website.

Exercise Discuss the pros and cons of using a cloud-based phone system provider.

Web Resources For additional information on RingCentral and the company's phone system solutions, see www.CloudBookContent.com/Chapter10/index.html.

FIGURE 10-9 RingCentral offers a fully functional cloud-based phone system.

Understanding Service-Level Agreements

When you sign a service agreement with a cloud-based solution provider, your agreement will normally contain a clause called a **service-level agreement (SLA)**. The SLA defines the level of service that the cloud-based company must provide. Common components of an SLA include MTBF, uptime percentage, throughput, and other performance benchmarks. Before you enter into an agreement, pay close attention to the details of the SLA.

Measuring Business Impact: The Essence of Risk Mitigation

Often the process of reducing risk will bring with it some sort of cost, perhaps for backups, system redundancy, and so on. As a result, a business cannot always eliminate all technology risks. Instead, the IT staff must evaluate which risks are most likely and which risks have the greatest potential impact on the company and its ability to continue operations. The risk mitigation process requires that the IT staff balance risks and potential impacts.

To start the risk mitigation process, make a list of the company's potential technology risks. Then estimate each risk's potential for occurrence and its business continuity impact, as shown in **TABLE 10-1**.

You may want to add a column that estimates the cost to reduce the risk. In this way, you can provide management with the key factors they should consider as they invest in resources to reduce the company's technology risks.

TABLE 10-1   RISK OCCURRENCE PROBABILITY AND BUSINESS CONTINUITY IMPACT

Risk	Occurrence Probability	Business Continuity Impact
User disk failure	Medium	Low
Server disk failure	Low	High
Network failure	Low	High
Database failure	Medium	High
Phone system failure	Low	Medium
Server power failure	High	High
Desktop power failure	High	Low
Desktop failure	Low	Low
Fire	Low	High
Flood	Low	High

Disaster Recovery Plan Template

Companies should have a **disaster recovery plan (DRP)** in place that details their planned operations. To get started with a DRP, you can use the following template as a guide.

COMPANY NAME: BUSINESS CONTINUITY AND DISASTER RECOVERY PLAN

PLAN OVERVIEW

Company Name is taking steps to provide risk mitigation, business continuity, and disaster recovery for its information technology and communications infrastructure. The following sections detail the operational plan and recommend responsible parties. When possible, the plan sections provide detailed contact information for the plan's responsible parties and stakeholders.

This plan is CONFIDENTIAL and is the property of *Company Name*.

PLAN GOALS AND OBJECTIVES

The goals of this business continuity and disaster recovery plan include the following:

- To ensure the safety of all *Company Name* employees
- To provide the ability to resume key business operations quickly and safely within the shortest possible amount of time following a disaster or business interruption
- To mitigate the impact of a disaster to *Company Name* stakeholders
- To reduce confusion with respect to operational steps and responsibility in the event of a disaster

DISASTER OR EVENT CATEGORIZATION

The *Company Name* recovery plan addresses three types of disaster or business interruption events:

- **Short term:** A day or less
- **Medium term:** A month or less
- **Long term:** A month or more, with the possible relocation of employees and facilities

DISASTER RECOVERY TEAM

Company Name has assigned the following key personnel to the disaster recovery team:

continues

COMPANY NAME: BUSINESS CONTINUITY AND DISASTER RECOVERY PLAN, continued

EMERGENCY CONTACT INFORMATION

Key contact	Individual	E-mail	Phone	Web
Emergency			911	
Telephone/VoIP	John Smith	JS@PhoneCompany.com	555-1212	www.PhoneCompany.com
Power/electrical	Alice Park	AP@PowerCompany.com	555-VOLT	www.PowerCompany.com
HVAC	Bill Davis	BD@HVAC.com	555-1212	www.HVAC.com
Facility contact	Jay Adams	JA@Facility.com	555-1212	www.Facility.com
Cloud provider	Jim Mills	JM@Cloud.com	555-1212	www.Cloud.com

RISK IDENTIFICATION

Tornado	Hurricane	Flood
Hail	Earthquake	Fire
Power failure (server, desktop)	Phone system	Database failure
Disk (server, desktop)	Theft	Disgruntled employee
Virus	Network failure	System failure (desktop, server)

RISK ANALYSIS

Risk	Occurrence Probability	Business Continuity Impact
User disk failure	Medium	Low
Server disk failure	Low	High
Network failure	Low	High
Database failure	Low	High
Phone system failure	Low	Medium
Server power failure	High	High
Desktop power failure	High	Low
Fire	Low	High
Flood	Low	High
Virus	High	High

continues

COMPANY NAME: BUSINESS CONTINUITY AND DISASTER RECOVERY PLAN, continued

RISK MITIGATION

Risk	Mitigation
User disk failure	*Company Name* will back up user disks to the Carbonite cloud-based backup system.
Server disk failure	*Company Name* will use RAID systems for all servers and will back up the server disks to the Carbonite cloud-based backup system.
Network failure	*Company Name* will bring two Internet providers into each facility and load balance the network traffic across the shared bandwidth.
Database failure	*Company Name* will replicate its existing database system to a remote database that resides in the cloud and will implement an automatic failover.
Phone system failure	*Company Name* will tie all company cell phones to the RingCentral cloud-based phone system.
Server power failure	*Company Name* will colocate a replicated copy of its servers within a cloud-based PaaS facility and will use load balancing to share traffic between the two. *Company Name* will implement an automatic failover between the servers.
Desktop power failure	*Company Name* will plug all desktop systems into UPS devices.
Fire	*Company Name* will house its servers within a cloud-based PaaS provider, which will act as fire suppression. *Company Name* will insure its desktop computers against loss from fire.
Flood	*Company Name* will house its servers within a cloud-based PaaS provider that does not reside within a flood zone. *Company Name* will insure its desktop computers against loss from flood.
Virus	*Company Name* will install antivirus software on all systems, place a firewall in front of the network, and prevent users from installing software.

CHAPTER SUMMARY

Since 9/11, a primary job of corporate IT staffs has been to ensure the availability of computing resources (applications, files, and even phone systems) not only on a day-to-day basis, but also in the event of a crisis or natural disaster. Business continuity refers to the policies, procedures, and actions taken by an organization to ensure the availability of critical business functions to employees, customers, and other key stakeholders. Disaster recovery describes the steps a business will take to restore operations in the event of a disaster (fire, flood, hurricane, tornado, or other event). By integrating cloud-based solutions, many companies have significantly reduced the cost of their business continuity programs while simultaneously reducing potential risks.

KEY TERMS

Business continuity
Disaster recovery plan (DRP)
Halon
Mean time between failure (MTBF)

Redundant array of independent
  (or inexpensive) disks (RAID)
Service-level agreement (SLA)
Uninterruptible power supply (UPS)
Virus

CHAPTER REVIEW

1. Define and describe business continuity.
2. Define and describe disaster recovery.
3. Discuss pros and cons of cloud-based backup operations.
4. Discuss threats to an IT data center infrastructure and provide cloud-based solutions to mitigate the risks.
5. Create a DRP for a company with which you are familiar.

Service-Oriented Architecture

"SOFTWARE ARCHITECTURE" DESCRIBES THE major components that comprise a system, their relationships, and the information the components exchange. The distributed nature of the cloud has provided an ideal platform to support service-oriented architecture (SOA), an architectural approach to building solutions through the integration of services. This chapter introduces SOA and its implementation through web services.

Learning Objectives

This chapter examines SOA. By the time you finish this chapter, you will be able to do the following:

- Define and describe SOA.
- Compare and contrast the roles of web services and web pages.
- List common examples of web services.
- Discuss the benefits of treating a web service as a black box.
- Discuss governance challenges in using web services.
- Discuss the role of the Web Service Description Language (WSDL) to describe a web service and its methods.

Understanding Service-Oriented Architecture

A software system consists of components that implement different aspects of the processing. There are many different ways to create the **architecture** for a system—its components and their relationships and interactions. **Service-oriented architecture (SOA)** is a system design upon which the solution is

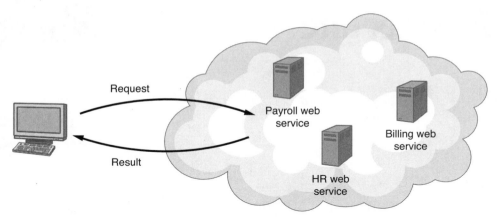

FIGURE 11-1 Within SOA, programs make remote-procedure calls to services that reside on servers distributed across the Web.

described in terms of one or more services. Normally, to promote reuse, the services are distributed on the Web. When a program must use a service, the program exchanges messages with the service, normally through the use of a remote-procedure (**method**) call, as shown in **FIGURE 11-1**. This chapter examines the use of web services to implement SOA design.

Web Services Are Not Web Pages

Across the Web, people use sites that perform specific tasks. For example, they book travel on Travelocity, buy books at Barnes & Noble, check their account balance at Bank of America, and order pizza from Domino's. These sites offer services to the user, but they are web pages, not web services. A web service is program code that resides on the Web and performs a specific task that other programs, not people, use. The following are examples of tasks performed by a web service:

- Return the weather conditions for a specific zip code
- Return real-time traffic conditions for a road or highway
- Return a stock price for a particular company
- Return driving directions to a specific location
- Return the country associated with an IP address

Programmers use web services within their programs to perform specific processing. To use a web service, a program exchanges messages across the

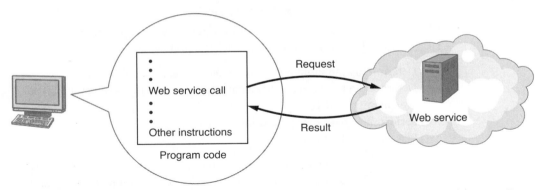

FIGURE 11-2 A program exchanges messages with a web service to call a specific method and then normally waits for the web service to return its result.

Internet with the web service that resides on a remote server. The program may pass parameter values to the service, such as a stock symbol of a company for which the program wants the stock price or the zip code of the area for which the program wants weather conditions. When a program calls a web service, normally the program will send its message to the web service via a function call and then wait, as shown in **FIGURE 11-2**, for the web service to return its result.

CASE 11-1 TEST DRIVING WEB SERVICES

As discussed, a web service is code that a program calls from across the Internet to perform a specific task. To help you understand how a program might use a web service, there are several simple programs (web applications) hosted on this book's companion website. In each case, the program creates a web page within which it displays information it receives from a web service.

Exercise Discuss potential pros and cons of using a web service to accomplish a specific task.

Web Resources To test drive several programs that use web services, visit www.CloudBookContent.com/Chapter11/index.html.

Many Companies Provide Web Services

When programmers create applications, often they need programs to perform tasks that involve another company, such as the following:

- Determining the shipping rate to send a package via UPS or FedEx
- Determining if a company has a particular product in inventory and, if so, the quantity available
- Performing credit card processing
- Placing an order for a product

To help programs perform such tasks, many companies provide web services. For example, FedEx and UPS provide web services that programs can use to integrate each company's shipping and tracking capabilities. Amazon provides web services that programs can use to integrate product searching and purchasing into their applications. Google provides web services that programs can use to access the site's search-engine capabilities.

Discovering Web Services

Before a developer can take advantage of an existing web service, he or she must know that the web service exists. Companies such as FedEx, UPS, Amazon, and Google usually have developer-specific web pages that provide documentation for their service offerings. Across the Web, developers may take advantage of registries within which other programmers store information about the web services they create. More than 10 years ago, when developers first began deploying web services, a large registry, known as Universal Description, Discovery, and Integration (UDDI), emerged. The goal of UDDI was to make it easier for a developer and a program to discover web services. Unfortunately, UDDI was never widely used and was shut down.

CASE 11–2 XMETHODS WEB SITE

As programmers develop web services, often they will share them with others—sometimes for free, sometimes not. At the XMethods website, shown in **FIGURE 11–3**, you can find a wide variety of web services available for use within programs. Even if you are not a developer, you should visit the site to gain a better understanding of the types of tasks performed by web services.

Exercise Visit the XMethods website. Describe three different web services listed that programmers might use within a business application.

Web Resources For more information on web services, visit www.CloudBookContent.com /Chapter11/index.html.

continues

CASE 11-2 XMETHODS WEB SITE, continued

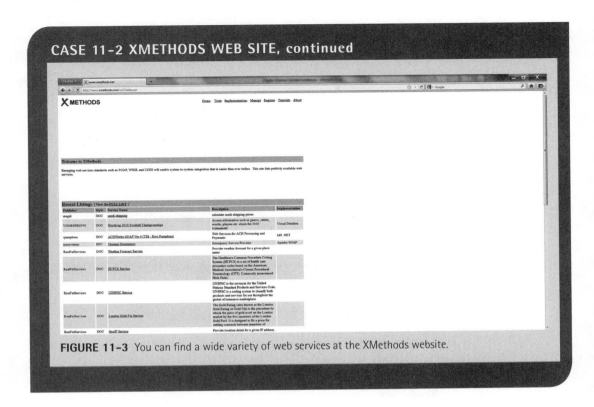

FIGURE 11-3 You can find a wide variety of web services at the XMethods website.

Understanding Web Service Performance

Primarily because of their distributed nature, web services provide advantages to developers, the most important of which is ease of code reuse. The cost of a web service's distributed processing is performance. Because web services require network operations, a web service will be considerable slower than a program's call to a function that resides on the same computer. Consider, for example, the following C# program that determines the square root of the values 1 to 1,000:

```csharp
using System;

namespace ConsoleApplication1
{
    class Program
    {
        static void Main(string[] args)
        {
            long StartingTicks = DateTime.Now.Ticks;
```

```
            for (double i = 0.0; i < 1000.0; i = i + 1.0)
            {
                double Discard = Math.Sqrt(i);
            }

            long EndingTicks = DateTime.Now.Ticks;

            long TicksRequired = (EndingTicks-StartingTicks) ;
            Console.Out.WriteLine("Ticks required: " +
              TicksRequired.ToString());
            Console.ReadLine();
        }
    }
}
```

The program simply tracks how long it takes to perform its processing and then displays output similar to the following:

Ticks required: 5

In this case, the square root processing takes 5 ticks (100 nanosecond intervals) to complete.

In contrast, consider the following C# program that uses a remote web service to calculate the square-root values:

```
using System;

namespace ConsoleApplication1
{
    class Program
    {
        static void Main(string[] args)
        {
            ServiceReference.ServiceSoapClient
                SquareRootReport = new
                ServiceReference.ServiceSoapClient();

            long StartingTicks = DateTime.Now.Ticks;

            for (double i = 0.0; i < 1000.0; i = i + 1.0)
            {
                double Discard = SquareRootReport
.SquareRoot(i);
            }
```

```
        long EndingTicks = DateTime.Now.Ticks;

        long TicksRequired = (EndingTicks -
          StartingTicks);

        Console.WriteLine("Ticks Required: " +
          TicksRequired);
        Console.ReadLine();
      }
    }
}
```

In this case, the program displays output similar to the following:

Ticks required: 10,562,000

As you can see, the message-passing overhead associated with calling the remote web service increases the processing to more than 10,000,000 ticks.

These examples illustrate that due to network overhead, a web service, despite its increased code reuse, is not always the best solution to a problem.

Web Service and Reuse

When programmers develop code, they break large, complex operations into smaller, more manageable tasks. Then they implement the well-defined tasks as functions. Ideally, each function should perform one task only. In this way, programmers can reuse the function code in other programs, which saves development and testing time and ultimately reduces costs. A common rule of programming is not to "reinvent the wheel," which means that if another programmer has written code that performs the task that your program needs, you should reuse that code.

Web services contain functions that perform specific tasks. Normally, the web service's functions will perform key tasks that many programs need. As a result, web services typically have a high level of code reuse.

Scaling Web Services

Chapter 19, *Application Scalability*, examines ways to scale cloud-based applications. Depending on its program demands, a web service may become a potential system bottleneck. An easy first solution is to scale up the web service by placing it on a faster server. If high utilization of the service continues, the developers may need to distribute copies of the web service onto additional servers and then use a load balancer, as shown in **FIGURE 11-4**, to distribute the program requests.

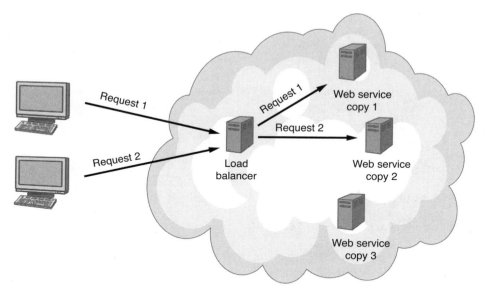

FIGURE 11-4 Using a load-balancing model, developers can scale a web service solution.

Web Services and Loose Coupling

As you have learned, a web service contains code that programs can call from across the Internet to perform a specific operation. **Coupling** describes the degree of dependence between a calling program and the web service. Ideally, to use a web service, a program only needs to know the location of the web service (its URL), the name of the functions (methods) the web service provides, and parameters the program can pass to the functions. In this way, programs and web services are said to be **loosely coupled**.

Because of a program's loosely coupled relationship to a web service, it is possible for a developer to update a web service with a newer version (perhaps a faster version) and for programs that use the service to use the new version immediately without requiring any modifications.

Treating a Web Service as a Black Box

The term **black box** describes a module for which the software developer does not care how the processing is performed, but instead, knows that the code, when provided valid inputs, will produce predictable results.

Based on a web service's loosely coupled relationship with a program that uses the service, the developer is confident that he or she can treat the web service as a black bos and not worry about how it performs a task. Instead, the developer trusts that, with valid input, the web service will function consistently.

Web Service Interoperability

One of the biggest advantages of web services is their **interoperability**. In other words, they can be called from programs using a variety of programming languages. Consider, for example, the following web service that provides two methods, Uppercase and Lowercase, which return the uppercase or lowercase equivalents of the character strings they receive:

```csharp
using System;
using System.Web.Services;

[WebService(Namespace = "http://tempuri.org/")]
[WebServiceBinding(ConformsTo = WsiProfiles
.BasicProfile1_1)]

public class Service : System.Web.Services.WebService
{
    public Service () {

        //Uncomment the following line if using
        //designed components
        //InitializeComponent();
    }


    [WebMethod]
    public string Uppercase(string source)
    {
        return source.ToUpper();
    }

    [WebMethod]
    public string Lowercase(string source)
    {
        return source.ToLower();
    }
}
```

This particular web service was written using the C# programming language within a .Net environment. The following C# program uses the methods the web service provides:

```
using System;

namespace ConsoleApplication1
{
    class Program
    {
        static void Main(string[] args)
        {
            ServiceReference1.ServiceSoapClient
                WebService = new
                ServiceReference1.ServiceSoapClient();

            Console.WriteLine(WebService
.Uppercase("hello") + " " +
                WebService.Lowercase("World"));
            Console.ReadLine();
        }
    }
}
```

When you compile and execute this program, it displays the following output:

HELLO world

Because they are interoperable, web services can be called from different programming languages. The following PHP script uses the web service:

```
<?php
$client = new SoapClient("http://localhost/service
.asmx?wsdl");
echo $client->Demo()->DemoResult;
echo "\n";
$params = array();
$params["source"] = 'Hello';
echo $client->Uppercase($params)->UppercaseResult;

echo ' ';
```

```
$params = array();
$params["source"] = 'World';
echo $client->Lowercase($params)->LowercaseResult;
?>
```

When you run this script, it displays the following output:

```
Hello, world
HELLO world
```

Web Service Description Language

A web service consists of one or more functions, each of which performs a specific task and normally returns a specific result. Within the web service, each function has a unique name and may receive zero or more parameter values. For example, a web service function called HousePayment might receive parameter values for the principal, interest rate, and length of the loan. Behind the scenes, the web service uses a **Web Service Description Language (WSDL)** file to describe the web service and its methods. Programs that use the web service will use the WSDL file to determine the available functions, parameter types, and more. The following statements, for example, contain the WSDL statements for the previous web service that provides the Uppercase and Lowercase methods. Within the WSDL, you can determine the methods supported, the values returned, and the types of parameters received:

```
<?xml version="1.0" encoding="UTF-8"?>

<wsdl:definitions xmlns:wsdl="http://schemas.xmlsoap.
org/wsdl/" targetNamespace="http://tempuri.org/"
xmlns:soapenc="http://schemas.xmlsoap.org/soap/
encoding/" xmlns:http="http://schemas.xmlsoap.org/
wsdl/http/" xmlns:tm="http://microsoft.com/wsdl/mime/
textMatching/" xmlns:soap="http://schemas.xmlsoap.org/
wsdl/soap/" xmlns:tns="http://tempuri.org/"
xmlns:mime="http://schemas.xmlsoap.org/wsdl/mime/"
xmlns:soap12="http://schemas.xmlsoap.org/wsdl/soap12/"
xmlns:s="http://www.w3.org/2001/XMLSchema"><wsdl:types>
<s:schema targetNamespace="http://tempuri.org/"
elementFormDefault="qualified"><s:element name
="Uppercase"><s:complexType><s:sequence><s:element
name="source" type="s:string" maxOccurs="1"
minOccurs="0"/></s:sequence></s:complexType>
```

```
</s:element><s:element name="UppercaseResponse">
<s:complexType><s:sequence><s:element
name="UppercaseResult" type="s:string" maxOccurs="1"
minOccurs="0"/></s:sequence></s:complexType>
</s:element>
<s:element name="Lowercase"><s:complexType><s:sequence>
<s:element name="source" type="s:string" maxOccurs="1"
minOccurs="0"/></s:sequence></s:complexType>
</s:element>
<s:element name="LowercaseResponse"><s:complexType>
<s:sequence><s:element name="LowercaseResult"
type="s:string" maxOccurs="1" minOccurs="0"/>
</s:sequence></s:complexType></s:element><s:element
name="Demo"><s:complexType/></s:element><s:element
name="DemoResponse"><s:complexType><s:sequence>
<s:element name="DemoResult" type="s:string"
maxOccurs="1" minOccurs="0"/></s:sequence>
</s:complexType></s:element></s:schema>
</wsdl:types><wsdl:message name="UppercaseSoapIn">
<wsdl:part name="parameters"
element="tns:Uppercase"/></wsdl:message><wsdl:message
name="UppercaseSoapOut"><wsdl:part name="parameters"
element="tns:UppercaseResponse"/>
</wsdl:message><wsdl:message name="LowercaseSoapIn">
<wsdl:part name="parameters" element="tns:Lowercase"/>
</wsdl:message><wsdl:message name="LowercaseSoapOut">
<wsdl:part name="parameters" element="tns:
LowercaseResponse"/></wsdl:message><wsdl:message
name="DemoSoapIn"><wsdl:part name="parameters"
element="tns:Demo"/></wsdl:message><wsdl:message
name="DemoSoapOut"><wsdl:part name="parameters"
element="tns:DemoResponse"/>
</wsdl:message><wsdl:portType name="ServiceSoap">
<wsdl:operation name="Uppercase"><wsdl:input message=
"tns:UppercaseSoapIn"/><wsdl:output message="tns:
UppercaseSoapOut"/></wsdl:operation><wsdl:operation
name="Lowercase"><wsdl:input message="tns:
LowercaseSoapIn"/><wsdl:output message="tns:
LowercaseSoapOut"/></wsdl:operation><wsdl:operation
name="Demo"><wsdl:input message="tns:DemoSoapIn"/>
<wsdl:output message="tns:DemoSoapOut"/>
```

```
</wsdl:operation></wsdl:portType><wsdl:binding
name="ServiceSoap" type="tns:ServiceSoap"><soap:
binding transport="http://schemas.xmlsoap.org/soap
/http"/><wsdl:operation name="Uppercase"><soap:
operation style="document" soapAction="http://tempuri
.org/Uppercase"/><wsdl:input><soap:body
use="literal"/></wsdl:input><wsdl:output><soap:body
use="literal"/></wsdl:output></
wsdl:operation><wsdl:operation name="Lowercase"><soap:
operation style="document" soapAction="http://tempuri
.org/Lowercase"/><wsdl:input><soap:body
use="literal"/></wsdl:input><wsdl:output><soap:body
use="literal"/></wsdl:output>
</wsdl:operation><wsdl:operation
name="Demo"><soap:operation style="document"
soapAction="http://tempuri.org
/Demo"/><wsdl:input><soap:body use="literal"/>
</wsdl:input><wsdl:output><soap:body use="literal"/>
</wsdl:output></wsdl:operation>
</wsdl:binding><wsdl:binding name="ServiceSoap12"
type="tns:ServiceSoap"><soap12:binding
transport="http://schemas.xmlsoap.org/soap
/http"/><wsdl:operation name="Uppercase"><soap12:
operation style="document" soapAction="http://tempuri.
org/Uppercase"/><wsdl:input><soap12:body
use="literal"/></wsdl:input><wsdl:output><soap12:body
use="literal"/></wsdl:output>
</wsdl:operation><wsdl:operation name="Lowercase">
<soap12:operation style="document" soapAction="http://
tempuri.org/Lowercase"/><wsdl:input><soap12:body
use="literal"/></wsdl:input><wsdl:output><soap12:body
use="literal"/></wsdl:output></
wsdl:operation><wsdl:operation
name="Demo"><soap12:operation style="document"
soapAction="http://tempuri.org/
Demo"/><wsdl:input><soap12:body use="literal"/>
</wsdl:input><wsdl:output><soap12:body
use="literal"/></wsdl:output></wsdl:operation>
</wsdl:binding><wsdl:service name="Service"><wsdl:port
name="ServiceSoap" binding="tns:ServiceSoap"><soap:
address location="http://localhost/service.asmx"/>
```

```
</wsdl:port><wsdl:port name="ServiceSoap12" binding=
"tns:ServiceSoap12"><soap12:address location="http://
localhost/service.asmx"/></wsdl:port></wsdl:service>
</wsdl:definitions>
```

Governing Web Services

Chapter 15, *Governing the Cloud*, examines the process of governing cloud operations to confirm that applications work correctly and are protected from potential malicious modification by an external source. A web service is program code that resides on a server that belongs to the company whose programs use the service, or on a server owned by a third party. Before a developer uses a web service within an application, the company's IT staff should ensure that the web service implementation and deployment satisfies their policies and procedures. These may include requirements such as the following:

- The solution must be developed and deployed by a reputable company.
- The solution cannot be dynamically changed or updated without the company's notification and approval.
- The solution must provide secure communications to avoid threats such as a man-in-the-middle attack.
- The solution must be scalable to meet potential demand.
- The solution must be able to be validated.

CHAPTER SUMMARY

Developers often refer to the major components of a software system as the system's architecture. To leverage the distributed nature of the cloud, developers make extensive use of SOA. Using this architecture, developers build systems by taking advantage of distributed web services, which may reside on a server anywhere across the Web. Traditionally, programs call the remote web service the same way it calls a function or subroutine, passing optional parameters to the service and waiting for an optional response. Today, companies such as Amazon and eBay offer a wide range of web services that perform specific tasks, which programmers can integrate into the applications they create. This chapter examined SOA and its implementation through web services.

KEY TERMS

Architecture

Black box

Coupling

Interoperability

Loosely coupled

Method

Service-oriented architecture (SOA)

Web Service Description Language (WSDL)

CHAPTER REVIEW

1. Define software architecture.

2. Define and describe SOA.

3. Compare and contrast a web page and a web service.

4. Search the Web for companies that offer web services and then describe three to five web services that programmers might integrate into the applications they create.

5. Discuss what it means for a web service to be interoperable.

Managing the Cloud

OFTEN, BY MOVING A solution to the cloud, IT managers shift a great deal of day-to-day management from their in-house department to the cloud-solution provider. That said, the IT manager must not relinquish oversight and responsibility for performance and data management. Instead, he or she must provide essential oversight of the key system operations.

Learning Objectives

This chapter examines essential cloud-management operations. By the time you finish this chapter, you will be able to do the following:

- Discuss components often found within a service-level agreement.
- Define and discuss vendor lock-in and specify steps a manager should take to reduce this risk.
- Discuss a manager's potential use of audit logs to identify system bottlenecks and resource use.
- List the specific aspects of the cloud deployment that a manager must oversee.

Know Your Service-Level Agreement

When you contract with a cloud-solution provider, part of your contract will contain a service-level agreement (SLA), which defines the levels of service the provider will meet. Common components of an SLA include the following:

- System uptime, normally expressed as a percentage, such as 99.9 percent
- Run-time monitoring capabilities and event notification
- Billing policy for various types of resource use (e.g., CPUs, disk space, and databases)
- Technical support operations (e.g., call-time delay and event response time)

177

- Data-privacy policy
- Multitenant systems and applications
- Customer and provider roles and responsibilities
- Backup policies and procedures
- Resolution steps in case provider fails to meet the service levels

CASE 12-1 APICA CLOUD LOAD PERFORMANCE TESTING

A key responsibility of cloud managers is to monitor system performance. Several sites in the cloud provide response time-based cloud performance monitoring; others provide **load testing**, which measures how a site will perform during high user demand. The Apica website, shown in **FIGURE 12-1**, provides both types of testing, as well as cache-utilization assistance, which the company says will significantly improve a site's responsiveness.

Exercise Discuss how a company might deploy load testing and the specific types of tests the process might include.

Web Resources For more information on Apica, visit www.CloudBookContent.com/Chapter12/index.html.

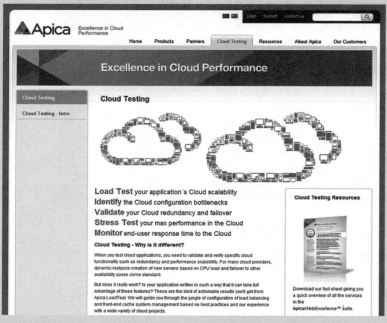

FIGURE 12-1 The Apica site offers performance monitoring, load testing, and assistance in configuring a site's cache settings.

Ensure and Audit System Backups

Chapter 6, *Data Storage in the Clouds,* discusses cloud-based backups in detail. Managers should consider different forms of backups. First, your company may back up user files from on-site computers to disks that reside within the cloud. Hopefully you will never require these backups; but regardless, you should periodically audit the backups, perhaps by checking that you can successfully restore randomly selected files of different users.

CASE 12-2 DISTRIBUTED MANAGEMENT TASK FORCE CLOUD-MANAGEMENT STANDARDS

The Distributed Management Task Force (DMTF) consists of hundreds of organizations and thousands of members who work to provide IT standards. As shown in **FIGURE 12-2**, the DMTF provides standards and recommendations for managing the cloud and virtual solutions.

Exercise Review the DMTF cloud-management recommendations. List the top 10 recommendations.

Web Resources For more information on the DTMF cloud-management standards, visit www .CloudBookContent.com/Chapter12/index.html.

FIGURE 12-2 The DMTF provides cloud-management standards and recommendations.

Second, if the cloud provider stores some or all of your company data, you must understand the provider's backup process (and include it in the SLA). For governance purposes, you should know if the data is encrypted, who has access to it, and if it is replicated to a remote facility. If it is backed up to another location, you must know where and how often.

Additionally, if the provider uses a database to store your company data, you need to know if and how the data is replicated and whether your company's information is stored in a private or multitenant database. You should also know the system's guaranteed uptime.

Know Your System's Data Flow

Often, developers and managers think of a cloud solution as a black box, which means that they know what the system does but not how it does it. Chapter 15, *Governing the Cloud*, discusses the role of internal controls in providing stakeholders with confidence, first and foremost, that a solution works correctly; second, that the solution cannot be manipulated by external factors; and third, that the solution is auditable.

Managers should create a detailed process-flow diagram that shows the movement of company data throughout the cloud solution. They should also identify within the dataflow various points for the placement of internal controls or auditing.

CASE 12–3 EMBOTICS CLOUD AND VIRTUALIZATION MANAGEMENT TOOLS

For many IT professionals, managing device virtualization and cloud deployment is a daunting task. To facilitate the process, Embotics offers V-Commander, an off-the-shelf-product that offers life cycle solutions for managing private cloud deployments and optimizing the underlying virtual devices. As shown in **FIGURE 12–3**, Embotics states that with its product an IT team can install the software and manage the cloud within one hour.

Exercise Discuss how cloud-management considerations may vary across the life cycle of a cloud-based solution.

Web Resources For more information on Embotics, visit www.CloudBookContent.com/Chapter12/index.html.

continues

CASE 12-3 EMBOTICS CLOUD AND VIRTUALIZATION MANAGEMENT TOOLS, continued

FIGURE 12-3 Embotics provides tools to assist in cloud management.

Beware of Vendor Lock-In

Relationships can go bad—even those with a cloud-solution provider. The agreement you sign with a cloud provider should stipulate exit procedures in case the provider fails to meet the service levels or breaches any other aspect of the contract.

IT managers must be able to control their company's data. In the event of a worst-case scenario, a manager must be able to export the company data, ideally to a file that can be imported by another provider. Managers should test this capability before a problem arises.

Vendor lock-in occurs when a provider does not support data export or when a provider's service is unavailable through others. Thus, the customer is "locked in" to the relationship with the vendor. If this happens, a company may have to put up with breaches of its SLA because it has no other place to move its data. Managers should consider the risk of vendor lock-in before they enter into a provider agreement.

Source-Code Escrow

Companies fail. Therefore, managers, should perform due diligence on a cloud-solution provider before they enter into an agreement. The manager may want to arrange a source code escrow agreement, which places a copy of the provider's

CASE 12-4 JITTERBIT CLOUD INTEGRATION

Many organizations use multiple cloud-based solutions provided by a variety of providers. Often, IT managers must integrate the various solutions, such as combining sales and financial data, or human resource and enterprise-resource planning solutions. Jitterbit, as shown in **FIGURE 12-4**, provides integration for cloud-based solutions without the need for programming. Jitterbit provides a drag-and-drop interface that allows a manager to define how applications integrate and share data. For companies with in-house developers, Jitterbit provides advanced scripting tools so that developers can incorporate business rules into the data-integration process.

Exercise Discuss challenges associated with integrating data from different cloud-based solutions.

Web Resources For more information on Jitterbit capabilities, visit www.CloudBookContent .com/Chapter12/index.html.

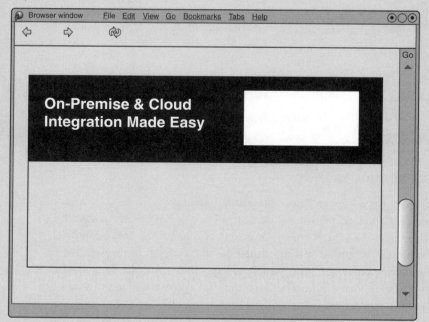

FIGURE 12-4 Jitterbit provides a drag-and-drop tool for data integration across cloud-based solutions.

programming language source code with a third-party escrow company. Then, if the solution provider fails, the company can acquire and deploy the source code, put it on its own system, and implement the provider's solution.

Determine Technical Support and Help Desk Procedures

Depending on the solutions it places in the cloud, a company may have various help desk support requirements. For example, in the case of a Solution as a Service (SaaS) solution, the cloud-solution provider may provide software technical support. For Platform as a Service (Paas) or Infrastructure as a Service (IaaS) solutions, however, the company may provide software technical support. There may also be shared support responsibilities. In all cases, an IT manager should ensure that the support specifics are defined within the SLA.

Determine Training Procedures

To be successful, large-scale cloud applications often require user training before, during, and after the integration. For SaaS solutions, the cloud-service provider normally provides user training. Depending on the application's processing, the company may need to augment the training with in-house instruction. The IT manager should stipulate the training responsibilities within the SLA.

CASE 12-5 NETUITIVE PREDICTIVE ANALYTICS AND CLOUD MANAGEMENT

Predictive analytics tools perform statistical analysis to predict future behavior. Netuitive integrates predictive analytics to provide IT managers with insights into how a solution will work under different conditions. Netuitive software can monitor a group of integrated or stand-alone cloud-based solutions. The software's self-learning capabilities allow the software to identify demand trends and more. As shown in **FIGURE 12–5**, Netuitive provides a dashboard and drill-down reporting.

Exercise Discuss factors a company might want to consider before using predictive analytics of a cloud-based solution.

Web Resources For more information on Netuitive predictive analytics, visit www.CloudBook Content.com/Chapter12/index.html.

continues

CASE 12-5 NETUITIVE PREDICTIVE ANALYTICS AND CLOUD MANAGEMENT, continued

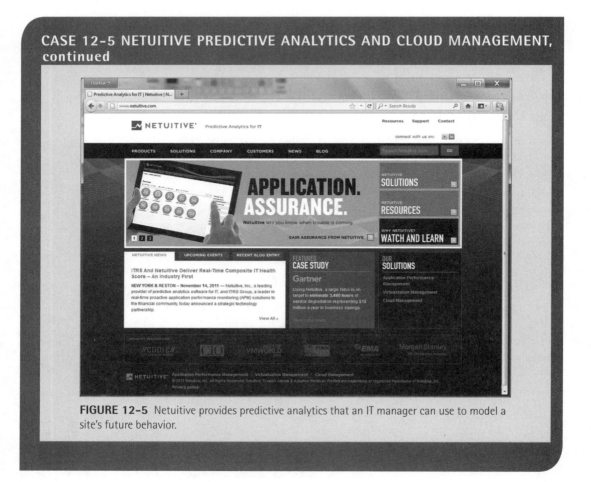

FIGURE 12-5 Netuitive provides predictive analytics that an IT manager can use to model a site's future behavior.

Know the Provider's Security Policies and Procedures

As discussed throughout this book, many clients are apprehensive about storing their data in the cloud. To reduce these concerns, IT managers should thoroughly understand the provider's security plans, policies, and procedures. Specifically, a manager should be aware of the provider's multitenant use, e-commerce processing, employee screening, and encryption policy. He or she should examine the provider's use of firewalls, intrusion detection, and security mechanisms. These security factors should be defined in the SLA.

Define the Data Privacy Requirements

If a company has specific data-privacy requirements, such as the Health Insurance Portability and Accountability Act (HIPAA) for health care or the Family Educational Rights and Privacy Act (FERPA) for student data, it should ensure that the SLA details the specific requirements.

CASE 12-6 NEW RELIC CLOUD-PERFORMANCE MONITORING

When it comes to cloud-performance monitoring, most managers spend 80 percent of their time monitoring 20 percent of a solution's code (see Chapter 19 and the Pareto Principle). New Relic, shown in **FIGURE 12-6**, provides monitoring software that will examine system performance to identify potential bottlenecks. New Relic software supports most common programming languages and can be easily integrated into a site.

Exercise Discuss common bottleneck locations within cloud-based solutions.

Web Resources For more information on New Relic cloud-performance monitoring, visit www .CloudBookContent.com/Chapter12/index.html.

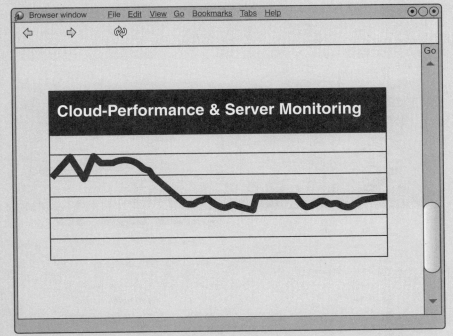

FIGURE 12-6 New Relic provides cloud-performance monitoring and bottleneck identification.

Know Specifics About the Economics of the Cloud and Return on Investment

Chapter 16, *Evaluating the Cloud's Business Impact and Economics*, examines the financial considerations for moving a solution to the cloud. An IT manager must evaluate the cloud's impact on capital as well as operational expenses. Managers should prepare a budget that compares the on-site costs to the cloud-based solution costs. Chapter 16 presents several online tools that can help managers produce such budgets.

CASE 12-7 STRANGELOOP SITE OPTIMIZATION

Across the cloud, developers strive for web pages that load in two or three seconds or less. There are a variety of site performance monitoring tools you can use to measure a site's responsiveness. That's the easy part. The hard part is making slow pages load faster. Often, that requires a company to take steps such as eliminating or compressing graphics, compressing text, and improving cache utilization. In the age of increasing bandwidth, many web managers may ask, "What's the big deal about a one- to two-second delay?" Research shows, however, that such delays are why customers log off of websites! Strangeloop, shown in **FIGURE 12-7**, provides a site-optimizing solution that companies can easily deploy to improve their site's performance.

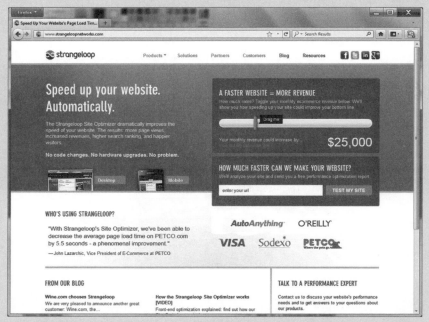

FIGURE 12-7 Strangeloop provides site-optimizing solutions that are easily integrated by cloud-based solutions.

continues

CASE 12-7 STRANGELOOP SITE OPTIMIZATION, continued

From the Strangeloop website, you can evaluate a specific site. For example, **FIGURE 12-8** shows a performance report created by Strangeloop.

Exercise Use the Strangeloop site to evaluate a site of your choice. Discuss the insights you gained from the report.

Web Resources For more information on Strangeloop reporting, visit www.CloudBookContent .com/Chapter12/index.html.

FIGURE 12-8 A site performance report created by Strangeloop.

Monitor Capacity Planning and Scaling Capabilities

Chapter 19, *Application Scalability*, examines capacity planning and scalability issues in detail. For SaaS solutions, the cloud-solution provider will scale the site to match user demand. An IT manager, however, must define in advance key response-time metrics the solution must provide and then include those measures within the SLA.

For PaaS and IaaS solutions, the IT manager must initially estimate the solution's capacity plan, which defines the resources the solution will need to operate satisfactorily. The IT manager should also estimate the site's potential growth and define, with the help of the solution provider, the plan for scaling the site resources as well as the related costs.

Several sites within the cloud provide system-performance reports that managers can use to measure current performance and the potential system benefit from scaling specific resources.

Monitor Audit-Log Use

To identify potential system bottlenecks, detect errors within the system, and identify system-resource use, the IT manager may examine various system log files. In a PaaS or IaaS solution, the manager can likely turn on the log file reporting that meets his or her needs. For a SaaS solution, the manager should discuss in advance with the cloud service provider the various logs that will be available and the costs of running them, both in terms of dollars and system performance.

CASE 12-8 UPTIME SOFTWARE

Too often, cloud-solution managers do not know that a system error has occurred until a user reports one. With Uptime, IT managers can easily monitor a wide range of servers and produce resource utilization reports similar to that shown in **FIGURE 12-9**. Companies can download, install, and use a trial version of the Uptime software from the company website.

Exercise Discuss how you would determine a return on investment for system-event notification, such as a system failure.

Web Resources For more information on Uptime, visit www.CloudBookContent.com/Chapter12/index.html.

continues

FIGURE 12-9 The Uptime site provides system monitoring and utilization reporting capabilities a site manager can easily implement.

Solution Testing and Validation

Just because a company provides a solution does not mean that the solution is error free. An IT staff using a cloud-based solution must test the solution and periodically audit key processing to confirm that the application is providing correct results. In particular, a cloud-service provider will often perform patch management and version updates. The IT staff should be aware of all system modifications and test accordingly.

CHAPTER SUMMARY

IT managers, by moving a solution to the cloud, shift considerable day-to-day management issues from their IT department to the cloud-solution provider. However, an IT manager must not relinquish the oversight and responsibility for performance and management. Instead, the manager must provide essential oversight of the key system operations. The manager's key tool for managing the cloud-service provider is the SLA, which should contain specifics about key performance issues, policies and procedures, and clear definitions of all levels of responsibility.

KEY TERMS

Load testing   Predictive analytics

CHAPTER REVIEW

1. Discuss key items that should be included in an SLA.

2. Define predictive analytics and discuss how an IT manager might use such analytics.

3. Discuss how an IT manager might use load testing on a site.

4. Define and discuss vendor lock-in and identify steps a company should take to mitigate this risk.

5. With respect to cloud-based solutions, list and discuss 5 to 10 operations or tasks an IT manager should oversee.

Migrating to the Cloud

FROM A TECHNICAL PERSPECTIVE, an application can be moved to the cloud quickly. There are a myriad of cloud-solution providers who will eagerly assist by giving you instant access to cloud-based servers, data storage, and support. That said, like all IT projects, the process of moving an application to the cloud, or the process of creating and deploying a new cloud application, should be well planned. This chapter examines issues that should be considered before you move an application to the cloud.

Learning Objectives

This chapter examines the process of moving applications to the cloud. By the time you finish this chapter, you will be able to do the following:

- Define requirements for migrating an application to the cloud.
- Describe the importance of backing up data before and after moving an application to the cloud.
- Appreciate the benefit of using experienced consultants to assist with a cloud migration.
- Describe an application in terms of its resource use.
- Define and describe vendor lock-in and discuss ways to avoid it.
- Describe the importance of training employees before, during, and after a cloud migration.
- Describe the importance of establishing a realistic cloud-deployment schedule.
- Discuss key budget factors impacted by the cloud.
- Discuss potential IT governance issues related to the cloud.
- Define and describe cloud bursting.

Define the System Goals and Requirements

All IT projects should begin with specific requirements. The process of taking an application to the cloud, known as **cloud migration**, is no exception. As you begin to define your solution's requirements, consider the following common issues:

- Data security and privacy requirements
- Site capacity plan—the resources that the application initially needs to operate
- Scalability requirements—the measurable factors that should drive scaling events
- System uptime requirements
- Business continuity and disaster requirements
- Budget requirements
- Operating system and programming language requirements
- Type of cloud—public, private, or hybrid
- Single tenant or multitenant solution requirements
- Data backup requirements
- Client device requirements, such as computer, tablet, or smartphone support
- Training requirements
- Help desk and support requirements
- Governance and auditing requirements
- Open source software requirements (some people believe that open source-based cloud solutions reduce the risk of vendor lock-in)
- Programming API requirements
- Dashboard and reporting requirements
- Client access requirements
- Data export requirements

After you define your application requirements, discuss each in detail with potential cloud-solution providers. Make sure you define all of your system requirements clearly within the Service-level agreement (SLA).

CASE 13-1 CLOUDSWITCH CLOUD MIGRATION

Many companies have enterprise-based applications that are widely used by their employees. These applications, therefore, are mission critical. CloudSwitch provides a download-able application that companies can install within their data center that securely maps the company's on-site applications to a cloud-based solution in a matter of minutes. In other words, CloudSwitch, shown in **FIGURE 13-1**, provides a way for companies running Windows or Linux solutions to migrate quickly to the cloud. The CloudSwitch migration program requires no programming or development. Additionally, CloudSwitch provides a suite of cloud-management tools that the IT staff can use to manage the solution after it moves to the cloud.

continues

CASE 13-1 CLOUDSWITCH CLOUD MIGRATION, continued

Exercise Most IT projects fail or come in over budget. Discuss steps you would take to reduce the risk of failure of a cloud-migration project.

Web Resources For more information on CloudSwitch, visit www.CloudBookContent.com /Chapter13/index.html.

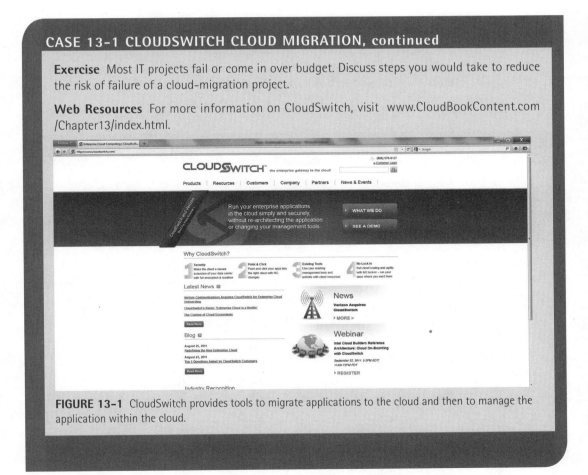

FIGURE 13-1 CloudSwitch provides tools to migrate applications to the cloud and then to manage the application within the cloud.

Protect Your Existing Data

Before you begin your application migration to a cloud provider, make sure that you back up your data so that you can revert, if necessary, to a known restore point. Then, be sure that you and the provider agree to the backup procedures that will be employed after they take control of your data. As discussed, it is easy to move a solution to a cloud provider. You need to ensure that it is equally easy to move out of the cloud if necessary

Furthermore, if your company has specific privacy requirements, such as those of the Health Insurance Privacy and Portability Act (HIPAA) for health care, or of the Family Educational Rights and Privacy Act (FERPA) for education, have your provider state explicitly, in writing, its data privacy policies and procedures.

Use an Experienced Cloud Consultant

Moving a solution to the cloud is a learning experience. The process has many options and a wide range of potential pitfalls. Many companies provide consultants who are experienced in the cloud migration process. Before you begin your

CASE 13-2 3TERA CLOUD SOLUTIONS

Formerly know as Computer Associates, CA Technologies provides a wide range of services and solutions to companies migrating to the cloud. To drive its cloud offerings, CA Technologies acquired 3Tera, a company that helps businesses move solutions to public and private clouds using a graphical user interface (GUI) tool. As shown in **FIGURE 13-2**, the 3Tera website offers a turnkey cloud-computing platform, driven by the company's AppLogic software, which allows large (enterprise) or small companies to migrate to the cloud through the use of the 3Tera virtual appliance, a device that behaves very much like a virtual machine. As user demand for an application grows, 3Tera can easily scale solutions.

Exercise Visit the 3Tera site and research the company's virtual appliance. Discuss how the appliance differs from a server.

Web Resources For more information on 3Tera, visit www.CloudBookContent.com/Chapter13/index.html.

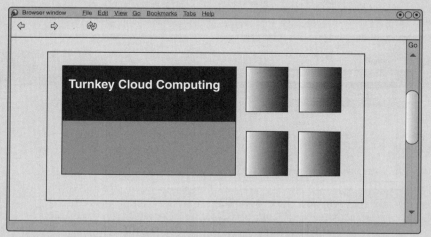

FIGURE 13-2 3Tera supports cloud migration through the use of its AppLogic software.

application's migration to the cloud, you should consider hiring a consultant. In most cases, you will find that this saves you money in the end by helping you avoid costly mistakes.

Know Your Application's Current Characteristics

Before you move your application to the cloud where you might face scaling issues, be sure that you monitor your application to identify its key performance indicators:

- **Demand periods:** Does the application have periods of high or low demand, such as 8 A.M. to 5 P.M.?
- **Average users:** How many users typically use the system simultaneously?
- **Disk-storage requirements:** What are the application's typical disk-storage needs? Are the files permanent or temporary? Are most operations read or write operations?
- **Database-storage requirements:** What are the application's database requirements? Is the database replicated in real time? What is the application's database read/write ratio?
- **RAM use:** What is the application's range of physical and virtual memory use?
- **Bandwidth consumption:** What is the application's bandwidth requirement?
- **Caching:** How does the application currently cache data?

Remember Vendor Lock-In

Vendor lock-in occurs when a vendor makes it difficult for a company to switch to another provider, even if the vendor has failed to fulfill the SLA. This lock-in may occur because the vendor is unable to export data completely or because the vendor provides services its competitors do not. A cloud-service provider should make it easy for clients to move to another provider in the event that the provider fails to meet one or more of the SLA requirements.

In the case of a Platform as a Service (PaaS) or Infrastructure as a Service (IaaS) provider, moving a company's applications and data should be relatively straightforward. Moving from a Software as a Service (SaaS) provider, however, may prove to be more difficult because of the specific capabilities of the vendor, upon which the company relies. To reduce the risk of vendor lock-in, many companies seek providers who support "open" solutions, which use open source software such as Linux, PHP, and MySQL.

CASE 13-3 KAYAKO HELP DESK SOLUTIONS

Change-management consultants often cite the integration of a trained help desk staff as key to an application's successful integration. Kayako, shown in **FIGURE 13-3**, provides a variety of key help desk tools that a company should consider before migrating a solution to the cloud. The following are features of the Kayako software:

- Support ticket management
- Ticket escalation support
- Live support desk chat software
- Voice over Internet protocol (VoIP) phone integration
- Remote computer access

Exercise Discuss a company's help desk requirements for SaaS, PaaS, and IaaS cloud integrations.

Web Resources For more information on Kayako help solutions, visit www.CloudBookContent.com/Chapter13/index.html.

FIGURE 13-3 Kayako provides cost-effective help desk tools to support software deployments.

Define Your Training Requirements

To reduce employee stress during an application's migration to the cloud and to increase employee productivity with the cloud-based tools, you should consider training before, during, and after the cloud migration. As you define your training requirements, consider the following:

- Employee preparedness for the SaaS solution
- Developer training on the solution application program interfaces (APIs)

- Administrator training for cloud-based operations
- IT-audit group training for corporate governance issues and internal controls
- Help desk support preparedness training
- Business continuity and disaster preparedness training

Given the cloud's cost-effective ability to deploy solutions, training may prove to be one of the most expensive aspects of the company's cloud migration.

CASE 13-4 RIGHTSCALE CLOUD APPLICATION MANAGEMENT

RightScale, shown in **FIGURE 13-4**, provides a fully automated cloud-management platform that lets companies deploy cloud-based solutions across one or more clouds. RightScale provides its cloud-management software as a SaaS solution that lets customers deploy and manage their solutions quickly. The RightScale website also features valuable videos, white papers, and forums that focus on cloud computing.

Exercise Discuss a scenario within which a company might have to manage multiple cloud solutions.

Web Resources For more information on RightScale, visit www.CloudBookContent.com /Chapter13/index.html.

FIGURE 13-4 RightScale provides support for application deployment to one or more clouds.

Establish a Realistic Deployment Schedule

Cloud-solution providers can quickly deploy solutions. Despite that, you should set a deployment schedule that provides sufficient time for training, testing, and benchmarking. Many organizations, when moving a new application to the cloud for the first time, will establish a beta-like release schedule that offers employees a prerelease opportunity to interact with the software and provide feedback. Furthermore, the testing period may provide time for the company to establish early system-performance benchmarks.

Review the Budget Factors

Chapter 16, *Evaluating the Cloud's Business Impact and Economics*, examines the steps you should perform to determine the return on investment (ROI) and total cost of ownership for a cloud-based solution. In Chapter 16, you will learn that the cloud's pay-for-use model significantly reduces a company's capital expenditures compared with what would normally be required to fund a data center. Furthermore, you will learn that because of a cloud provider's economies of scale, the providers can normally offer solutions at lower cost than a company would normally pay for the same on-site solution.

Before you move to the cloud, you should consider key budget factors, which may include the following:

- Current data center costs breakdown, including the following:
  - Rent
  - Power and air conditioning
  - Colocation costs
  - Server costs
  - Data storage costs
  - Network costs
- Current payroll costs for existing site administrators and projections for possible staff reduction opportunities
- Current costs for software licenses that may shift to the cloud, and the (lower) projected cloud-based costs for the software
- Current payroll costs for patch management and software version updates
- Current hardware maintenance costs

In Chapter 16, you will find many cloud-based tools to help you analyze the cloud's potential economic impact on your company.

CASE 13-5 GOGRID CLOUD HOSTING

GoGrid is a very large IaaS solution provider that provides scalable solutions to thousands of customers. At GoGrid customers can acquire on-demand solutions for physical, virtual, or hybrid servers at cost-effective pricing levels. Additionally, GoGrid offers solutions for load balancing, colocation, and cloud-based data storage.

Exercise Discuss the pros and cons of using a large cloud provider instead of a smaller provider.

Web Resources For more information on GoGrid, visit www.CloudBookContent.com /Chapter13/index.html.

Identify IT Governance Issues

Chapter 15, *Governing the Cloud*, examines the IT governance process and how the cloud extends the governance requirements for your IT staff. Before you migrate an application to the cloud, consider the following governance requirements:

- Identify how the cloud solution aligns with the company's business strategy.
- Identify and define the internal and external controls the company will need within the application, and at what control points, in order to validate that the application is performing correctly and is free from possible external modification.
- Describe risks the IT staff is trying to mitigate and ways the cloud can help.
- Describe who within the company will have access to data within the cloud and how they will get it.
- Determine who within the cloud provider's organization will have access to data within the cloud and how they will get it.
- Discover how the cloud provider logs errors and system events and how you can access them.
- Determine how and when the cloud provider performs system updates and patches.
- Discover which performance-monitoring tools are available for your use.

Understanding Cloud Bursting

One of the cloud's biggest advantages is its ability to scale on the fly to meet user demand. Some companies that run on-site applications have started to use the cloud as a way to scale their applications on demand. When the on-site application encounters increased user demand, the application expands into the cloud through a process called **cloud bursting**, as shown in FIGURE 13–5. When the user demand declines, the application leaves the cloud. Cloud bursting is most common for seasonal demand, or event-driven demand, such as the load on Google Maps when an earthquake or other natural disaster occurs.

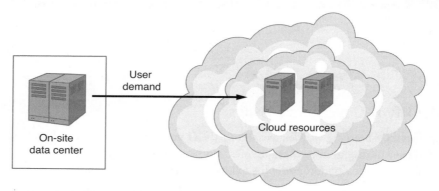

FIGURE 13–5 Cloud bursting lets a company extend an on-site application into the cloud to scale temporarily to meet user demand.

CHAPTER SUMMARY

An application can be moved to the cloud quickly—cloud-solution providers are eager to assist with cloud-based servers, data storage, and support. In other words, the technical aspects of moving a solution to the cloud are not difficult. The challenge, for most businesses, is to ensure that the company is properly trained, has established policies and procedures for cloud operations, and has put in place necessary governance requirements. As with all IT projects, proper planning and defining the requirements is essential before a company begins moving an application to the cloud or creating and deploying a new cloud application.

KEY TERMS

Cloud bursting

Cloud migration

Vendor lock-in

CHAPTER REVIEW

1. List and describe common system requirements one should consider before moving an application to the cloud.

2. Discuss why a company should consider using a consultant to oversee a cloud migration and list specific skills you would expect the consultant to have.

3. List and discuss resource utilization characteristics one should monitor for an application prior to moving the application to the cloud.

4. List possible training requirements for an SaaS solution integration, a PaaS application migration, and an IaaS application migration.

5. List and describe budget considerations one should evaluate before moving an application to the cloud.

6. List and describe IT governance considerations one should evaluate before moving an application to the cloud.

7. Define and describe cloud bursting.

Mobile Cloud Computing

IF YOU ASK A roomful of cloud computing experts whether the cloud is driving the growth of mobile computing or mobile computing is driving the growth of the cloud, the results will be mixed. In any case, within a few years, mobile computing will be a trillion-dollar-a-year business. This chapter examines various aspects of mobile computing and the underlying use of the cloud.

Learning Objectives

This chapter examines mobile computing in the cloud. By the time you finish this chapter, you will be able to do the following:

- Describe the evolution of mobile computing.
- Discuss the different generations of cell phones.
- Discuss the ecosystem that comprises the mobile web.
- Describe the roles of phone network operators, transcoders, and proxies.
- Compare and contrast web pages, applications, and widgets.
- Discuss the importance of HTML5 with respect to mobile development.
- Describe mobile development considerations.

The Evolution of Mobile Computing

If you list inventions that have had the biggest impact on society, from the automobile to airplanes to television and the telephone, the cell phone may (or likely eventually will) top the list. It is important to note that in less than 30 years the cell phone has evolved from a heavy cumbersome device, as shown in **FIGURE 14-1**, to a small handheld device with more than 1 billion users. Today, the liveliest sector of the mobile phone market is "smartphones," which integrate computing capabilities, and often a web browser, which allows the phones to provide a wide range of solutions. Beyond traditional phone calls, users use smartphones to do the following:

- Browse websites, including Google, Facebook, eBay, and more
- Place face-to-face video calls to phones and computers
- Perform GPS-based navigational operations
- Exchange text messages
- Perform e-commerce operations
- Run a myriad of applications (apps)

FIGURE 14-1 In less than 30 years, the cell phone has gone from a cumbersome device used by early adopters to a handheld device used worldwide.

Understanding the G in 3G and 4G

When you discuss phone capabilities, you will hear terms such as 3G and 4G. In the simplest sense, the G stands for generation. A 4G phone, therefore, is a fourth-generation phone. Although there are standards with respect to the potential speeds associated with each generation, the speed of most devices today depends upon the location (some cities support faster speeds), the provider network, and the phone technology, as well as whether the user is moving or stationary. **TABLE 14-1** describes the key generational attributes.

TABLE 14-1	THE COMMON GENERATIONS OF CELL PHONES
Generation	**Capability**
1G	First-generation phones supported analog communication.
2G	Second-generation phones introduced digital communication.
3G	Third-generation phones supported faster speeds, which, in turn, made web browsing and e-mail readily available.
4G	Fourth-generation phones support near Wi-Fi speed, which enables rich media and video streaming.

The Mobile Cloud Ecosystem

An **ecosystem** is an environment that consists of living and nonliving things with which one interacts. Many cloud-based companies use the term ecosystem to describe the user's environment. To that end, you might describe the mobile-cloud ecosystem as consisting of the following:

- Phone class, which may be voice or face-to-face
- Web browsing
- Apps and widgets
- Voice commands and voice recognition
- Display screens
- Transmission speeds for upload and download operations
- Keyboard interface
- Touchscreens

The **mobile cloud** consists of apps and web pages that originate from sites within the cloud from which users download, or with which they interact via a mobile device. If you are creating a mobile solution, you should consider how your solution interacts with or supports the various mobile-device ecosystem components.

Introducing the Mobile Players

To understand mobile data communication, you should understand the players. To start, the operator, or network, is the company that makes the mobile network available. Within the United States, mobile operators include Verizon and AT&T. In the simplest sense, the operator owns the cell tower through which the data communication occurs. Most operators will provide internal groups that support developers in bringing mobile solutions to the market.

Within most mobile networks, operators will place special servers, called transcoders, which examine the content a mobile device is downloading from a website. The **transcoder**, in turn, may change the document content, such as changing a PNG graphic to a GIF graphic to improve the download performance or device display. If you are developing mobile content, you must be aware of how the transcoder may change the content. FIGURE 14-2, for example, shows how a transcoder (in this case a Google transcoder) might modify the content of a website.

Unfortunately, standards for transcoders are still being developed. As a result, you may see differences, in some cases considerable ones, among the content produced by different transcoders.

Many operators may include proxy servers (proxies) which perform operations on behalf of a device. By serving as an intermediary, a **proxy** provides a level of security that separates the device from the web server with which the device is interacting.

A

B

FIGURE 14–2 Within a mobile network, a transcoder may modify web content to a form and layout more suitable for a mobile device.

Pages, Apps, and Widgets

When developers build mobile solutions, they can approach their solution in one of three ways. First, they can build a web page, ideally targeted for a mobile display. As users browse the Web using mobile browsers built into their phones, the contents of the web page appear.

Second, developers can build an **app**, which typically is a device-specific program that users download and install (either free or for a price) onto a device. The app, in turn, displays an icon on the device, which users click to start the app. FIGURE 14-3 illustrates a page from which users can access hundreds of thousands of apps that have been created for the iPhone.

Third, developers can create a **widget**, which is much like an app that the user downloads and installs to his or her mobile device. A widget differs from an app in that the widget is always active. A clock widget's icon, for example, might constantly display the current time, a weather widget's icon, in turn, might display changing weather conditions, and a map widget may constantly update its icon to show the user's location. In other words, a widget is always running and may possibly be communicating. Having many active widgets at one time might affect a device's performance.

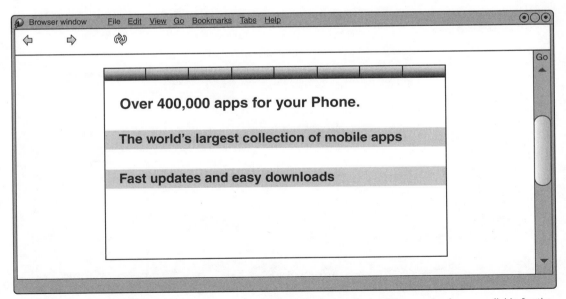

FIGURE 14-3 From business apps, to games, to education, there are hundreds of thousands of apps available for the iPhone.

CASE 14-1 W3C MOBILE PAGE CHECKER

Web developers should be familiar with the W3C website and its outstanding development tutorials and tools. When it comes to malformed HTML tags, mobile web browsers, because of their compact size (code size), tend not to be as forgiving as desktop browsers. Before you launch your mobile pages, you should validate your code using the S3C Mobile Checker at www.w3c.org/mobile, as shown in **FIGURE 14-4**.

Within the W3C Mobile Checker site, you simply enter the URL (web address) of the page you want to examine. The W3C Mobile Checker, in turn, analyzes the page's HTML and displays a summary similar to the one shown in **FIGURE 14-5**.

Exercise Select several traditional web or mobile web pages you commonly visit and use the W3C Mobile Checker to evaluate the pages. Report your findings.

Web Resources For more information on the W3C Mobile Checker, visit www.CloudBookContent .com/Chapter14/index.html.

FIGURE 14-4 The W3C Mobile Checker provides warnings and error messages that developers can use to improve the quality of their mobile web pages.

continues

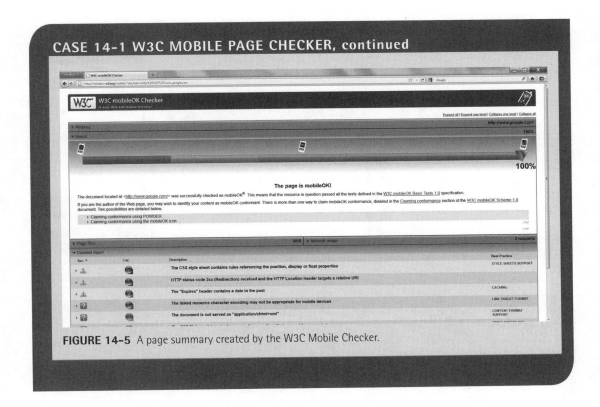

FIGURE 14-5 A page summary created by the W3C Mobile Checker.

Revisiting the Role of HTML5

HTML is the markup language that developers use to build pages for display on the Web and mobile web. When a user browses the Web, either with a computer or mobile device, a web browser downloads and interprets the HTML tags to build the display page the user sees. **FIGURE 14-6**, for example, shows a simple HTML page and its resultant display within a web page and mobile device.

HTML5 is the fifth major release of HTML. HTML5 is important because developers can use it to create multimedia pages similar to what they previously created using Flash. Unlike Flash-based pages, which handheld browsers could not display, HTML5 multimedia pages display on all devices. In this way, HTML5 opens a vast new area of development for mobile devices.

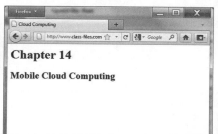

FIGURE 14-6 An HTML markup file and its display within a web browser and mobile device.

CASE 14-2 CISCO IBSG PRESENTATION: "WHEN MOBILE AND CLOUD COLLIDE"

Cisco is one of the key network solution companies driving the infrastructure upon which the cloud resides. Within Cisco, the Internet Business Solutions Group (IBSG) studied mobile solutions and their use of the cloud. The group created five key predictions, which they titled "When Mobile and Cloud Collide." You can view the presentation from the Web Resources link below.

Exercise Discuss whether you believe the cloud is driving mobile or mobile is driving the cloud.

Web Resources For more information on the IBSG mobile cloud predictions, visit www .CloudBookContent.com/Chapter14/index.html.

Mobile Development Considerations

Chapter 18, *Coding Cloud-Based Applications*, looks at the details of creating a cloud application—it is the chapter for coders and developers. Many people play different roles in the development of a mobile solution (project manager, sales and marketing, technical support, coder, tester, and more). If you work on a mobile solution, remember the following development considerations:

- **The mobile web is not the traditional web**: You should not expect to use your traditional web pages as mobile solutions. You should optimize your web solutions and then optimize your mobile solutions.
- **Fast is good**: Mobile data communication is still slower than most computer-based data communication solutions. As such, you should optimize your mobile web layout and design to maximize download performance.
- **Remember your goals and requirements**: As you design your mobile solutions, keep your original goals and requirements in mind to ensure that your solution matches your business strategy.
- **You cannot support everything**: Pick your largest market segment (or device) and focus your initial efforts there.
- **Do not treat mobile content as an afterthought; create, do not convert, mobile content**: Do not simply convert your traditional web content for use on the mobile web. Instead, design your mobile content for optimal performance and market impact.
- **Handle different display sizes differently**: Mobile applications should query the browser or device to determine the supported display size and then provide matching display content dynamically.

CASE 14-3 WEBKIT OPEN SOURCE BROWSER

As you drill down through the specifics of mobile web browsers, you will find that many run the WebKit open source browser. You can learn more about this browser and download the source code at the WebKit website, www.webkit.org, shown in **FIGURE 14-7**.

Exercise Research several commonly used phones (based on market share). Indicate whether the phones use the WebKit open source browser.

Web Resources For more information on the WebKit open source browser, visit www.CloudBookContent.com/Chapter14/index.html.

continues

CASE 14-3 WEBKIT OPEN SOURCE BROWSER, continued

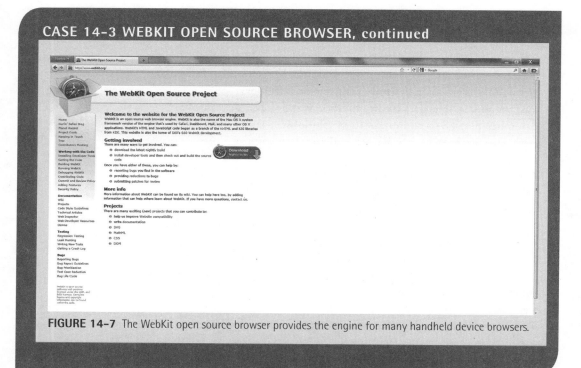

FIGURE 14-7 The WebKit open source browser provides the engine for many handheld device browsers.

CASE 14-4 MOBIREADY PAGE CHECKER

Developers will often customize web pages for mobile delivery. As you develop your pages, you should test their content against the mobiReady page checker, shown in **FIGURE 14-8**. As you enter a URL on the mobiReady page, the site will evaluate your page content and display a detailed report, similar to that shown in **FIGURE 14-9**. Based on the report feedback, you can adjust your page components.

Exercise Select several traditional and mobile web pages that you use regularly. Use the mobiReady readiness test to examine the sites. Report your findings.

Web Resources For more information on the mobiReady site checker, visit www.CloudBookContent.com/Chapter14/index.html.

continues

CASE 14–4 MOBIREADY PAGE CHECKER, continued

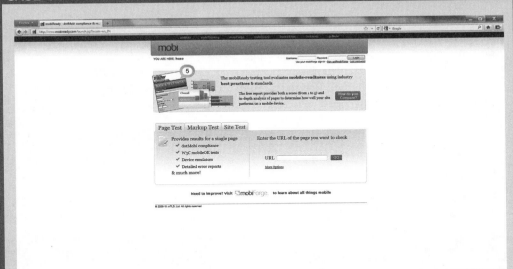

FIGURE 14–8 The mobiReady page checker examines key aspects of mobile page content.

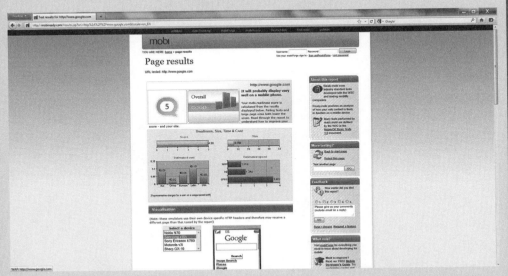

FIGURE 14–9 This report by mobiReady indicates not only that the site will display nicely on a mobile phone, but also that there are areas that need improvement.

CASE 14-5 THE ".MOBI" TOP-LEVEL DOMAIN

Developers will often create separate web pages for mobile-device display. To direct users to those pages, developers have several options. First, they can have their web software detect the device type, such as a computer or phone, and then download the appropriate pages dynamically. Second, many developers will place the letter "m" before their site domain name (creating a subdomain), such as m.somesite.com or even mobile.somesite.com. Third, just as sites use the domain types .com, .org, and .edu, many mobile-based sites now use the ".mobi" domain type, such as www.somesite.mobi.

Developers can purchase a .mobi-based domain name at most domain name registry sites.

Exercise Assume you are launching a mobile web page. Discuss how you might make your HTML pages available to site users.

Web Resources For more information on the .mobi domain type, visit www.CloudBookContent .com/Chapter14/index.html.

CHAPTER SUMMARY

It is not clear whether mobile computing is driving the growth of the cloud, or vice versa. Either way, the use of the cloud and the use of mobile devices continues to grow exponentially. This chapter examined various mobile-computing factors and their underlying impact on cloud-based solutions. Today, most businesses understand the need to have a mobile-computing presence. Many of the early players, however, came to the cloud with a conversion of their traditional web-based content. To maximize the user experience, developers must design solutions specifically within the mobile ecosystem in mind. Whether a solution is a mobile web page, an app, or a widget, many of these solutions will utilize underlying cloud-based resources.

KEY TERMS

App
Ecosystem
Mobile cloud

Proxy
Transcoder
Widget

CHAPTER REVIEW

1. Define and describe the mobile web.
2. Describe the different generations of cell phones.
3. Describe how smartphones differ from ordinary cell phones.
4. Select a mobile or traditional website that interests you. Describe the site in terms of the ecosystem that makes up the site's user experience.
5. Describe how web pages differ from apps and how apps differ from widgets.
6. Discuss why developers say that HTML5 will drive mobile solutions.
7. Describe some development best practices for designing solutions for the mobile cloud.

Governing the Cloud

FOLLOWING THE DOT-COM CRASH and corporate scandals such as Enron, Tyco, and WorldCom, pressures emerged from the government, shareholders, and numerous other stakeholders for companies to increase their financial oversight to reduce opportunity for fraud and to restore confidence in corporate financial reporting. The need for better corporate governance became an issue for all public companies. Because most of the data that drive corporate financial reports originate within data centers, the new era of governance has brought greater visibility and a greater need for controls to IT departments.

Learning Objectives

This chapter examines corporate and IT governance and the new challenges introduced by cloud migrations. By the time you finish this chapter, you will be able to do the following:

- Define and describe corporate governance.
- Define business strategy and provide examples of strategic goals.
- Discuss how companies use the Capability Maturity Model to measure their current capabilities.
- Define and describe internal controls.
- Define and describe IT governance.
- Discuss the various types of governance a company must perform.
- Discuss the role of Sarbanes-Oxley in corporate IT governance.
- Discuss factors to consider when developing governance procedures for the cloud.

Understanding Corporate Governance

Corporate governance combines the processes, policies, laws, and controls that affect how a company operates. The governance guides the company's decision-making and administrative processes. Corporate governance, as shown in **FIGURE 15-1**, is complex and involves people, processes, systems, and more.

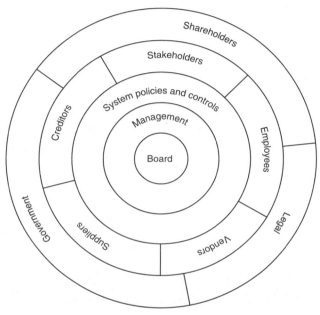

FIGURE 15-1 Components of the corporate governance process.

Understanding Business Strategy

A strategy is a plan of action designed to achieve one or more particular goals. A **business strategy** comprises the plans a company executes to achieve business goals, which may include the following:

- Maximizing shareholder value
- Reducing or managing costs to maximize profits
- Providing a high-quality work environment to attract and retain employees
- Maintaining a high degree of customer satisfaction
- Supporting environmentally friendly operations
- Developing a sustainable, competitive advantage
- Providing accurate reporting of company operations

Measure What Is Important

After a business defines its strategic plans, it must determine ways to measure progress toward each goal. The initial measurement will establish a baseline for the company's current level of operations, and future measurements will establish the company's level of improvement.

CASE 15-2 CAPABILITY MATURITY MODEL

As companies begin to govern IT operations, they must identify their current level of capability. The company might apply measures with respect to software development, security, operations, user support, and more.

The Capability Maturity Model (CMM) was developed at Carnegie Mellon University to help businesses measure and improve their current capabilities. Over time, as a business matures and its skills improve, a company's CMM scores should increase. As scores increase, so too should the predictability and reliability of the business.

To help businesses integrate the CMM process, Carnegie Mellon created the Capability Maturity Model Integration (CMMI) process. In fact, the CMMI group has defined processes for common industry activities, such as acquisitions, security, software design, and system design.

Within CMM, there are five levels of maturity, as shown in **TABLE 15–1**.

A company evaluates its processes using the levels to define its current capabilities and then sets goals for moving the processes to the next level.

Exercise Select an organization that you know or one where you can interview a manager. Identify the organization's key operational tasks. Using the CMM, rate the company's current capabilities.

Web Resources For more information on the CMM, visit www.CloudBookContent.com/Chapter15/index.html.

continues

CASE 15-2 CAPABILITY MATURITY MODEL, continued

TABLE 15-1   MATURITY LEVELS WITHIN THE CMM

Level	Description	Characteristics
1	Initial	Processes are typically changing. Those that are static are likely undocumented. Many operations are reactive.
2	Repeatable	Some processes are repeatable, ideally with consistent results. Many defined systems are still lacking.
3	Defined	Many processes are now static and documented. Some processes are under evaluation for improvement opportunities.
4	Managed	Most processes are controlled and adjusted to improve quality.
5	Optimized	Focus is on continuous improvement of existing processes.

Inspect What You Expect

Once a company defines its business goals and metrics, it must inspect the underlying factors that drive business results. In other words, rather than take its financials at face value, the company should examine the sources from which the values are derived to ensure that each is accurate and free from fraud. This inspection process is known as **auditing**.

The auditing process can be internal (done by the company) or external (done by a third party), as shown in **FIGURE 15-2**.

Understanding Internal Controls

The auditing process will identify key stages within processes that the auditor should inspect. To support the process, the company should put in place its own **internal controls** (policies and procedures) at each of these key stages, as shown in **FIGURE 15-3**.

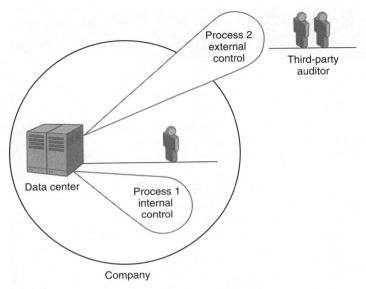

FIGURE 15–2 Companies must audit the source of the values they measure and report using internal or external auditors.

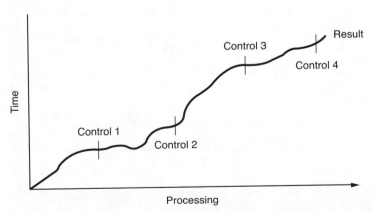

FIGURE 15–3 Internal controls allow a company auditor to inspect data values at key stages.

CASE 15-3 COMMITTEE OF SPONSORING ORGANIZATIONS OF THE TREADWAY COMMISSION

A key aspect of corporate governance is internal controls. In general, an internal control is a process that provides assurance that the objectives of a company's operational goals and legal compliance requirements are being met, as well as confidence in the accuracy of the reporting of operations. The Committee of Sponsoring Organizations of the Treadway Commission (COSO) has defined a model that companies can use to evaluate their internal controls.

The original COSO model's framework consisted of five key components, defined in **TABLE 15-2**.

To meet the demand for companies to address risk management, the COSO framework has been expanded to support eight components, as listed in **TABLE 15-3**.

To download a variety of documents focused on internal controls and risk management, or to order publications available for purchase, visit www.coso.org, as shown in **FIGURE 15-4**.

Exercise Select a company with which you are familiar. List five potential internal controls you would expect to see in place within the company's IT group.

Web Resources For more information on COSO and internal controls, visit www.CloudBook Content.com/Chapter15/index.html.

TABLE 15-2   THE ORIGINAL FIVE KEY COMPONENTS OF THE COSO MODEL

COSO Component	Description
Control environment	The organization creates an environment supportive of controls, which includes ethical operations, managerial integrity, and compliant operations.
Risk assessment	Opportunities and existing processes are evaluated with respect to potential risks and ways to mitigate the risks.
Control activities	Business operations include control activities such as approvals, authorizations, reviews, and audits.
Information and communication	Reliable and truthful communication flows up, down, and across the organization, as well as out from it.
Monitoring	Existing processes and internal controls are monitored on a consistent basis.

continues

CASE 15-3 COMMITTEE OF SPONSORING ORGANIZATIONS OF THE TREADWAY COMMISSION, continued

TABLE 15-3   THE COMPONENTS OF THE EXPANDED COSO MODEL

COSO Component	Description
Internal environment	The organization creates an environment supportive of controls, which includes ethical operations, managerial integrity, and compliant operations.
Objective setting	The business establishes defined and measurable objectives for operations.
Event identification	The business watches for, recognizes, and responds to events that will impact operations.
Risk assessment	Opportunities and existing processes are evaluated with respect to potential risks and ways to mitigate the risks.
Risk response	Management accepts risks based upon a consistent approach to risk tolerance.
Control activities	Business operations include control activities such as approvals, authorizations, reviews, and audits.
Information and communication	Reliable and truthful communication flows up, down, and across the organization as well as out from it.
Monitoring	Existing processes and internal controls are monitored on a consistent basis.

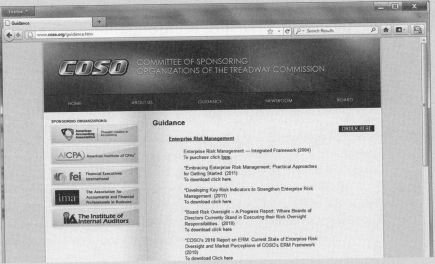

FIGURE 15-4 The COSO website provides documents on internal controls and risk management. You can also order publications through the website.

CASE 15-4 CONTROL OBJECTIVES FOR INFORMATION AND RELATED TECHNOLOGY

Control Objectives for Information and Related Technology (COBIT) is an IT governance framework defined by the Information Systems Audit Control Association (ISACA). COBIT defines dozens of processes an IT manager and staff can use to plan, acquire, implement, deliver, support, monitor, and evaluate IT solutions. COBIT, whose first version was released in 1996, has evolved to support current IT capabilities and governance needs. COBIT is used by small business owners to structure their IT processes and by larger companies and organizations (public and governmental) to align IT and business strategies to conform with regulations such as Sarbanes-Oxley and to implement IT best practices. You can purchase the COBIT guide from the ISACA website.

Exercise COBIT defines processes a company's IT staff should consider when performing common operations. Assume you must write the COBIT processes for selection of a cloud provider. List the processes you would recommend.

Web Resources For more information on COBIT, visit www.CloudBookContent.com/Chapter15/index.html.

Extending Governance to Information Technology

Within most companies, the data from which the company creates its reports originates from data within the company's IT department. As you might expect, much of corporate governance is based upon IT-related factors.

Furthermore, over the past decades, companies have invested heavily in IT solutions that drive a variety of company-wide (enterprise) applications. Unfortunately, many IT projects fail due to poor management, incorrect requirements, or misalignment of the IT solution with the company strategy. Put simply, companies make large investments in IT solutions; to succeed, the projects must be governed.

IT governance is a subset of corporate governance that includes the policies, procedures, and controls that relate to IT use and deployment, performance, return on investment, and risk mitigation. As shown in **FIGURE 15-5**, IT governance is one of many key types of governance a company must consider.

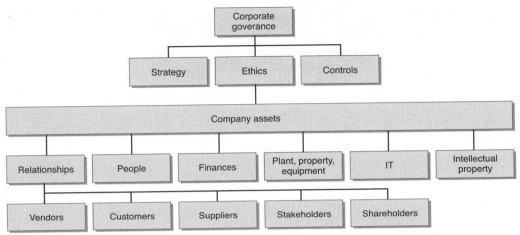

FIGURE 15-5 IT governance is one of many key types of governance a company must consider.

CASE 15-5 SARBANES-OXLEY

In 2002, in the aftermath of the dot-com crash and corporate scandals that included Enron, Tyco, and WorldCom, Senator Paul Sarbanes of Maryland and Representative Michael Oxley of Ohio cosponsored a Senate bill entitled the Public Company Accounting Reform and Investor Protection Act and a House bill entitled the Corporate Auditing, Accountability, and Responsibility Act. Once passed, the law became known as Sarbanes-Oxley.

The law's goal was to improve confidence in the truthfulness of company reporting by requiring greater transparency and controls of the data that companies report. The law put in place criminal penalties for corporate officers who violated or failed to comply with the law.

As you would expect, Sarbanes-Oxley had a large impact on financial groups within an organization who report a company's financials. The law also had a large impact on corporate IT groups, who had to implement auditable controls on the processes, data, and applications that produced the information that drove the financial reports.

In general, Sarbanes-Oxley was a major catalyst in driving the origin of IT governance and the related processes. For more information on Sarbanes-Oxley, download a copy of the act shown in **FIGURE 15-6**.

continues

CASE 15-5 SARBANES-OXLEY, continued

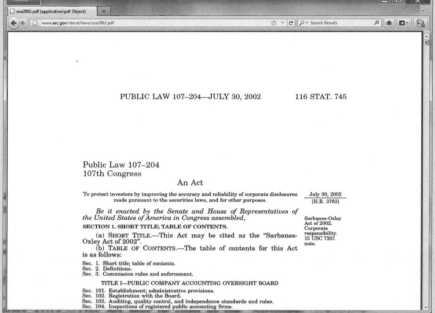

FIGURE 15-6 Individuals responsible for IT governance of an organization should review the complete Sarbanes-Oxley Act of 2002, which is available on the Web.

Exercise Using the Web, research Sarbanes-Oxley. Provide a list of five reasons why Sarbanes-Oxley should remain in effect and five reasons why it should be abolished.

Web Resources For more information on Sarbanes-Oxley, visit www.CloudBookContent.com/Chapter15/index.html.

CASE 15-6 IT GOVERNANCE INSTITUTE

The IT Governance Institute (ITGI) was formed in 1998 to assist businesses in aligning IT solutions with business strategies. The institute conducts research on the global practices and perceptions of IT governance. The institute makes many of its best practices, case studies, and research papers available for sale or download from its website, as shown in **FIGURE 15-7**.

continues

CASE 15-6 IT GOVERNANCE INSTITUTE, continued

Exercise Assume you must make a presentation on IT governance to a company's board of directors. Prepare a 10-slide PowerPoint presentation that introduces the key aspects of IT governance.

Web Resources For more information on the ITGI, visit www.CloudBookContent.com /Chapter15/index.html.

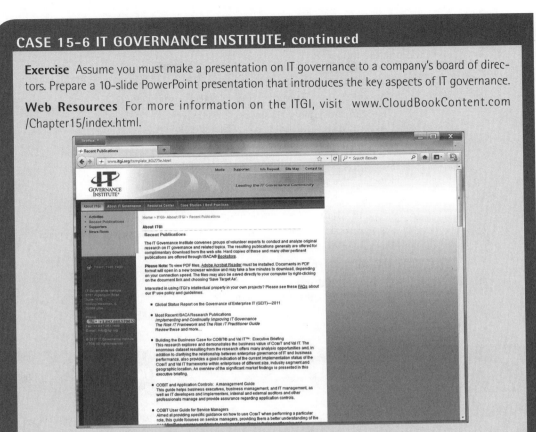

FIGURE 15-7 You can find a wide range of research articles on IT governance at the ITGI website.

Cloud Computing Governance

When a company moves to the cloud, the company must further extend its IT governance. First and foremost, the company must ensure that on-site and within-the-cloud solutions align with the company's business strategies. If the IT resource development and deployment does not align with company strategies, the IT initiatives are destined to fail. Then, the company must govern the cloud deployment. That is, the company must create policies, procedures, and controls that not only ensure strategic alignment, but also provide confidence in the accuracy and security of the cloud-based solutions.

A key place to begin the cloud-governance process is with the service-level agreement (SLA). Specific questions to consider with respect to the agreement include the following:

- Who within the company can access the service?
- Who within the cloud provider can access the service?
- What can those who can access the service do?
- Is the solution multitenant?
- How is the service secured?
- How is the service replicated or colocated?
- How can the service be tested and validated?
- What is the service uptime?
- How and when is the service maintained?
- What controls can be implemented and at what stages of the service?
- How are errors and exceptions logged?
- How can performance be monitored?
- What is the upgrading and versioning process?
- What auditing support is provided?

CASE 15-7 CLOUDAUDIT AUTOMATED AUDIT, ASSERTION, ASSESSMENT, AND ASSURANCE API (CODENAME A6)

In the future, many cloud service providers will offer automated auditing capabilities that companies can use as part of their cloud-governance procedures. The CloudAudit/A6 working group consists of cloud-compliance administrators, developers, security personnel, auditors, and others. The group's goal is to develop an application program interface (API) that developers can use and cloud service providers will support, to allow the developers to monitor key cloud issues.

For more information on CloudAudit/A6, visit the cloudaudit.org website shown in **FIGURE 15-8**.

Exercise Discuss the importance of having audit capabilities for cloud-based solutions.

Web Resources For more information on CloudAudit/A6, visit www.CloudBookContent.com /Chapter15/index.html.

continues

CASE 15-7 CLOUDAUDIT AUTOMATED AUDIT, ASSERTION, ASSESSMENT, AND ASSURANCE API (CODENAME A6), continued

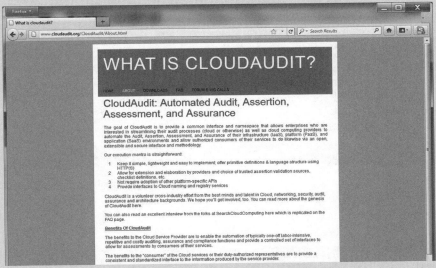

FIGURE 15-8 The CloudAudit/A6 working group is defining an API that developers will use to automate the auditing of key cloud operations.

CHAPTER SUMMARY

After the dot-com crash and corporate scandals such as Enron, Tyco, and WorldCom, businesses were pressured by the government, shareholders, and various other stakeholders to increase their financial oversight to reduce opportunity for fraud and to restore confidence in financial reporting. As a result, corporate governance became an issue for all public companies. Because IT departments create and store most of the data that drive corporate financial reports, the new era of governance has brought greater visibility and a greater need for controls to IT departments. IT governance consists of the policies and procedures the IT staff uses to control data and applications within a data center. With the advent of cloud-based solutions, IT governance now extends to the cloud.

KEY TERMS

Auditing

Business strategy

Corporate governance

Internal control

IT governance

CHAPTER REVIEW

1. Define corporate governance.

2. Discuss the events that led up to the need for increased corporate governance.

3. Define business strategy. List five possible business strategies.

4. Discuss the purpose of the Capability Maturity Model.

5. Define auditing.

6. Define internal control and provide an example of a control.

7. Discuss the role Sarbanes-Oxley has played with respect to corporate governance.

8. Define IT governance.

9. List factors one should consider with respect to governing the cloud.

Evaluating the Cloud's Business Impact and Economics

SO FAR, YOU HAVE learned that the cloud is bringing with it new business models and economics. Large companies are saving costs, reducing staff, and improving system scalability by moving from on-site data centers to the cloud. Small companies are leveraging pay-on-demand models to "right-size" their computing needs quickly and cost effectively. The cloud business model and its economic opportunities for all businesses, large and small, is the subject of this chapter.

Learning Objectives

This chapter examines the impact of the cloud business model on businesses and the resulting economic opportunities. By the time you finish this chapter, you will be able to do the following:

- Discuss the total cost of ownership for an IT solution.
- Compare and contrast the capital expenses and operational expenses of an IT solution.
- Describe supply-side savings made available through large-scale, cloud-based data centers.
- Describe and discuss the efficiencies gained to providers through multi-tenant applications.
- Describe and discuss the "right-sizing" process.
- Identify the primary costs of a data center.
- Describe how Moore's law relates to the cloud.

CASE 16-1 CLOUD ECONOMICS

Economics is the study of the production, distribution, and consumption of goods and services. One of the best overviews of cloud economics, published in November 2010, was written by two employees at Microsoft, Rolf Harms and Michael Yamartino. The document provides an overview of the cloud, a historical perspective, and an easy-to-follow discussion of its impact on business (see **FIGURE 16-1**).

Exercise Select an industry-changing event in history, such as the automobile assembly line, the first commercial airline flight, or the advent of radio or television, and compare the rate of adoption, societal impact, and economic impact with that of the cloud.

Web References For more information on the Microsoft "Economics of the Cloud" paper, visit www.CloudBookContent.com/Chapter16/index.html.

FIGURE 16-1 The authors of an influential white paper on the economics of the cloud compare the current state of cloud computing with the early days of "horseless carriages," when no one could predict how the modern automobile industry would evolve.

Business Economics 101

To understand the business and economics impact of the cloud, first you should understand several key terms. The following sections examine key business concepts and their impact associated with the cloud.

Total Cost of Ownership

Computer hardware and software have associated direct and indirect costs. For example, when you purchase a network-attached disk drive, you incur the direct cost of the hardware device, plus, possibly, a warranty. Before you purchased the device, you likely spent time researching it, shopping, and finally placing your order, which then required tax and shipping expenses. After the device arrived, you spent time installing, configuring, and testing it. Finally, the device was ready for use and began to consume power and generate heat. Admittedly, for the one disk drive in this case, the indirect cost may be small. The point is that you can establish a series of costs before the acquisition, at the time of the acquisition, and following the acquisition.

These different costs combined constitute the **total cost of ownership (TCO)**—the total direct and indirect costs, including capital and operating expenses, of owning a particular piece of equipment or other capital good. When you examine the economics of the cloud, you need to consider the total cost of ownership of an on-site solution compared with that of the cloud.

When you calculate the total cost of ownership for various computers, hardware, network, and software solutions, you should consider the following items:

- Software (server, desktop, notebook, tablet, and mobile)
  - Prepurchase research
  - The actual software purchase or licensing
  - Installation
  - Training
  - Version and patch management
  - License management
  - Security considerations
  - Administration
- Hardware (server, desktop, notebook, tablet, and mobile)
  - Prepurchase research
  - The actual hardware purchase
  - Installation
  - Testing
  - Footprint and space
  - System downtime
  - Electricity and air conditioning
  - Insurance
  - Replacement costs of failed components

- Decommission, removal, and disposal of previous equipment
- Cost of scaling solutions to new demands
- System maintenance
- Data storage
  - Prepurchase research
  - The actual device purchase
  - Installation
  - Testing
  - Security considerations
  - Backup operations
  - Footprint and space
  - Electricity and air conditioning
  - Maintenance
  - Replacement costs of failed components
- Network equipment
  - Internet access (Internet service provider)
  - Prepurchase research
  - The actual component acquisition
  - Installation
  - Training
  - Security considerations
  - System downtime
  - Maintenance
  - Administration

CASE 16-2 AMAZON TOTAL COST OF OWNERSHIP SPREADSHEET

To help users calculate and then compare the total cost of ownership for a cloud-based solution, collocated solution, and on-site solution, Amazon provides the Excel spreadsheet shown in **FIGURE 16-2**. Using this spreadsheet, you can perform a detailed analysis of the costs related to each solution.

Exercise Assume you must deploy a 2,000-server solution for a new technology company. Using the Amazon spreadsheet, calculate and compare the total cost of ownership for using Amazon web services, a colocated data center, and an on-site solution.

Web Resources For more information on the Amazon total cost of ownership spreadsheet, visit www.CloudBookContent.com/Chapter16/index.html.

continues

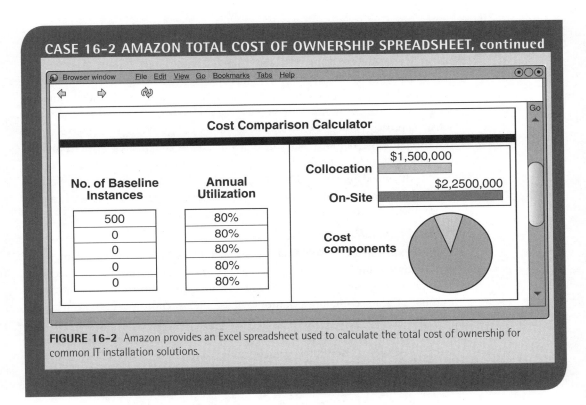

CASE 16-2 AMAZON TOTAL COST OF OWNERSHIP SPREADSHEET, continued

FIGURE 16-2 Amazon provides an Excel spreadsheet used to calculate the total cost of ownership for common IT installation solutions.

Economies of Scale

Economies of scale describes the cost savings that a company may experience (up to a point) by expanding. Assume, for example, that a data center has two system administrators who oversee 100 servers. Each administrator is paid $50,000. The cost per server for system administration becomes the following:

Administrative costs	= $50,000 + 50,000
	= $100,000
Administrative cost per server	= $100,000 / 100
	= $1,000

Assuming the servers are running similar operating systems, the two administrators may be able to oversee as many as 1000 servers. In that case, the cost per server for system administration becomes the following:

Administration cost per server	= $100,000 / 1,000
	= $100

In this case, by scaling the number of servers, the company can reduce the per-server administrative costs. Furthermore, the company may reduce its per-server software licensing costs and other expenses due to the larger volume of servers.

Because of their size, cloud-based data centers experience significant economies of scale. As cloud-based data centers supply computing resources, providers can offer supply-side savings. Additionally, because many cloud-based providers use a multi-tenant approach, perhaps a software as a solution (SaaS) that uses virtual servers or an infrastructure as a solution (IaaS) data center that houses multiple clients, the providers gain efficiencies and cost reductions, some of which can be passed on to the customer.

As discussed, one of the largest costs within the data center is power. Because larger data centers can combine power across multiple customers, they can purchase power at better rates than smaller data centers can.

Capital Expenditures

Capital expenditures (CAPEX) are large expenditures, normally for a plant, property, or large equipment. Companies make large capital expenditures to meet current or future growth demands. Because capital expenditures have value over a number of years, companies cannot expense the expenditures in full during the current year. Instead, using a process called expense capitalization, the company can deduct a portion of the expense over a specific number of years. Different asset types, such as buildings, vehicles, and computers, are capitalized over various lengths of time, based on rules of the U.S. Internal Revenue Service.

Traditionally, a company would have to make a large capital investment for a data center facility, its computers, power supplies, air conditioning, and so on.

For many companies, the cloud eliminates the need for a large data center and the corresponding capital expenditures. Instead, companies that use the cloud experience operational expenses.

Operational Expenses

Operational expenses (OPEX) are expenses that correspond to a company's cost of operations. Within a data center, for example, operating expenses include the following:

- Power and air conditioning
- Rent and facilities
- Equipment maintenance and repair
- Internet accessibility
- Software maintenance and administration
- Insurance

When a company migrates its IT solutions to the cloud, it incurs a fee for the cloud-based services it consumes. However, because of the cloud-service provider's economies of scale, the operational cost of using the cloud will likely be lower than what the company would pay for an on-site data center.

CASE 16-3 MICROSOFT OPERATIONAL EXPENSE CALCULATOR

To help companies compare their operational costs to those of the Windows Azure plat-form as a service (PaaS), Microsoft provides the Windows Azure pricing calculator, shown in **FIGURE 16–3**.

Exercise Assume you must deploy a system with the following attributes:

- 5,000 hours of medium computing capability
- 75 GB of relational database support
- 1 TB of disk storage
- 2 GB of data transfer
- Four 2048 MB caches

Use the Windows Azure pricing calculator to determine the corresponding monthly operating expenses.

Web Resources For more details on the Windows Azure pricing calculator, visit www.Cloud BookContent.com/Chapter16/index.html.

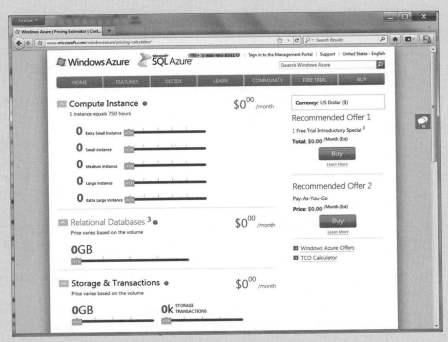

FIGURE 16–3 The Windows Azure pricing calculator.

Return on Investment

Return on investment (ROI) is a measure of the financial gain (or return) on an investment, such as a new piece of equipment. For example, assume that a company can repeatedly save $10,000 based on a $50,000 investment. The company's first-year ROI would become

$$
\begin{aligned}
\text{Return on investment (ROI)} \quad &= \text{Income (or savings) / Cost} \\
&= 10,000 \: / \: 50,000 \\
&= 0.20 \text{ or } 20 \text{ percent}
\end{aligned}
$$

Assume that company can repeatedly save $7,000 by making a $25,000 investment. The company's first-year ROI would become

$$
\begin{aligned}
\text{Return on investment (ROI)} \quad &= \text{Income (or savings) / Cost} \\
&= 7,000 \: / \: 25,000 \\
&= 0.28 \text{ or } 28 \text{ percent}
\end{aligned}
$$

The higher the ROI, the better. Using an ROI in this way, a company can compare two or more investment opportunities.

Traditionally, before investing in a large data center, a company would determine the ROI. Because one typically does not have a large investment within cloud-based solutions (cloud solutions normally have monthly operational expenses), calculating the ROI for cloud-computing solutions can be difficult.

Company IT personnel will instead evaluate the benefits of the monthly cloud investment based on factors including the following:

- **Rapid scalability**: Customers can make and implement scaling decisions quickly.
- **Reduced total cost of ownership**: By leveraging the cloud-service provider's economies of scale, the customer's total cost of ownership will normally be less.
- **Improved business continuity and disaster recovery**: The cloud becomes an operational insurance policy for fail-safe operations.
- **Increased cost controls**: Customers normally pay only for the resources they consume and may be able to align that increased resource consumption with increased revenues.
- **Enhanced ability to "right-size"**: Companies can monitor system utilization and scale resource use up or down to align resources with demand.

CASE 16-4 CLOUD COMPUTING RETURN ON INVESTMENT CALCULATOR

To help IT personnel estimate the ROI for using cloud-based services, www.GetApp.com provides a cloud computing migration calculator, as shown in **FIGURE 16-4**. Using the calculator, you enter your current costs for various IT components, the facility, operating system licenses, servers, data storage, and more. Then, for each item, you specify the potential cost reduction realized by using the cloud. The calculator, in turn, determines your potential savings and ROI for the cloud migration.

Exercise Assume you must deploy a system with the following attributes:

- 7,200 hours of computing capability—24/7 monthly operations
- 100 GB of relational database support
- 1 TB of disk storage
- 5 GB of data transfer

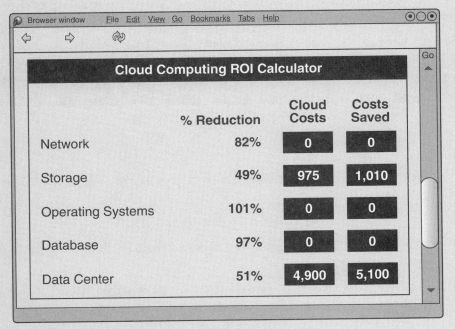

	% Reduction	Cloud Costs	Costs Saved
Network	82%	0	0
Storage	49%	975	1,010
Operating Systems	101%	0	0
Database	97%	0	0
Data Center	51%	4,900	5,100

FIGURE 16-4 The cloud computing ROI calculator.

continues

CASE 16-4 CLOUD COMPUTING RETURN ON INVESTMENT CALCULATOR, continued

Assume you have the current data center expenses:

- Facilities rent: $100,000 a year
- Power/AC: $5,000 a month
- System administration: $250,000 a year
- Operating system server site licenses: $25,000 a year
- Network costs: $80,000 a year
- Disk storage costs: $25,000 a year
- Disaster recovery: $50,000 a year
- Developer costs: $400,000 a year
- Operational IT costs: $150,000 a year

Use the www.GetApp.com ROI calculator to determine the corresponding monthly operating expenses and potential cloud savings.

Web Resources For specifics on calculating and analyzing the ROI for cloud computing, visit www.CloudBookContent.com/Chapter16/index.html.

Profit Margins

A company's **profit margin**, often simply called the margin, is a ratio of the company's income to revenue:

Profit Margin = (Income / Revenue) * 100

Assume, for example, a company has $500,000 of revenue and the following expenses:

Non-IT related expenses	$300,000
IT data center expenses	$150,000

Total expenses	$450,000

To calculate the company's income or profit, you simply subtract the expenses from the revenues:

Profit = Revenues – Expenses
      = $500,000 – $450,000
      = $50,000

Then, you can calculate the company's profit margin as follows:

Profit margin   = (Income / Revenue) * 100
                 = (50,000 / 500,000) * 100
                 = 10 percent

Assume that by migrating its IT data center to the cloud, the company can reduce its IT expenses to $75,000. The company's margin, in turn, would improve as follows:

Non-IT related expenses $300,000
IT data center expenses $ 75,000

Total expenses $375,000

Profit   = Revenues – Expenses
              = $500,000 – $375,000
              = $125,000

Profit margin = (Income / Revenue) * 100
              = (125,000 / 500,000) * 100
              = 25 percent

One way to determine the benefit of moving to the cloud is to evaluate a company's on-site profit margins compared with the cloud-based profit margins.

Moore's Law and the Cloud

Gordon Moore, one of the cofounders of Intel, identified a computing trend during the 1960s that remains true today:

The number of transistors that can be placed on an integrated circuit doubles every two years.

This observation is known as Moore's law. We find that computing power and disk storage capacity also double at nearly this rate. The result is that a capital investment in computing devices has a very short effective life expectancy. The systems we buy today may be only half as fast as those we will purchase two to three years from now.

By shifting computer resources to the cloud, companies eliminate the need to update their own data center equipment, which may drive a considerable cost savings. Today, within the cloud environment, you can think of the services provided (SaaS, PaaS, and IaaS) as a commodity.

Understanding Right-Sizing

A goal of most computer systems is high CPU utilization. If CPUs have low activity, processing resources are wasted. However, if a CPU is running at

100 percent, performance will suffer due to increased process switching. Thus, the goal is a high level of utilization, but not maximum utilization.

As a company moves new products to the cloud, it has no way of knowing what the level of utilization will be. If a company launches solutions with too few servers, the solution's performance will suffer. If a company provides more servers than necessary, it will pay for unused resources.

The virtual and easily scalable nature of the cloud makes it easy for companies to "right-size" their resource needs. **Right-sizing** is the process of aligning computing resources (processors, servers, disk capacity, and so on) with user demand and requirements. With the company's optimal CPU utilization come optimal related costs within the cloud's pay-as-you-go environment. Within the cloud environment, a customer may pay for one hour of processing by 50 servers—or the same for 50 hours of processing by one server. In other words, it is easy to "right-size."

Defining a Large Data Center

Throughout this chapter, we have referred to "large data centers" and their economies of scale. A large data center may house from 500,000 to several million square feet of space, and may initially cost several billion dollars. **FIGURE 16-5**

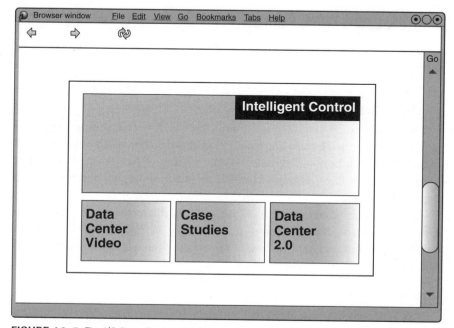

FIGURE 16-5 The I/O Data Center website.

shows the I/O Data Center website. Visit the site to gain a better understanding of the size and scope of a large data center.

Other Economic Key Performance Indicators

Beyond the traditional total cost of ownership, the shift from capital to operational expenses, and ROI, TABLE 16-1 describes several **key performance indicators** that should be considered before initiating a cloud deployment.

TABLE 16-1 ADDITIONAL KEY PERFORMANCE INDICATORS TO CONSIDER	
Metric/Indicator	**Measure**
System availability	Through system redundancy and colocation, cloud-based service providers typically provide 99.9 percent uptime and system availability. Because cloud service providers maintain the operating system and support software, companies normally experience little downtime for system patch or version upgrades. Most cloud service providers guarantee system availability as part of their SLA.
Processor utilization	Because cloud-based providers can scale processors on demand, a company does not have to deploy a large number of processors to meet potential demand. Instead, a company can estimate initial demand and then scale up or down accordingly and dynamically to drive a more efficient processor utilization.
Time-of-day utilization	Many applications experience spikes during specific times of the day. For example, a human resource (HR) solution will normally experience traffic during business hours and then little traffic during off times. Because cloud service providers can dynamically scale resources to meet user demand, the solutions can scale processor power up or down as necessary throughout the day.

continues

TABLE 16-1 ADDITIONAL KEY PERFORMANCE INDICATORS TO CONSIDER, continued	
Resource demand/utilization (RAM, disk and database)	Many companies find that their resource demand models their time-of-day utilization. A cloud service provider may be able to scale resources to best align user demand with costs.
Time to market	Most companies can turn on a cloud service solution immediately, without the cost and time involved in establishing a data center (small or large); acquiring, installing, and testing hardware and software; and hiring system administrators.
Opportunity costs	There are costs associated with an activity's potential that a company must forgo when selecting an alterative. For example, if a company invests in an on-site data center, the company may have to forgo an advertising and marketing initiative that could increase revenues.
User experience	Hiring, onboarding, and training skilled IT employees is usually an expensive investment. Most cloud service providers have an experienced team of administrators and security personnel.
Market disruption	Being first to market can have disruptive benefits. By utilizing cloud-based resources, a company may become more nimble and faster to market than a company that integrates an on-site data center.

Marketing the Cloud

As with all products and services, the rate at which users migrate to the cloud follows a common pattern. **FIGURE 16-6** illustrates a typical adoption cycle. It is interesting to note that the innovators and early adopters comprise only 50 percent of the eventual market. Judged by that, the cloud still experiences significant growth from the late majority and laggards.

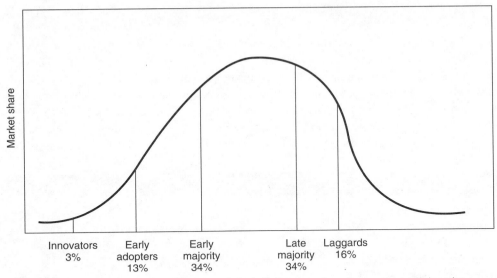

FIGURE 16-6 The cloud's market adoption cycle is similar to that of most new product and service offerings.

CHAPTER SUMMARY

The cloud brings new business models and economics. By moving to infrastructure as a service, large companies can save costs, reduce staff, and improve system scalability. Through SaaS and PaaS, small companies are leveraging pay-on-demand models to "right-size" their computing needs quickly and cost-effectively. This chapter examined the cloud business model and related economic opportunities. Specifically, you learned how companies are converting large capital expenditures to monthly operational expenses and how the cloud service provider's economies of scale result in savings to companies that pay for the cloud services.

KEY TERMS

Capital expenditures (CAPEX)
Economics
Economies of scale
Key performance indicators
Operational expenses (OPEX)
Profit margin

Return on investment (ROI)
Right–sizing
Total cost of ownership (TCO)

CHAPTER REVIEW

1. Define and describe total cost of ownership. List at least 10 items to consider when determining a data center's total cost of ownership.

2. Define and describe a capital expense. How are capital expenses different from operational expenses?

3. Define and describe economies of scale and provide a cloud-based example.

4. Define and describe "right-sizing" as it pertains to cloud computing.

5. Define Moore's law and discus how it might influence cloud migration.

6. Given company revenues of $2.5 million and expenses of $2.1 million, calculate the company's profit and profit margin.

Designing Cloud-Based Solutions

THROUGHOUT THIS BOOK, WE have looked at a variety of cloud-related issues, from scalability to security to economics and business models. In Chapter 18, *Coding Cloud-Based Applications*, we will build and deploy several simple cloud-based solutions. In this chapter, we look at many design considerations a developer should consider when designing a cloud-based solution.

Learning Objectives

This chapter examines cloud-based solution designs. By the time you finish this chapter, you will be able to do the following:

- Compare and contrast functional and nonfunctional system requirements.
- Understand why developers should delay selecting an implementation platform during the design phase.
- Discuss considerations designers should evaluate when they design a system to meet specific nonfunctional requirements.

Revisit the System Requirements

Before you begin the design process, you must ensure that you have a complete set of system requirements. If the system requirements were defined by another individual or group, you should review the requirements and then walk through your understanding of them with the group and ideally the stakeholder who served as the expert for the requirements specification. Identifying errors, omissions, and misunderstandings early in the design process will save considerable time and money later.

System requirements fall into one of two categories: functional requirements and nonfunctional requirements. The **functional requirements** specify what the system does—that is, the specific tasks the system will perform. Normally, the functional requirements are provided by the system or business analyst to the designer within the specification of the things that the system needs to do. In contrast, nonfunctional requirements specify how the system will work behind the scenes. **Nonfunctional requirements** are often called quality requirements and include common factors such as performance, reliability, and maintainability. As a designer with a strong working knowledge of the cloud environment, you can exhibit considerable influence on the system's design to meet the nonfunctional requirements. Much of this chapter examines specific design considerations for nonfunctional requirements.

When to Select a Development Environment

Many developers want to be quick to select the platform upon which they will develop and implement the solution. That is, they want to start thinking about .Net, Linux, C#, or Ruby. When designing solutions, however, you should hold off on the implementation details as long as you can. Your design goal is to understand the requirements (functional and nonfunctional) fully and then to evaluate alternative solutions and implementations. If you focus too soon on platform capabilities, the platform may begin to dictate your design, not only for a specific requirement, but also for the requirements that follow.

Knowing the capabilities of a platform is important; but it is wise to hold off deciding on one until you have your requirements and potential solutions on the table.

Design Is a Give-and-Take Process

Designing a system is challenging. Budgets and time constraints mean you cannot solve every problem. That said, you need to consider the common design issues and then help the stakeholders prioritize the solutions they desire. As you evaluate your system's nonfunctional requirements, remember the 80/20 rule (Often 80 percent of a program's processing takes place within 20 percent of the code). You will want to focus your system design on the issues that will produce the greatest impact for the stakeholders.

Designing for Accessibility

Depending on the processing a system performs, a designer may need to create an interface that maximizes user access or may have to lock down the system and control which users can access specific features. For a public solution, such as a consumer website, maximizing user access not only makes great marketing sense, but also may be required by law (see the Americans with Disabilities Act website at www.ada.gov). In contrast, for a secure site, controlling user access can range from ensuring the security of the login process to some type of biometric user authentication.

CASE 17-1 VOICEPAY CLOUD-BASED USER AUTHENTICATION

Authenticating a mobile device user can be challenging. Often, mobile users will precon-figure different pages to "remember" them in order to simplify login processes. If a user loses the device, another person may be able to access those pages. VoicePay, shown in **FIGURE 17-1**, has an interesting voice-based biometric authentication capability. When a user wants to make a purchase or log in to a specific site, the user calls VoicePay and speaks. The system, in turn, uses the user's voice profile to authenticate him or her. The user does not have to provide a username, password, or other confidential information—all he or she has to do is speak. As mobile device use continues to grow exponentially, biometric solutions such as those offered by VoicePay will become mainstream.

Exercise List and describe other potential uses for voice-based user authentication.

Web Resources For more information on VoicePay, visit www.CloudBookContent.com /Chapter17/index.html.

FIGURE 17-1 Using biometric voice recognition to identify users at VoicePay.

CASE 17-2 WEB ACCESSIBILITY INITIATIVE

As discussed, designing for user access is not just good business—for most web-based companies, it is a matter of law. To help designers understand potential solutions and user needs, the World Wide Web Consortium (W3C) has developed guidelines within its Web Accessibility Initiative pages, as shown in **FIGURE 17-2**. Before you begin a user interface design, you should review these accessibility issues and requirements.

Exercise   Research and discuss lawsuits that companies have lost for failing to support web accessibility for all users.

Web Resources   For more information on the W3C Web Accessibility Initiative, visit www .CloudBookContent.com/Chapter17/index.html.

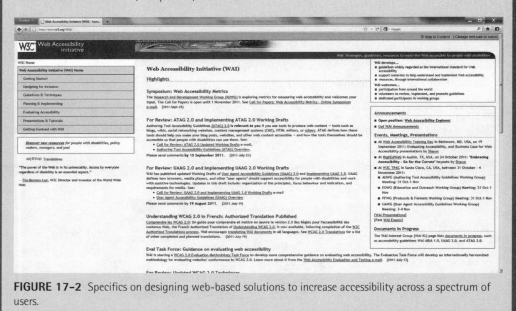

FIGURE 17-2 Specifics on designing web-based solutions to increase accessibility across a spectrum of users.

Designing for Audit

Chapter 15, *Governing the Cloud*, examined the cloud's impact upon the IT governance process. As you design a cloud-based solution, you must first identify critical processing points at which you will want to place an internal control to confirm that the solution's processing is correct and free from outside manipulation. You may design such controls to be active, meaning the code may generate a processing exception should unexpected results occur; or, the control may be passive, possibly logging events to a file or saving snapshots of data.

In either case, it is important that you identify your audit processing needs early so that the appropriate controls can be integrated into the implementation process and you can discuss and confirm your processing needs with a potential cloud-solution provider.

Designing for Availability

As part of their service-level agreement (SLA), most cloud-based providers guarantee system availability, normally specifying a percentage of uptime, such as 99.9 percent. For most applications, 99.9 percent uptime is acceptable (this means that the system is down 0.1 percent of the time, or 525 minutes each year). It is important that you identify your system's uptime requirement and then, likely through the use of redundant colocated servers, design a solution that meets your needs.

Designing for Backup

With the myriad of inexpensive high-capacity data-storage solutions available within the cloud, loss of user data should not occur. If you are designing your own solution, you must consider not only ways to back up your data (and databases), but also the impact of each method on your system availability should you need to bring down the system to restore a backup.

Designing redundant data-storage solutions will always involve a cost-versus-risk trade-off. The issue is not whether you back up data—data backups should be a given, always. The issue is aligning acceptable risk mitigation with cost.

If you are designing a solution for which a third party (such as a software as a solution (SaaS) provider) will manage your data, you need to understand the company's backup policies and procedures, and even then you will probably still want to integrate your own.

Designing for Existing and Future Capacity

Chapter 19, *Application Scalability*, examines the capacity planning process. If you are moving an existing on-site solution to the cloud, you should monitor the application closely to fully understand its processing attributes, such as user demand, CPU utilization, RAM use, and data-storage consumption. Knowing your system's current resource use, you can better guess (it is difficult to predict system demand accurately) your system's cloud resource needs.

With this knowledge, you can design for scalability—the ease of integrating additional computing resources. As you will learn in Chapter 19, there are two primary ways you can scale an application. First, you can scale the application up (called vertical scaling) by moving the application to a faster, more powerful processor. Second, you can scale an application out (called horizontal scaling) by distributing different tasks across different servers. As you design a solution, you should identify opportunities to leverage horizontal scaling. At a minimum, you should design your solution in such a way that you do not restrict future horizontal scaling potential.

Designing for Configuration Management

Ideally, cloud-based solutions may be used at any time, from any place, with any device. In practice, however, this means that developers must consider a variety of operating systems, browsers, and device-specific GUIs. Operating systems and browsers often require patches to address security issues, and, eventually, each will face new version releases. If you are designing your own solution, you will want to layer configuration solutions on top of your system. In this way, you will reduce the impact to a computer-based user when changes are made to a handheld device interface or vice versa.

If your system design includes the use of an SaaS provider, you need to know that company's patch management and versioning policies and procedures.

Designing for Deployment

Chapter 8, *Virtualization*, examined ways that desktop virtualization is changing how solutions are delivered. From an operating system on demand, to thin client (browser-based) solutions, developers have a myriad of ways to deploy a system. As you design a solution, you should identify each potential user type and its environment attributes (such as operating system, device type, and browser). Then, you need to consider not only how you will deploy the initial solution to the user, but also how you will deploy system upgrades.

Designing for Disaster Recovery

Chapter 10, *Disaster Recovery and Business Continuity and the Cloud*, examined considerations for reducing the risk from a disaster and increasing the likelihood that a business is able to continue operating after such an event. When designing a solution with respect to disaster recovery and business continuity, you must balance risks and costs. It is likely impossible and unnecessary to protect a system from all potential events. Instead, you must determine each event's likelihood and business impact and then seek to provide an affordable solution that mitigates risks. Fortunately, the cloud's affordable and distributable resources provide developers with considerable flexibility.

Designing for the Environment (Green Computing)

Green computing describes environmentally friendly IT operations. For example, replacing an application that prints reams of paper reports with a browser-based performance dashboard is an example of a green-computing initiative. As you have learned, within a data center, the biggest environmental impact is the power consumption to drive devices and air conditioners. As more companies migrate to platform as a service (PaaS) and infrastructure as a service (IaaS) providers, many smaller (and possibly less efficient) data centers are being accumulated into larger, state-of-the-art facilities.

As the capabilities of cloud-based collaboration tools continue to increase, travel for face-to-face meetings will decrease, resulting in a lower business-related carbon footprint. That said, as solutions are made available any place, any time, and from any device, the net result is a huge number of handheld devices that are never powered off.

As green-computing practices continue to emerge, designers will be pressured to consider the environmental impact of their designs.

Designing for Interoperability

Cloud-based solutions are emerging for a wide range of applications. Whereas just a few years ago, a company might have used one cloud-based solution for a customer relationship management (CRM) requirement, or a solution for an HR application, today, many companies use a wide range of cloud-based solutions. To simplify the user interaction with such solutions, many companies strive to integrate the solutions and often even to share data across solutions. In the past, companies would buy and install **middleware** software to facilitate the exchange of data between solutions. Today, there are cloud-based middleware solutions that let companies tie together two cloud-based solutions, often without the need for programming development.

As you design cloud-based solutions, or when you work with an SaaS provider, consider ways you may need to integrate data between applications and then design accordingly.

Designing for Maintainability

Designing and building software solutions is an expensive process. Usually, the most costly phase of the software development life cycle is the system maintenance phase. To maximize code reuse and to increase code maintainability, software engineers are taught to create highly functional (cohesive) and independent (loosely coupled) software modules. Chapter 11, *Service-Oriented Architecture*, discussed the role of cloud-based web services to make solutions readily available to a variety of applications. By decomposing an application into highly cohesive, loosely coupled modules and then deploying those solutions to applications such as web services, developers not only increase component reuse, but they also make the resulting systems easier to maintain by centralizing key processing as a distributed solution.

If you are using an SaaS solution, you need to keep the long-term nature of your relationship in mind. Many people argue that cloud solutions are initially inexpensive but may cost you more in the long run.

Designing for Performance

Speed matters. Across the cloud, you can find a myriad of companies that will monitor your system performance and will estimate a percentage of users who will leave your site if the pages do not load within 2 to 3 seconds. As you design the performance aspects of your solution, first you need to identify the 20 percent of your system that will be used 80 percent of the time. Then, you need to focus your initial performance optimizations there. Chapter 19, *Application Scalability*, looks at ways you can scale a solution to meet user demand. Designing for performance and designing for scalability are two different issues. Designing for performance means optimizing what you have. Designing for scalability means designing for the future integration of additional computing resources. The following are some ways that you can design for performance:

- Reduce the use of graphics on key pages.
- Optimize the graphics file format for all images.
- Compress large text blocks before downloading the text to a browser.
- Utilize data and application caching.
- Fine-tune disk and database I/O operations.
- Reduce, when possible, network operations.
- Fine-tune secure data communication transactions.

As you design solutions, evaluate them for potential bottlenecks as well as for optimization points. Understand that you may not, due to time or budget constraints, have the ability to optimize everything.

Designing for Price

Budgets are a fact of life. As you design, you must be aware that your design decisions have financial implications. A solution that was inexpensive to deploy may prove costly to maintain or vice versa. Just as you would consider the performance or security aspects of each component you design, you must also consider each component's short-term and long-term budget impact.

Designing for Privacy

As discussed throughout this book, many users are not comfortable with the idea of putting their data in the cloud. Cloud-based solutions must protect a user's data privacy. If you are developing a healthcare solution with HIPAA requirements, an education solution with FERPA requirements, or an e-commerce solution that stores credit card information, you will need to design your solution in a way that protects data not only from external access, but also from internal users such as developers and administrators.

Most designers understand the importance of backing up user data and replicating key databases. It is important to note, however, that each data backup creates a potential opportunity for a user, administrator, or hacker to gain access to the data.

Designing for Portability

Portability is a measure of the ease with which a solution can be moved, typically from one platform to another. Ideally, you should design your system so that you can easily move the solution from one cloud provider to another. Many developers argue that by using open source tools to create an application you increase the application's portability. In reality, within the cloud, developers using .Net will find many hosting opportunities beyond Microsoft—it's a big cloud and solution providers want to service all developers. If you are designing your own solutions, be aware that using a provider-specific application program interface (API), which may not be available through other providers, may create a form of vendor lock-in. Likewise, if you use an SaaS provider, be aware that each unique or custom capability integrated into your solution may bind you to that provider.

Designing for Recovery

We have discussed the need to design a solution to support disaster recovery and business continuity needs. Additionally, you should design your solution with consideration for how you will recover from more common events, such as server failure, user error, power outages, and so on. Your recovery design should tie closely to your backup design and your system redundancy design.

Designing for Reliability

Computing devices (disks, servers, routers, and so on) will eventually fail. You have learned that many devices have an associated mean time between failures (MTBF) attribute that you can use to estimate the device's potential life expectancy. As you design your solutions, you must identify potential signal points of failure and then design potential system redundancy or establish an acceptable system downtime.

Designing for Response Time

When you design a solution, you should keep the user experience in mind. As discussed, users are conditioned to expect fast system response. In fact, a large percentage of users will leave a site if they have to wait more than a few seconds for pages to download and display. As you design a solution, you need to consider not only the page download times, but also the system response time after a user performs an operation, such as submitting a form. Across the cloud, there are companies that specialize in testing the user experience. These companies will evaluate a system from different geographic locations, using different connection speeds, and with a variety of browsers. Your response time design efforts may be closely related to your site's capacity plan design.

Designing for Robustness

Robustness is a measure of a site's ability to continue operations in the event of an error or system failure, such as a server failure or database error. Again, as you design you should strive to identify and eliminate single points of failure. Furthermore, you should consider automating a system resource utilization monitor that alerts administrators before a system's resources become critically low.

Designing for Security

Chapter 9, *Securing the Cloud*, looks at a variety of cloud-based security issues developers must consider, including the following:

- Software patch installations and software version management
- HR vetting of cloud-based personnel
- Early awareness of security incidents and appropriate responses
- Data privacy issues and considerations
- Jurisdictional issues for a remote cloud-service provider
- Multitenant solution issues
- Cloud-provider failure or collapse
- Defense mechanisms for common low-level network attacks
- Data wiping for shared-storage space
- Physical security considerations

For each component you design, you must evaluate the component's potential security exposure. Again, in some cases you will need to balance risk and cost.

Designing for Testability

Cloud-based solutions will likely have a large number of functional and nonfunctional requirements. As you design a solution, you need to keep in mind how you will test various aspects of your design. As you might guess, the system's nonfunctional requirements are often the most difficult to test. Depending on a system component's purpose and functionality, some developers will use a methodology called test-driven design by which they first design and implement one or more test cases and then build a solution that can satisfy the test.

Designing for Usability

To be of use a system must be usable. **Usability**, in the world of IT, is understood as a measure of a system's ease of use. As you design a solution, you must keep the user foremost in your mind. Because of the importance of meeting system usability requirements, many designers will model or create a prototype of the user experience so they can receive user feedback early in the design process.

CHAPTER SUMMARY

Cloud-based systems will have functional requirements, which specify the tasks the system must perform, and nonfunctional requirements, which define the behind-the-scenes operational requirements the system must satisfy. This chapter focused primarily on considerations a designer must evaluate when addressing a system's nonfunctional requirements for a cloud-based solution. Designers must balance a large number of operational requirements with budget and time considerations. Initially, a designer should list the known requirements and then work with the stakeholders to focus on the requirements that will have the biggest positive ROI.

KEY TERMS

Functional requirements
Green computing
Middleware
Nonfunctional requirements

Portability
System requirements
Usability

CHAPTER REVIEW

1. Compare and contrast functional and nonfunctional requirements and provide an example of each.
2. Discuss why a designer should avoid selecting an implementation platform for as long as possible during the design process.
3. Discuss various trade-offs a designer may need to make with respect to nonfunctional requirements.
4. Discuss why the system maintenance phase is often the most expensive phase of the software development life cycle.

Coding Cloud-Based Applications

BEHIND THE SCENES, DEVELOPERS who create new cloud-based applications or who move existing applications to the cloud are truly driving the cloud's explosive growth. Creating a cloud-based application is very similar to building a traditional web-based application. Developers normally use a programing language such as PHP, Ruby, Perl, Pty, or C#, along with HTML and CSS, and a database. As discussed in Chapter 3, *Platform as a Service (PaaS)*, many cloud-solution providers offer tools that developers need to build and deploy a solution. In this chapter, we will look at two of the most widely used developer platforms: Google App Engine and Windows Azure. In addition, many companies now offer tools that nonprogrammers can use to create and display a solution without coding. We'll look at one such tool, Yahoo! Pipes, and its ability to help users create a mashup.

Learning Objectives

This chapter examines coding cloud-based applications. By the time you finish this chapter, you will be able to do the following:

- Use Yahoo! Pipes to create a mashup.
- Create and deploy a cloud-based application using Google App Engine.
- Create and deploy a cloud-based application using Windows Azure.

Creating a Mashup Using Yahoo! Pipes

Across the cloud, different sites provide different content offerings. A mashup is a page that combines several such independent pieces of content. As shown in

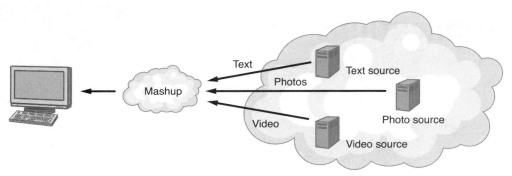

FIGURE 18-1 A mashup combines content from several sources onto the same page.

FIGURE 18-1, a mashup may be created and delivered by a server, or a browser may use JavaScript to combine the content.

Yahoo! Pipes is a cloud-based application that provides a graphical user interface (GUI) that programmers can use to combine content (create a mashup) by dragging and dropping content sources onto a canvas. Later, when a user views a pipe, the user will see the corresponding content. **FIGURE 18-2**, for example, illustrates the user view of a pipe that combines news feeds from a wide range of sources.

Pipes are so named because they let developers connect the data flowing from one source into the data processed by another. **FIGURE 18-3**, for example, illustrates the pipes to create the news feed previously shown.

FIGURE 18-2 Yahoo! Pipes allows developers to combine content from multiple sources into a single mashup.

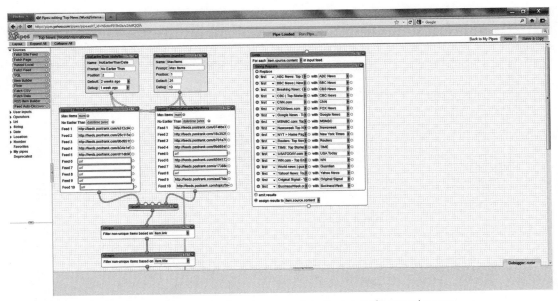

FIGURE 18-3 Yahoo! Pipes flow the content from one source into the input of a second source.

Similarly, **FIGURE 18-4** illustrates a pipe that combines movie reviews with photos from Flickr and videos from YouTube.

FIGURE 18-4 Using Yahoo! Pipes to mash content from several sites to create a movie review.

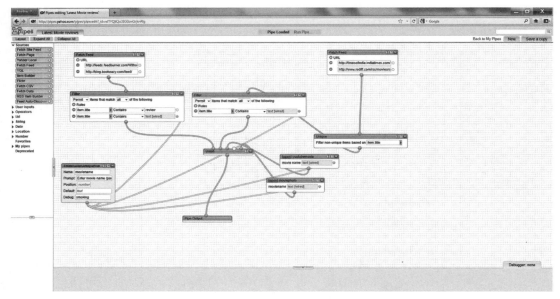

FIGURE 18-5 Using Yahoo! Pipes to combine text, image, and video data into a user interface.

Again, the developer created this pipe by connecting data sources, as shown in **FIGURE 18-5**.

Creating a Simple Yahoo! Pipe

To create your own Yahoo! Pipe, visit pipes.yahoo.com, as shown in **FIGURE 18-6**.

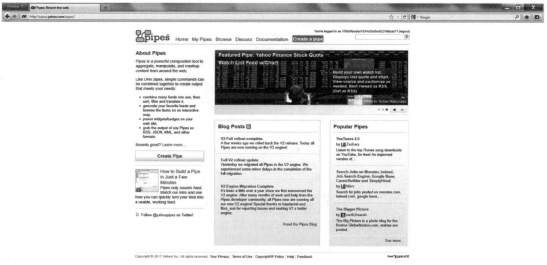

FIGURE 18-6 To create a pipe, start at pipes.yahoo.com.

FIGURE 18-7 To create a Yahoo! Pipe, users drag and connect data sources within the Yahoo! Pipe canvas.

Within the page, log in to Yahoo! and click the Create Pipe button. Your browser, in turn, will display the pipe canvas and the data sources that you can use to create your pipe, as shown in **FIGURE 18-7**.

In this example, you will create a pipe called FindIt, which prompts the user to enter an item (store, restaurant, or other destination) and a geographic area (city, state, or zip code) as shown in **FIGURE 18-8**.

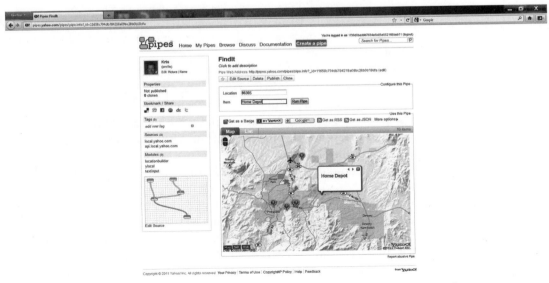

FIGURE 18-8 The user interface of a Yahoo! Pipe, which prompts the user for an item and location.

FIGURE 18-9 Using a Yahoo! Pipe to display locations that offer pizza.

After the user types in the item and location, the page will display the location of items that match. For example, **FIGURE 18-9** lists locations within Prescott, Arizona, that offer pizza.

To create your Yahoo! Pipe, perform the following steps:

1. From the left side of the screen, drag a Text Input object from the User Input group onto the canvas.
2. Label the Name of the Text Input object as Item and set the prompt to Item.
3. From the Sources group, drag a Yahoo! local object onto the canvas. Within the object, change the "Within" field to "20 miles."
4. Using your mouse, drag the circle found at the bottom of the Text Input box into the Find field of the Yahoo! Local box. The canvas will display a pipe, as shown in **FIGURE 18-10**.
5. From the Location group, drag and drop a Location Build object onto the canvas.
6. From the User Input group, drag another Text Input object onto the canvas. Label the object's Name as Location and set the prompt to Location.
7. Using your mouse, drag the circle from the new text box into the Location field of the Location Builder object. The canvas will display a second pipe, as shown in **FIGURE 18-11**.

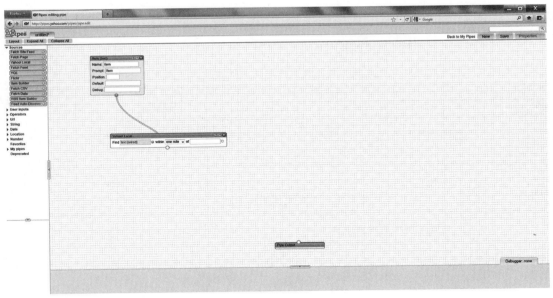

FIGURE 18-10 Using a pipe to connect objects within a Yahoo! Pipe.

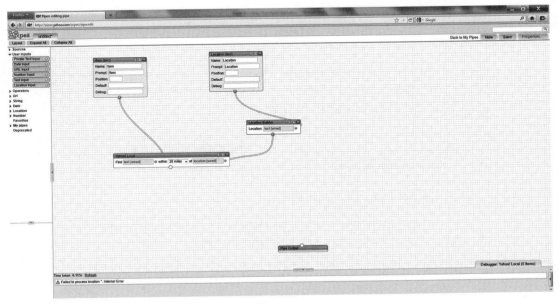

FIGURE 18-11 Creating a second pipe to connect objects.

8. Using your mouse, drag the circle from the Yahoo! Location box to the Pipe Output object. The canvas will display the third and final pipe, as shown in **FIGURE 18-12**.

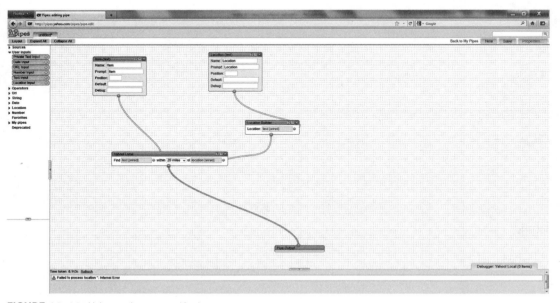

FIGURE 18-12 Using a pipe to specify the user output.

9. Click the Save button and specify a name under which to save your pipe.
10. Click the Properties button. Your browser will display a link that you can use to run your pipe (display the pipe's output).

Later, if you share the URL to your pipe with other users, they can use it to search for a wide range of items. **FIGURE 18-13**, for example, shows the pipe's input screen and output results for pipe search.

Using Google App Engine

Using **Google App Engine**, developers can deploy applications that run on the Google infrastructure. Google maintains the servers, scales the applications, and performs the behind-the-scenes server administration. Developers can get started with Google App Engine at no charge. As an application's demand increases, Google allows developers to pay only for the resources they consume. Developers normally build Google App Engine solutions using Java, Python, or PHP.

FIGURE 18-13 Displaying the results of a Yahoo! Pipe.

Creating a Hello, World! Application with Google App Engine

To start, create the following simple Python application, which displays the text "Hello, world!" to the user:

```
print "Content-type: text/html\n\n"
print "<html>Hello, world!</html>"
```

After you have the application working locally, you can upload the application to the Google App Engine. Visit appengine.google.com and log in to a Google account. Then select the Create Application button. You may need to authenticate yourself to Google further before you can continue.

Downloading the Google App Engine Software Development Kit

Depending on the programming language you are using to develop your application, you will need to download and install the corresponding Google App Engine **software development kit (SDK)**. For this example, you would download the Python SDK. The SDK, in turn, provides utility programs you can use to upload your program into the Google App Engine.

Deploying a Simple Google App Engine Example

To begin, open a command line window as shown in **FIGURE 18-14** and locate the file folder that contains the appcfg.py script, which was created by the SDK installation.

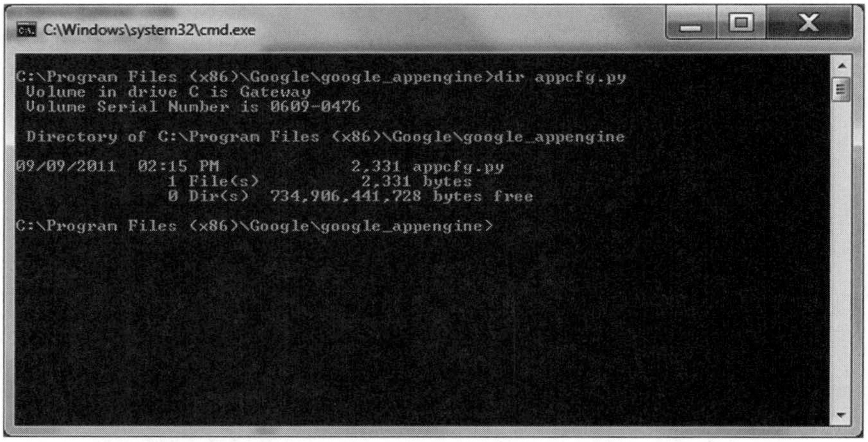

FIGURE 18-14 Using a command line window, locate the appcfg.py script that you will use to upload your Python script to the Google App Engine.

For this example, create a folder within the folder that contains appcfg.py named Hello, within which you store the Hello.py script:

```
print "Content-type: text/html\n\n"
print "<html>Hello, world!</html>"
```

Next, within the same folder, create a file named app.yaml, which Google will use to configure your application. Use the following script, replacing the value 2a2a2a2a2a2a2abbb with the application ID you received from Google:

```
application: 2a2a2a2a2a2a2abbb
version: 1
runtime: python
api_version: 1

handlers:
- url: /.*
  script: hello.py
```

Then, run the appcfg.py script, as shown in **FIGURE 18-15**, to upload your application.

You can then test your application from Google's appspot website, as shown in **FIGURE 18-16**.

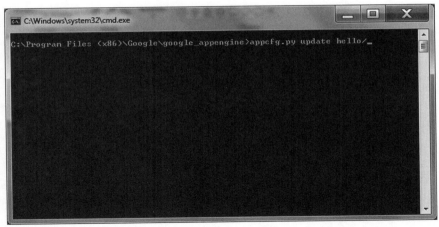

FIGURE 18–15 For a Python script, the appcfg.py script will upload the application into the Google App Engine.

FIGURE 18–16 Running a Python script deployed to the Google App Engine.

Creating a More Advanced Google App Engine Application

To assist developers in creating applications, Google provides a variety of application program interfaces (APIs). The following code uses a Google API to display specifics about the current user:

```
from google.appengine.api import users
from google.appengine.ext import webapp
from google.appengine.ext.webapp.util import
run_wsgi_app

class MainPage(webapp.RequestHandler):
    def get(self):
        user = users.get_current_user()
        if user:
            self.response.headers['Content-Type'] =
'text/html'
```

```
            self.response.out
.write('<HTML><BODY>Hello, nickname:' + user
.nickname() + '<br/>E-mail:' +
            user.email() + '<br/>User ID:' +
user.user_id() + '</BODY></HTML>')
        else:
            self.redirect(users.create_login_
url(self.request.uri))

application = webapp.WSGIApplication([('/',
MainPage)], debug=True)

def main():
  run_wsgi_app(application)

if __name__ == "__main__":
  main()
```

If you place this code into your previous Hello.py script, you can then rerun the previous appcfg.py script to upload the application into the Google App Engine.

When you later run the script, Google will prompt you to log in. Then the page will display your user specifics, as shown in FIGURE 18-17.

Creating a Windows Azure "Hello, World!" Application

For .Net developers, creating a Windows Azure application is a natural extension of their previous ASP.NET development. The developers will use the Visual Studio to create and deploy their applications. Eventually, support for Windows Azure will be integrated into Visual Studio. At the time of this writing, however, developers must download and install a Windows Azure software development kit as well as tools for Visual Studio. In addition, developers must register at the Windows Azure site—which they can do free of charge. At the Windows Azure site, developers will find tutorials to guide them through the process of creating and deploying a cloud-based application.

FIGURE 18-17 Displaying a user's Google specifics.

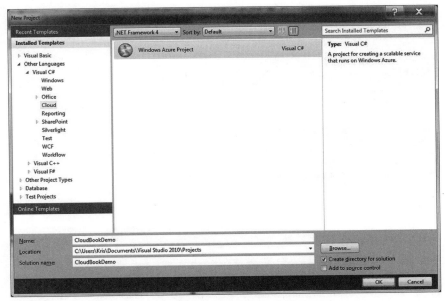

FIGURE 18-18 Creating a cloud-based project hosted on Windows Azure.

After you install the Windows Azure SDK and Visual Studio support tools, start Visual Studio and create a new project. Within Visual Studio's list of installed templates, select Cloud, as shown in **FIGURE 18-18**.

Within the New Windows Azure Project dialog box, select the ASP.NET Web Role entry, as shown in **FIGURE 18-19**.

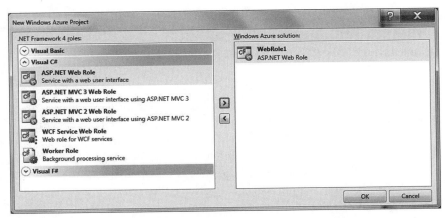

FIGURE 18-19 Using the ASP.NET Web Role to create your cloud application.

A

B
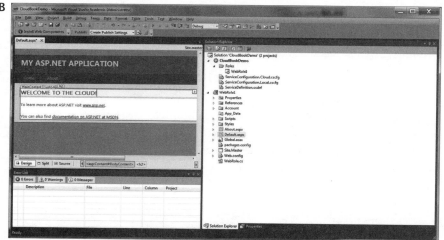

FIGURE 18-20 Modify the Default.aspx file's contents and screen display.

Next, within Visual Studio, edit the Default.aspx file to change the text from Welcome to ASP.NET! to Welcome to the Cloud, as shown in **FIGURE 18-20**.

Select the Project menu Package option. Visual Studio will display the Package Windows Azure Application dialog box. Select OK. Your screen will display a window that contains the package files, as shown in **FIGURE 18-21**. Note the name of the folder within which the package files reside. You will need the files later to upload your application to Windows Azure.

Log in to the Windows Azure site, as shown in **FIGURE 18-22**.

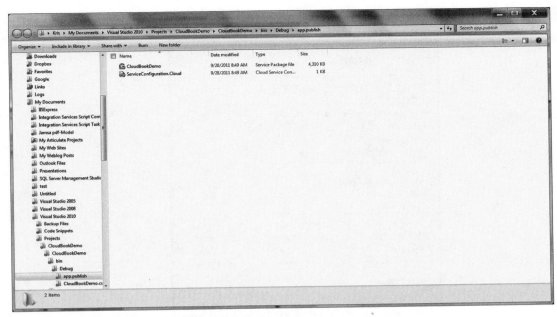

FIGURE 18-21 Displaying package files within Visual Studio.

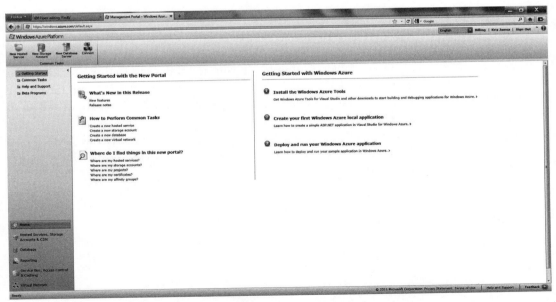

FIGURE 18-22 To upload a program, you must first log in to the Windows Azure site.

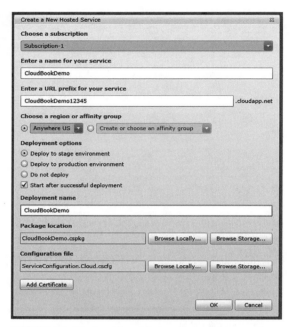

FIGURE 18-23 Providing Windows Azure with specifics about your application.

Click the New Hosted Services button. Your screen will display a dialog box similar to that shown in **FIGURE 18-23**, which you must complete.

Using the folders within which you stored the application's package files, complete the dialog box fields. Windows Azure, in turn, will begin the upload process, eventually displaying specifics about the application, as shown in **FIGURE 18-24**.

Using the URL provided in the Windows Azure project specifics, deploy your application. Your browser, in turn, should display the cloud-hello message, as shown in **FIGURE 18-25**.

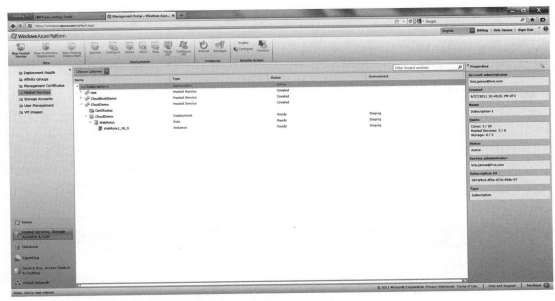

FIGURE 18–24 Loading an application into the Windows Azure platform.

FIGURE 18–25 Successfully deploying an application within Windows Azure.

CHAPTER SUMMARY

Cloud use is driven by new applications, which means that developers who create new cloud-based applications or who move existing applications to the cloud are the ones truly driving the cloud's explosive growth. In general, creating a cloud-based application is similar to building a traditional web-based application. That is, developers will use a programing language such as PHP, Ruby, Perl, Pty, or C#, along with HTML and CSS, and a database. In addition, many cloud-solution providers offer tools that developers need to build and deploy a solution without having to code. Such applications should accelerate the rate at which applications enter the cloud. In this chapter, you learned how to use Google App Engine and Windows Azure to deploy a cloud-based application. In addition, you learned how Yahoo! Pipes allows users to create mashups without the need for code.

KEY TERMS

Google App Engine   Yahoo! Pipes
Software development kit (SDK)

CHAPTER REVIEW

1. Using Yahoo! Pipes, create a pipe that displays the names of pizza restaurants within a given zip code.

2. Using Google App Engine, create a page that displays the following Python script:

```
print "Content-type: text/html\n\n"
print "<html>Cloud Computing, Chapter 18</html>"
```

Application Scalability

SCALABILITY REFERS TO AN application's ability to add or remove resources dynamically based on user demand. Throughout this book, you have learned that one of the greatest advantages of cloud-based applications is their ability to scale. Anticipating user demand is often a "best guess" process. In the past, developers had to release site resources (servers, CPUs, disk space) capable of meeting the anticipated initial user demand, plus growth. Often developers could not accurately project the demand, and frequently they released too few or too many resources.

Learning Objectives

This chapter examines the resource-scaling process. By the time you finish this chapter, you will be able to do the following:

- Define and describe scalability.
- Define and describe the Pareto principle.
- Compare and contrast scaling up and scaling out.
- Understand how the law of diminishing returns applies to the scalability process.
- Describe the importance of understanding a site's database read/write ratio.
- Compare and contrast scalability and capacity planning.
- Understand how complexity can reduce scalability.

CASE 19-1 THE PARETO PRINCIPLE (80/20 RULE)

Whether you are developing code, monitoring system utilization, or debugging an application, you need to consider the **Pareto principle**, also known as the 80/20 rule, or the rule of the vital few and the trivial many. The Pareto principle accurately describes different scenarios such as the following:

- 80 percent of development time is spent on 20 percent of the code.
- 80 percent of errors reside in 20 percent of the code.
- 80 percent of CPU processing time is spent within 20 percent of the code.
- 80 percent of system use comes from 20 percent of the users.

If you consider the Pareto principle, you may find that you do not need to optimize all of an application's code. Instead, you can focus your effort on 20 percent of the code that users use most often.

Exercise Consider system performance monitoring. What other relationships, such as disk space use or database space use, may relate to the Pareto principle?

Web Resources For more information on the Pareto principle, visit www.CloudBookContent .com/Chapter19/index.html.

Reviewing the Load-Balancing Process

Cloud-based solutions should scale on demand. This means that if an application's user demand reaches a specific threshold, one or more servers should be added dynamically to support the application. Likewise, when the demand decreases, the application should scale down its resource use. When an application uses multiple servers, one server, as shown in **FIGURE 19-1**, must perform the task of load balancing.

The load-balancing server receives client requests and distributes each request to one of the available servers. To determine which server gets the request, the load balancer may use a round-robin technique, a random algorithm, or a more complex technique based upon each server's capacity and current workload. For an application to exploit load balancing fully, the application developers must design the application for scaling.

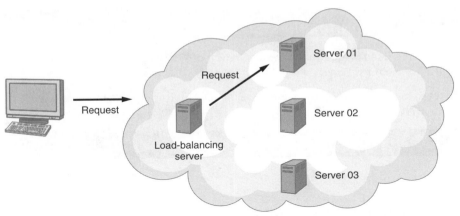

FIGURE 19-1 The load-balancing server distributes workload across an application's server resources.

CASE 19-2 GANGLIA MONITORING SYSTEM

If you are using Linux-based servers, you should consider deploying the Ganglia Monitoring System to monitor your system use. Ganglia is an open-source project created at the University of California, Berkeley. The software monitors and graphically displays the system utilization, as shown in **FIGURE 19-2**.

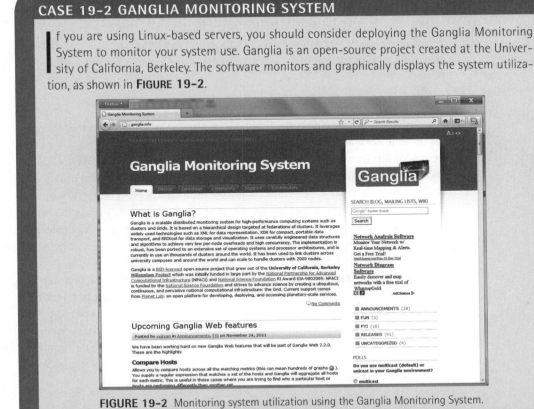

FIGURE 19-2 Monitoring system utilization using the Ganglia Monitoring System.

continues

CASE 19-2 GANGLIA MONITORING SYSTEM, continued

Exercise Examine the Ganglia Monitoring System. Which of the system's features are most critical to cloud administrators? Why?

Web Resources For more information on the Ganglia Monitoring System, visit www .CloudBookContent.com/Chapter19/index.html.

Designing for Scalability

Often developers take one of two extremes with respect to designing for scalability—they do not support scaling or they try to support unlimited scaling. In general, developers should focus their effort somewhere in the middle. In other words, they should design and build the application with the expectation that it will scale to a point, possibly beyond reasonable expectations. It is important to note that most applications do not experience, and therefore do not need to support, overnight success.

Scaling Up, Scaling Out, or Both

Before you discuss or plan for scaling, it is important to understand that there are two ways to scale a solution. First, you can scale up an application (known as **vertical scaling**) by moving the application to faster computer resources, such as a faster server or disk drive. If you have a CPU-intensive application, moving the application to a faster CPU should improve performance. Second, you can scale out an application (known as **horizontal scaling**) by rewriting the application to support multiple CPUs (servers) and possibly multiple databases. As a rule, normally it costs less to run an application on multiple servers than on a single server that is four times as fast.

Assume, for example, that your application makes extensive use of a web service to perform complex processing. If the web service becomes a **bottleneck**, a place where system traffic slows because of lack of resources, you could host the web service on a faster server (by scaling up) or you could place the web service on multiple servers, which the application may call in a round-robin fashion (by scaling out). As shown in **FIGURE 19-3**, over time, a developer may use both vertical and horizontal scaling.

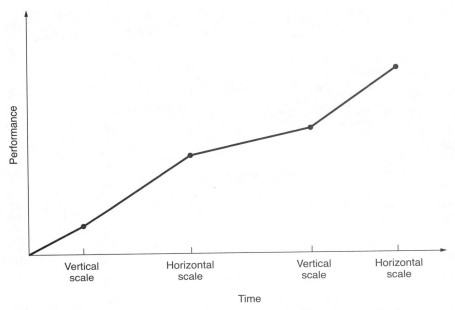

FIGURE 19–3 Developers often use vertical and horizontal scaling to meet application demands.

CASE 19-3 WEBPAGETEST

Before you consider scaling, you should understand your system performance and potential system bottlenecks. www.webpagetest.org evaluates your site and creates a detailed report, as shown in **FIGURE 19–4**. The report helps you identify images you can further compress and the impact of your system caches, as well as potential benefits of compressing text.

Exercise Use WebPagetest to evaluate two or more websites. Discuss how the report's findings align with your user experience.

Web Resources For more information on WebPagetest, visit www.CloudBookContent.com /Chapter19/index.html.

continues

CASE 19-3 WEBPAGETEST, continued

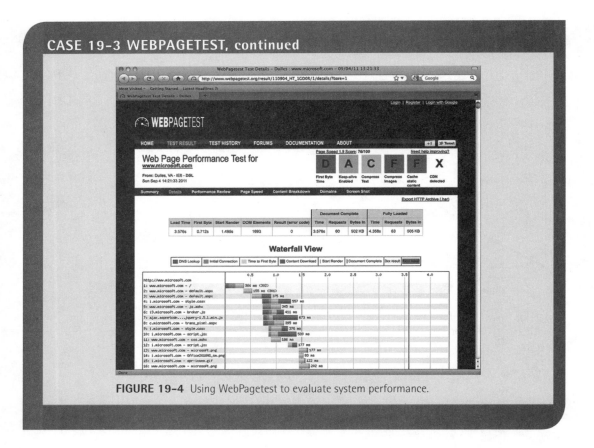

FIGURE 19-4 Using WebPagetest to evaluate system performance.

Minimize Objects on Key Pages

Across the Web, developers strive for site pages that load in 2 to 3 seconds or less. If a web page takes too long to load, visitors will simply leave the site. With that in mind, you should evaluate your key site pages, particularly the home page. If possible, reduce the number of objects on the page (graphics, audio, and so on), so that the page loads within an acceptable time.

Selecting Measurement Points

As you analyze your site with respect to scalability, you will want your efforts to have a maximum performance impact. To begin, identify the potential bottlenecks within the system, both with respect to CPU utilization and database use. If, for example, you scale part of the system that is not in high demand, your scaling will not significantly affect system performance. As you consider your measurement points, keep the 80/20 rule in mind and strive to identify the 20 percent of your code that performs 80 percent of the processing.

CASE 19-4 ALERTRA WEBSITE MONITORING

Often, system administrators do not know that a site has gone down until a user contacts them. Alertra, shown in **FIGURE 19–5**, provides a website monitoring service. When it detects a problem, it sends an e-mail or text message to the site's administrative team. Companies can schedule Alertra to perform its system checks minute-by-minute or hourly.

Exercise Discuss the benefits of having a real-time site monitor and describe how you would justify the investment of using such a site.

Web Resources For more information on the Alertra Website Monitoring service, visit www .CloudBookContent.com/Chapter19/index.html.

FIGURE 19–5 Alertra notifies system administrators about a cloud-based system error or failure.

Analyze Your Database Operations

As you know, load balancing an application that relies on database operations can be challenging, due to the application's need to synchronize database insert and update operations. Within most sites, most of the database operations are read operations, which access data, as opposed to write operations, which add or update data. Write operations are more complex and require database synchronization.

You may be able to modify your application so that it can distribute the database read operations, especially for data that are not affected by write operations (static data). By distributing your database read operations in this way, you horizontally scale out your application, which may not only improve performance, but also improve resource redundancy.

CASE 19-5 PINGDOM WEBSITE MONITORING

Pingdom provides real-time site monitoring with alert notification and performance monitoring. It notifies you in the event of system downtime and provides performance reports based on your site's responsiveness. As shown in **FIGURE 19-6**, Pingdom provides tools you can use to identify potential bottlenecks on your site.

Exercise Discuss the potential bottlenecks that are common to all cloud-based sites.

Web Resources For more information on Pingdom Website Monitoring, visit www .CloudBookContent.com/Chapter19/index.html.

FIGURE 19-6 Pingdom performance reports identify system bottlenecks.

Evaluate Your System's Data Logging Requirements

When developers deploy new sites, often they enable various logging capabilities so they can watch for system errors and monitor system traffic. Frequently, they do not turn off the logs. As a result, the log files consume considerable disk space, and the system utilizes CPU processing time updating the files. As you monitor your system performance, log only those events you truly must measure.

CASE 19–6 GOMEZ WEB PERFORMANCE BENCHMARKS

Many times developers want to compare their site's benchmarks with those of other sites. This is where Gomez comes into play. Gomez provides site benchmarking for web and mobile applications. It provides cross-browser testing as well as load testing. In addition, as shown in **FIGURE 19-7**, Gomez performs real-user monitoring, which focuses on the user experience with respect to the browser influence, geographic location, communication speed, and more.

Exercise Discuss the importance of performing real-user monitoring.

Web Resources For more information on Gomez Web Performance Benchmarks, www .CloudBookContent.com/Chapter19/index.html.

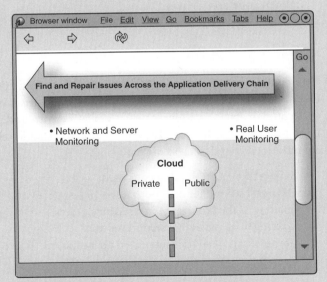

FIGURE 19-7 Using Gomez Web Performance Benchmarks to measure the user experience.

Revisit Your Service-Level Agreement

As you plan for your site's scalability, take time to review your service-level agreement (SLA) with the cloud-solution provider. The SLA may specify performance measures that the provider must maintain, which, in turn, provides the resources to which your application can scale. As you review your SLA, make sure you understand the numbers or percentages it presents. For example, many solution providers claim 99.9 percent uptime and availability. If you do the math, you will see that if your site is down 0.1 percent of the time, it equals

$(0.1\%)(365 \text{ days/year})(24 \text{ hours/day})(60 \text{ minutes/hour}) = 525$ minutes per year (nearly 10 hours)

Capacity Planning Versus Scalability

Scalability defines a system's ability to use additional resources to meet user demand. In contrast, capacity planning defines the resources your application will need at a specific time. The two terms are related, yet different. When you first design a system, for example, you might plan for 10,000 users accessing the system between 6:00 A.M. and 6:00 P.M. Starting with your user count, you can then determine the number of servers needed, the bandwidth requirements, the necessary disk space, and so on. In other words, you can determine the capacity your system needs to operate.

When your user demand exceeds your system capacity, you must scale the system by adding resources.

Scalability and Diminishing Returns

If an application is designed to scale (vertical, or scaling up to faster resources is easy), the question becomes "How many resources are enough?" Keep in mind that you will start a scaling process to meet performance requirements based upon user demand. To measure performance, you should select benchmarks that are most meaningful, such as the following:

* Support for 5,000 simultaneous users
* CPU utilization that does not exceed 50 percent
* Loading of the home page in 3 seconds or less
* Loading of all pages in 5 seconds or less
* Completions of all user submitted operations in 10 seconds or less

With your selected benchmarks in place, you can begin to measure the performance effects of scaling. At first, adding a faster processor, more servers, or increased bandwidth should have measurable system performance improvements. However, you will reach a **point of diminishing returns**, as shown in **FIGURE 19-8**, when adding additional resources does not improve performance. At that point, you should stop scaling.

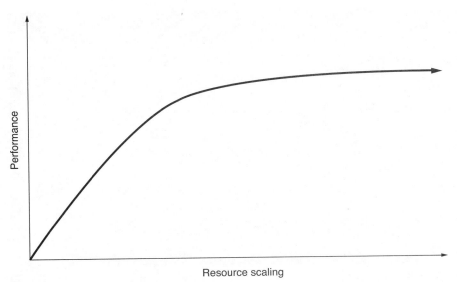

FIGURE 19–8 You will reach a point of diminishing returns, at which point further scaling does not significantly improve application performance.

Performance Tuning

Your goal is to maximize system performance. By scaling resources, you will, to a point, increase performance. In addition to managing an application's resource utilization, developers must examine the application itself, beginning with the program code and including the objects used, such as graphics and the application's use of **caching**. Caching is the use of a faster disk drive or faster random access memory to store items that are used repeatedly by the application in order to improve system performance

This process is known as **performance tuning**. To start the process, look for existing or potential system bottlenecks. After you correct those, you should focus on the 20 percent of the code that performs 80 percent of the processing—which will provide you the biggest return on your system tuning investment.

Complication Is the Enemy of Scalability

As you design solutions, remember that as complexity within a system increases, so too does the difficulty of maintaining the underlying code, as well as the overhead associated with the complex code. Furthermore, as an application's complexity increases, its ability to scale usually decreases. When a solution begins to get complex, it is worth stopping to evaluate the solution and the current design.

CASE 19-7 KEYNOTE CLOUD MONITORING

Keynote, as shown in **FIGURE 19-9**, is one of the world's largest third-party monitors of cloud and mobile applications. In fact, the company performs more than 100 billion site measurements each year. Keynote uses thousands of measurements that come from computers dispersed across the globe. In addition to providing notification of site downtime, Keynote provides a real-time performance dashboard.

Exercise Discuss the importance of testing a cloud solution's performance from computers dispersed across the globe.

Web Resources For more information on Keynote Cloud Monitoring, visit www.CloudBookContent.com/Chapter19/index.html.

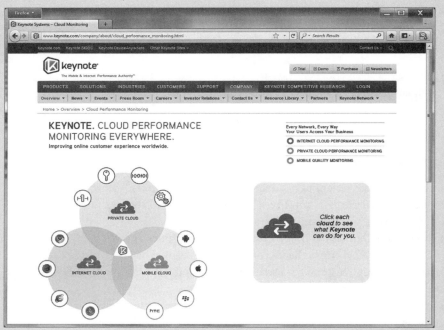

FIGURE 19-9 Keynote Cloud Monitoring provides site performance in real time.

Often, complexity occurs because a solution is trying to handle all possible conditions—some of which may never occur. If you design the solution for the common conditions (the 80/20 rule) in a simple way, your code will be easier to modify in the future, perhaps to support horizontal scaling.

CHAPTER SUMMARY

An application's scalability corresponds to its ability to add or remove resources dynamically based on user demand. One of the greatest advantages of cloud-based applications is their ability to scale. Unfortunately, often it is difficult for developers to identify what an application's user demand will be. Often, developers will release site resources (servers, CPUs, disk space) capable of meeting the anticipated initial user demand, plus growth. When developers are wrong, however, the project will have too few or too many resources. This chapter examined ways applications can scale up to faster processors or scale out to utilize more resources.

KEY TERMS

Bottleneck

Caching

Point of diminishing returns

Horizontal scaling

Pareto principle

Performance tuning

Vertical scaling

CHAPTER REVIEW

1. Define scalability.
2. List five to ten potential relationships that align with the Pareto principle, such as how 80 percent of sales come from 20 percent of customers.
3. Compare and contrast vertical and horizontal scaling.
4. Explain the importance of the database read/write ratio.
5. Assume a site guarantees 99.99 percent uptime. How many minutes per year can the site be down?

The Future of the Cloud

THROUGHOUT THIS BOOK, YOU have examined the most recent cloud-based solutions and applications. With many cloud solutions already seemingly quite cutting edge, it is hard to imagine how the cloud will evolve in the near and far term.

Learning Objectives

This chapter examines the future of the cloud and cloud-based applications. By the time you finish this chapter, you will be able to do the following:

- Describe how the cloud will influence future operating systems.
- Describe how the cloud enables location-aware applications.
- Describe how the cloud will change the way people watch TV.
- Describe how the cloud may enable the use of intelligent fabrics.
- Describe how the cloud will enable communication among smart devices.
- Describe how the cloud will drive mobile solutions and mobile solutions will drive the cloud.
- Discuss the role of HTML5 in enabling new mobile applications.
- Describe the role of home-based clouds.

CASE 20-1 FUTURE OF CLOUD COMPUTING

Janna Quitney of Elon University and Lee Rainie of the Pew Research Center's Internet & American Life Project surveyed cloud experts and produced "The Future of Cloud Computing," shown in **FIGURE 20-1**. The report includes opinions and insights as to how the cloud will evolve over the next 10 years.

Quitney also heads Elon University's Imagining the Internet Center, shown in **FIGURE 20-2**, where you will find surveys, articles, and videos that look at the Internet's past and future. Much of the discussion provides insights into the cloud's future as well.

Finally, the Pew Research Center's Pew Internet & American Life Project provides surveys and articles on the cloud—from where it has come to where it is going.

Exercise   Read the predictions on the cloud's future. Argue for one prediction and against another.

Web Reference   For more information on the predictions of the cloud's future, visit www .CloudBookContent.com/Chapter20/index.html.

FIGURE 20-1 "The Future of Cloud Computing," published by Quitney and Rainie, provides insights into the evolution of cloud computing.

continues

CASE 20-1 FUTURE OF CLOUD COMPUTING, continued

FIGURE 20-2 The Imagining the Internet site is filled with evaluations of the Internet's past and predictions of its future.

How the Cloud Will Change Operating Systems

Operating systems exist to allow users to run programs and store and retrieve data from one user session to the next. As discussed in Chapter 8, *Virtualization*, most server operating systems now support and will continue to support hypervisors that allow multiple (and possibly different) operating systems to run simultaneously. Virtualized servers will continue to play a large role in driving the behind-the-scenes operation of the cloud.

As also discussed in Chapter 8, many organizations are going to an operating-system-on-demand model for which servers download a user's operating system, applications, and environment settings to any computer the user logs in to. With the advent of more programs that run within a browser, there

CASE 20-2 HOW THE CLOUD WILL IMPACT PLAYERS SUCH AS MICROSOFT

Microsoft is heavily invested in all aspects of computing, including the cloud. Microsoft's CEO, Steve Ballmer, has publicly stated that Microsoft, like other companies, is "betting the exact quote is betting *our* company on the cloud company on the cloud." Windows (and SQL Azure) provide a platform as a server (PaaS) solution for .NET developers, Office 360 provides a powerful software as a service (SaaS) solution, Microsoft servers are integrating virtualization support, and the huge revenue generator that is the Windows operating system faces risks from a "thin" and possibly downloadable operating system. (A **thin operating system** is one that performs only the minimal tasks needed for a user to run programs and save and retrieve information.)

Accordingly, Microsoft has formed a group named Cloud Computing Futures, which focuses on scalable computing, data center solutions, and cloud-based software infrastructures. The cloud, therefore, is not just an industry changer; it is making key players rethink their strategies.

Exercise Describe the cloud's potential biggest benefit for Microsoft and the cloud's biggest threat to Microsoft.

Web Reference For more information on the cloud's impact on Microsoft's future, visit www.CloudBookContent.com/Chapter20/index.html.

may be much less need for powerful desktop operating systems, such as Windows and Mac OS. If you doubt that statement, note the rapid user adoption of smartphones that feature scaled-down operating systems and applications.

Location-Aware Applications

A **location-aware application** utilizes data from the GPS (global positioning system) capabilities built into mobile devices to integrate an individual's location into the processing it performs. As GPS capabilities are built into more devices, applications will begin to deliver more location-aware solutions. For example, a stroll through a mall may result in coupons being pushed to your handheld device. Grocery store aisles may become interactive zones with retailers able to deliver "bid-based" coupons in real time to influence your purchases.

Using the cloud and location-aware solutions, you will be able to track not only the packages you ship, but also stolen cars, lost luggage, misplaced cell phones, missing pets, and more.

CASE 20-3 COUPIOUS MOBILE COUPONS

Users of computers and handheld devices are becoming on-demand consumers: They want what they want, when and where they want it. Coupious Mobile Coupons provides insights into the future of coupon clipping. The site, shown in **FIGURE 20–3**, currently delivers on-demand, location-aware coupons to states along the east coast of the United States.

Exercise Discuss ways on-demand coupons may change how shoppers make purchases.

Web Resources For more information on Coupious Mobile Coupons, visit www.CloudBook Content.com/Chapter20/index.html.

FIGURE 20–3 Through sites such as Coupious Mobile Coupons, users receive coupons on their smart devices from the cloud based on their current location.

Intelligent Fabrics, Paints, and More

The ability to connect devices to the cloud from any place, at any time, will open the door to a wide range of cutting-edge applications. At the obvious end, devices that once had to be read by utility or city employees, such as electric meters and parking meters, will connect to the Web and create a report. At the cutting edge, intelligence will be built into the fabrics of our clothes, bedding, and furniture. These **intelligent fabrics** will provide a wide range of services including the following:

- Automatically adjust room temperature when body temperature becomes too warm or too cold.
- Notify rooms when we enter or leave so that lights, music, and other devices are automatically controlled.
- Monitor body functions such as blood pressure, blood sugar levels, stress, and more, and notify the person and adjust the environment to affect those functions.
- Notify others when an elderly person has fallen.
- Provide deterrence against mosquitoes and other insects.

FIGURE 20-4 presents the Textronics website, which provides a wide range of wearable electronics.

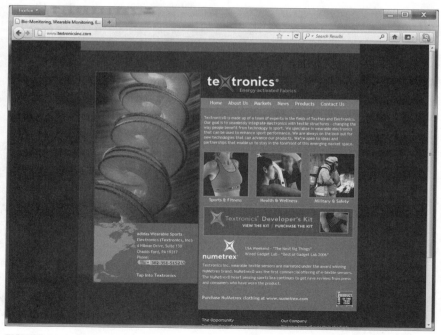

FIGURE 20-4 Through developments at companies such as Textronics, in the near future our clothing may interact with our environment through the cloud.

Similarly, new paints being developed change form based on environmental conditions. Currently, paints can change color on roads to indicate the presence of ice. In the future, intelligent paint may report driving conditions back to the cloud.

CASE 20-4 ABOVE THE CLOUDS: A BERKELEY VIEW OF CLOUD COMPUTING

Reliable Adaptive Distributed Systems Laboratory from the University of California, Berkeley, has published a paper that not only provides a view of where cloud computing is going, but also is an excellent summary and overview of the key cloud-computing concepts. The paper, as shown in **FIGURE 20–5**, is available on the Web and is a must-read. It addresses the following questions:

- What is cloud computing, and how is it different from previous paradigm shifts such as SaaS?
- Why is cloud computing poised to take off now, whereas previous attempts have foundered?

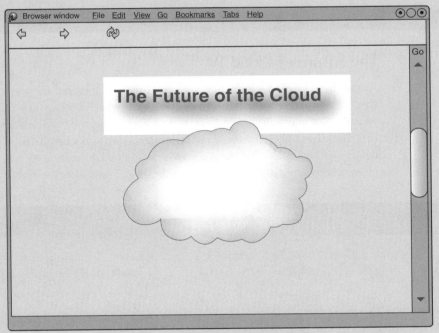

FIGURE 20–5 "Above the Clouds" is a must-read for those wanting to become cloud technology experts.

continues

CASE 20-4 ABOVE THE CLOUDS: A BERKELEY VIEW OF CLOUD COMPUTING, continued

- What does it take to become a cloud provider, and why would a company consider becoming one?
- What new opportunities does cloud computing drive or make possible?
- How might we classify current cloud computing offerings, and how do the technical and business challenges differ depending on where in the spectrum a particular offering lies?
- What, if any, are the new economic models enabled by cloud computing, and how can a service operator decide whether to move to the cloud or stay in a private data center?
- What are the top 10 obstacles to the success of cloud computing—and the corresponding top 10 opportunities available for overcoming those obstacles?
- What changes should be made to the design of future application software, infrastructure software, and hardware to match the needs and opportunities of cloud computing?

Exercise Read the "Above the Clouds" paper and answer the questions listed above.

Web Resources For more information on "Above the Clouds," visit www.CloudBookContent .com/Chapter20/index.html.

The Future of Cloud TV

As you have learned, companies such as Hulu are changing the way consumers watch TV. With greater bandwidth available everywhere, DVDs will soon fall by the wayside. Not only will TV viewers watch shows on demand in their homes, in their cars (backseats only, let's hope), and on airplanes, but also a new breed of projection devices will make any flat surface a TV screen. Furthermore, users will be able to interact with content, perhaps changing the outcome of a story in real time.

CASE 20-5 PREDICTING CLOUD TV'S FUTURE

As shown in **FIGURE 20-6**, Cisco's Internet Business Solutions Group (IBSG) has developed a presentation that predicts the future of TV based on cloud-based delivery.

Exercise Discuss how TV companies need to change their business models to adapt to cloud-based content delivery.

Web Resources For more information on the predictions of the cloud's impact on TV, visit www.CloudBookContent.com/Chapter20/index.html.

continues

CASE 20-5 PREDICTING CLOUD TV'S FUTURE, continued

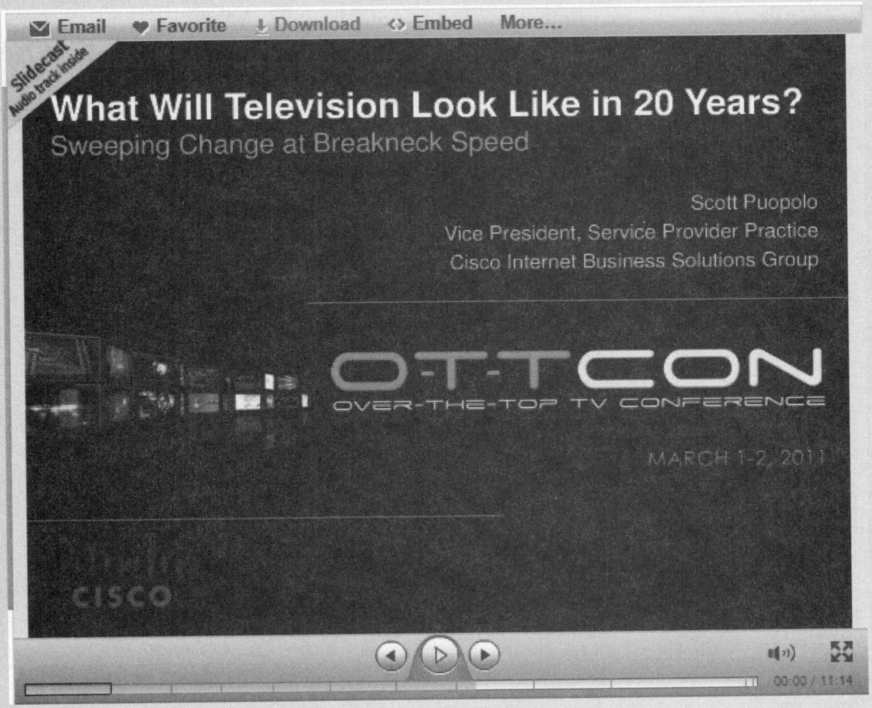

FIGURE 20-6 Cisco's IBSG predicts how the cloud will change TV.

Courtesy of Cisco Systems, Inc. Unauthorized use not permitted. www.slideshare.net/ CiscoSystems/future-of-tv-ott-con-ibsgfinal0228. (accessed 8/3/11).

CASE 20-6 FUTURE OF CLOUD COMPUTING

CloudTimes is a San Francisco-based web publisher that provides the latest news on all aspects of cloud computing. Bookmark and visit cloudtimes.org, shown in **FIGURE 20-7**. Recently, CloudTimes published 10 predictions about the future of cloud computing, which you should consider and evaluate.

Exercise Read the 10 predictions by CloudTimes about the future of cloud computing. Argue for one prediction and argue against one prediction.

continues

CASE 20-6 FUTURE OF CLOUD COMPUTING, continued

Web Resources For more information on the 10 predictions on cloud computing by CloudTimes, visit www.CloudBookContent.com/Chapter20/index.html.

FIGURE 20-7 The 10 predictions about the future of cloud computing by CloudTimes.

Future of Cloud-Based Smart Devices

For years, futurists have forecast the day when a refrigerator would automatically create your grocery list and send the list to the store so your essentials could be delivered. The cloud's ability to provide Internet access and at any time makes such processing a reality. Some devices may initially be "intelligent" with respect to their ability to control power consumption, possibly avoiding power use during peak times and costs.

Using the cloud for communication, devices can coordinate activities. For example, your car may notify your home automation system that you are down

CASE 20-7 POWER-AWARE APPLIANCES

Every household has appliances such as a refrigerators, water heaters, dishwashers, washers, dryers, and so on. If these devices are replaced with **smart appliances**—ones that are "energy aware"—they can control their power demand during peak times and in the process, save the consumer money. The Pacific Northwest National Laboratory has created a video that discusses such appliances.

Exercise Discuss three appliances that may benefit from power-control capabilities.

Web Resources For more information on power-aware appliances, visit www.CloudBook Content.com/Chapter20/index.html.

the block and instruct it to light the house, turn on your favorite music, and prompt the refrigerator for a list of ready-to-cook meals.

Cloud and Mobile

The cloud is going to drive mobile applications. No, wait. Mobile applications will drive the growth of the cloud. Cloud-based mobile applications are going to experience explosive growth!

CASE 20-8 MOBILE CLOUD: TOP FIVE PREDICTIONS

Cisco is a key player in the hardware and network technology that drives the cloud. Cisco's IBSG is a strategic consulting group that examines new and emerging technologies that utilize the Web. The group has developed five predictions about the future of mobile cloud computing, "When Mobile and Clouds Collide." You read about these predictions in Chapter 14, but here they are again, shown in **FIGURE 20-8**.

Exercise Discuss whether you think the cloud will drive the growth of mobile computing more than mobile computing will drive the growth of the cloud, or vice versa.

Web Resources For more information on the predictions of the cloud's impact on mobile computing, visit www.CloudBookContent.com/Chapter20/index.html.

continues

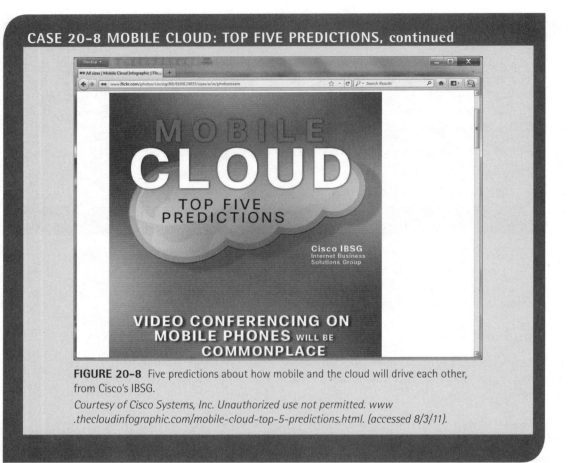

CASE 20-8 MOBILE CLOUD: TOP FIVE PREDICTIONS, continued

FIGURE 20-8 Five predictions about how mobile and the cloud will drive each other, from Cisco's IBSG.

Courtesy of Cisco Systems, Inc. Unauthorized use not permitted. www .thecloudinfographic.com/mobile-cloud-top-5-predictions.html. (accessed 8/3/11).

How HTML5 Will Drive Mobile Applications

Mobile applications are one of the fastest growing IT market segments. Today, mobile developers have several choices. First, they can implement a simple HTML-based site that both a computer and a mobile device can display. Second, they can build separate pages for computers and mobile devices. Or, third, they may need to implement a computer page, an iPhone-specific page, and pages for other devices such as the Android.

The primary problem facing developers is that many computer-based websites use Flash-based applications, and Flash does not work on mobile devices. As such, developers cannot simply build a single website that works on all devices. Or rather, they could not until the advent of **HTML5**.

Across the Web, the content that users view within a browser must eventually become HTML, the hypertext markup language. HTML5 is the 20th anniversary update release of HTML, which supports capabilities previously available only through Flash-based development. Using HTML5, developers can create multimedia content suitable for all devices. As a result, HTML5 will further drive the success of mobile applications.

Faster Time to Market for Software Applications

The cloud streamlines many expensive and time-consuming development steps. Companies no longer have to raise the capital required to fund a large data center. Instead, they can leverage a PaaS solution. Furthermore, companies no longer have to pay expensive upfront licensing fees for various software tools such as database management systems. Instead, they can leverage pay-on-demand solutions. Finally, companies no longer have to guess their site's adoption rate so that they can provide the underlying computing resources. Instead, they can let their cloud-based applications scale to meet demand. The net result: Developers will release software solutions at a faster pace, bringing the solutions to a market that expects high functionality and demands lower cost.

Home-Based Cloud Computing

Today, most households have wireless network capabilities that allow family members to connect to the Web and access sites and content they desire. With the advent of smart devices, intelligent fabrics, and greater use of radio frequency identification (RFID) devices, family members will expect on-demand personalized technology solutions. When a teenager enters his or her room, for example, the music will play louder, lights may dim, and the computer might initiate specific Skype connections. If a parent enters the room, the volume will lower, lights will turn on, and the Skype page might change to an SAT prep application. In other words, families will use cloud-based devices to customize their environments and experiences. Within such an environment, families will want to restrict processing to within the home—meaning that they will not want neighbors to receive signals generated by their devices and clothing. That implies the ability to encrypt a wide range of signals within the home. To that end, you should expect to see cloud-based, in-home devices that store family files, maintain appliance settings, download and store movies and TV shows, and more.

CHAPTER SUMMARY

This book examines many recent cloud-based solutions and applications. For those who are new to the cloud, many existing cloud solutions will seem quite cutting edge. As you have learned in this chapter, we have just begun to scratch the surface with respect to ways new technologies can use the cloud to communicate, coordinate, and develop applications that take into account our location, body feedback, and more. From mobile-device applications to new operating systems to an integration of smart appliances and devices, the cloud is really just beginning to form.

KEY TERMS

HTML5   Smart appliance
Intelligent fabrics   Thin operating system
Location-aware application

CHAPTER REVIEW

1. List and describe five ways you think the cloud will change the future of TV.
2. List and describe five potential uses for intelligent fabric.
3. List and describe five ways the cloud will influence the mobile application market, or vice versa.
4. Discuss the importance of HTML5.
5. Discuss how the cloud will impact future operating systems.
6. List and describe three potential location-aware applications.
7. List and describe five ways intelligent devices may work together.

Glossary of Key Terms

Amazon Web Services (AWS)   Amazon.com's cloud solution, which provides scalable hosting solutions to developers and enterprises for moving applications to the cloud.

App   Software application that users download and install to their phone to perform specific tasks.

Application program interface (API)   Group or library of related programming solutions that developers can use within the programs they create. For example, one API might provide developers with prepackaged code they can use to perform common Internet tasks. Another might provide developers with code they can use to encrypt or decrypt a document.

Architecture   Components that comprise a system, their relationships, and their interactions.

Auditing   Process of examining and verifying a financial record or control.

Black box   Software component for which developers can ignore how the component performs its processing, knowing instead that the component will produce correct results for required inputs.

Blog   Web log; users with little or no web development experience can publish content in a blog.

Bottleneck   Place within a solution or system that due to insufficient resources, slows the flow of system performance.

Business continuity   Steps taken by a business to ensure its continued operations in the event of a system failure, disaster, or other disruptive event.

Business strategy   Plans executed by a company to achieve its business goals.

Caching   Items that are used repeatedly by an application to improve system performance are stored by using a faster disk drive or faster RAM.

Capital expenditures (CAPEX)   Large expenditures, often for a plant, property, or large equipment (PPE), which have value over a number of years. As such, companies cannot write off the expenditures in full during the current year and must instead use a process called expense capitalization, which allows the company to deduct a portion of the expense over a number of years.

Cloud-based block storage device   Device that stores data in raw (unformatted) blocks of bits, up to a terabyte. Usually it does not provide a file system to manage the data stored within a block or blocks.

Cloud-based database   Web-based database system that scales to meet system demands, integrates automatic backups, and allows developers access from within their programs through an API.

Cloud bursting   Scaling of an on-site solution temporarily into the cloud to meet user demand, typically in response to seasonal or event-driven demand.

Cloud computing   Abstraction of virtualized web-based computers, resources, and services that support scalable IT solutions.

Cloud Data Management Interface (CDMI)   Developing standard by the Storage Networking Industry Association that defines how applications will interface with cloud-based storage devices behind the scenes.

Cloud file system (CFS)   System that allows users and applications to directly manipulate files that reside on the cloud.

Cloud migration   Process of moving one or more applications to the cloud.

CloudNAS   Trade name of a particular cloud-based NAS (network-attached storage) solution.

Collaboration Two or more people working together to achieve a goal.

Colocation Positioning of additional computers and/or communications equipment at a remote (offsite) location for load balancing, redundancy, or improved business continuity.

Common Internet File System (CIFS) A protocol that defines a standard for remote file access using a large scale of computers at a time.

Community cloud Cloud solution shared by two or more organizations, normally with shared concerns, such as schools within a university.

Corporate governance Processes, policies, laws, and controls that affect the way a company operates.

Coupling Degree of dependence between a calling program and the web service.

Customer-relationship management (CRM) Term used to describe the various aspects of locating, recruiting, managing, and growing a company's customer base.

Data integration Process of combining data from two or more solutions.

Data wiping Process performed by cloud-based storage devices that overwrites (wipes) a file's contents when a file is deleted. Then, another application that allocates the deleted file's storage locations cannot access the deleted file's contents.

Denial-of-service attack Hacker attack that attempts to consume resources on a system in such a way that slows the system or makes its resources unavailable to users.

Disaster recovery plan (DRP) Plan that details the steps taken by an organization to resume business operations following an event such as a natural disaster or terrorist attack.

Economics Study of the production, distribution, and consumption of goods and services.

Economies of scale Cost savings gained through expansion. Because of its buying power and ability to use resources across multiple customers, a cloud-based service provider normally has greater economies of scale than an on-site data center.

Ecosystem Environment that consists of living and nonliving things with which one interacts.

Federated identity management (FIDM) Technologies and protocols that combine to allow the exchange of identity attributes across autonomous systems.

File system Part of the operating system that oversees file and folder (directory) access.

Functional requirements Requirements that specify tasks a system must perform.

Google App Engine Development tools that assist with the deployment of cloud-based applications that run within the Google infrastructure.

Green computing Environmentally friendly IT operations, such as reducing a device's power demands when it is inactive.

Grid computing Large-scale use of computers connected by a network (the grid) to perform parallel processing on complex tasks.

Guest-hopping attack Hacker attack that attempts to gain access to (hop onto) another guest operating system from within a peer-level guest operating system running on the same server.

Guest operating system Operating system that resides within a virtualized environment. For example, a virtual desktop might use Windows and Linux as guest operating systems.

Halon Chemical used in data-center fire suppression systems, which stops a fire by removing the level of oxygen in the room.

Horizontal scaling Process of scaling out; that is, distributing a system's processes across multiple resources.

Hybrid cloud Solution that comprises a combination of two or more public, private, or community clouds.

Hyperjacking attack   Hacker attack that targets the hypervisor within a virtualized server or desktop.

Hypervisor   Software within a virtual system that oversees and manages the virtualization process.

HTML5   Fifth release of the hypertext markup language, which provides device-independent support for multimedia capabilities previously available through Flash-based applications.

iCloud   Apple's cloud-based solution, which facilitates the exchange of music, photos, videos, and documents.

Identity (or identification) as a service (IDaaS)   Cloud-based approach to managing user identities, including usernames, passwords, and access. Sometimes referred to as "identity management as a service."

Infrastructure as a service (IaaS)   Scalable, cloud-based collection of server, data storage, and network hardware upon which a company can install and manage its operating system and database management software in order to host their applications within the cloud.

Instant messaging (IM)   Originally a text-based method for users to communicate; today, IM supports text, audio, and video interaction.

Integrated development environment (IDE)   Software system for application developers that provides a user interface that allows access to key software-development activities, such as editing, compiling, and testing.

Intelligent fabrics   Clothing that includes technology and computing devices within the fabric that can be used to monitor body temperature, blood pressure, and other vitals. The technology may be used to broadcast an individual's position to location-aware applications.

Internal control   Policy put in place by a business to provide confidence and assurance on the accuracy of the data reported by the company.

Interoperability   Measure of a software component's ability to support different platforms and programming languages.

IT governance   Processes, policies, and controls that affect the way an IT staff operates to maximize a company's ROI and to align its business strategy and IT operations.

Key performance indicators   Business ratios and results measured and evaluated by a company to understand the state of the business and its operations.

Load testing   Simulation of user demand on a site.

Location-aware application   Application that utilizes GPS-based data to integrate an individual's location into the processing performed by the application, such as location-specific delivery of coupons and home environment processing.

Loosely coupled   Ideal relationship between programs and the web services they call on, in which the program need only know the location of the web service (its URL), the name of the functions (methods) the web service provides, and parameters the program can pass to the functions.

Man-in-the-middle attack   Hacker attack that attempts to intercept messages between a user and a system, insert, and then send messages on behalf of the user or the system.

Mashup   Software solution built from a combination of two or more other solutions.

Mean time between failures (MTBF)   Measure of the estimated time a device will operate without failing.

Method   Function that performs a specific task.

Middleware   Software that sits between two applications to facilitate the exchange of data.

Mobile cloud   Applications and web pages that originate from sites within the cloud with which users download or interact via a mobile device.

Multitenant solution SaaS or PaaS solution for which two or more customers may share computing resources simultaneously. Many SaaS solutions use a multi-tenant architecture.

Network-attached Storage (NAS) Storage devices that can be accessed over a computer network rather than being directly connected to the computer.

Network File System (NFS) A system that allows directories and files to be shared with others over a network.

Nonfunctional requirements Requirements a system must meet to complete its functions, such as performance, response time, and security.

Operational expenses (OPEX) Expenses that correspond to a company's cost of operations.

Packet sniffing Process of examining network packets that travel past a system within a wired network or through the air within a wireless network.

Pareto principle Rule of 80/20 that describes relationships between two items, such as 80 percent of a company's sales are generated by 20 percent of its customers.

Performance tuning Process of modifying different aspects of a system or the supporting hardware to improve system performance.

Platform Combination of hardware and software resources that yields a run-time environment, such as a Windows- or Linux-based environment.

Platform as a service (PaaS) Software and hardware that provides an operating system (such as Windows or Linux) upon which developers can create and deploy solutions, without the need to administer the underlying system software. Examples include the Google App Engine and Microsoft Azure.

Point of diminishing returns Point at which adding resources fails to change a system's performance or output.

Portability Measure of a system's ease of moving from one platform to another.

Predictive analytics Tools that perform statistical analysis in order to predict future behavior.

Private cloud Solution in which the underlying hardware and software is owned by a specific entity (company) for use by the entity and its customer.

Profit margin Measure of a company's profitability and effectiveness, calculated by dividing a company's net income by its revenues.

Provisioning Process of creating a user account on a system; removing the account is called deprovisioning.

Proxy Person or entity that performs a task on behalf of another. Within the mobile web, proxies may perform a server-based interaction on behalf of a mobile user to provide a layer of security between the server and device.

Public cloud Solution available to the general public, such as Google Docs.

Redundancy A system design that duplicates components to provide alternatives in case one component fails.

Redundant array of independent (or inexpensive) disks (RAID) Collection of disk drives across which a file system stores information about a file, as well as recovery information the system can use to recover the file should one or more of the disk drives fail.

Reliability Measure of a system's ability to process without errors or failure.

Return on investment (ROI) Business analysis ratio that lets a company compare the potential return of two or more investments, calculated by taking the revenue (or savings) divided by the cost of the investment.

Right-sizing Process of aligning computing resources (e.g., processors, servers, and disk capacity) with user demand. Because cloud-based providers can scale up or down quickly, based on user demand, they make it easier for companies to right-size resources.

Robust   Ability to function in the event of errors, such as a server failure.

Scalability   Ability to increase or decrease resource use (such as servers or data storage) on demand, as processing needs require. Scalable applications can scale up (increase) resources when there is high user demand and scale down (decrease) resources when there is low demand.

Security Assertion Markup Language (SAML)   Language that applications use to package a user's security credentials.

Service-level agreement (SLA)   Clause within a service provider's contract that specifies the level of service (such as system uptime or MTBF).

Service-oriented architecture (SOA)   System design upon which the solution is described in terms of one or more services, usually distributed on the Web.

Single sign-on (SSO)   Process that allows a user to log into a central authority and then access other sites and services for which he or she has credentials.

Smart appliance   Appliance such as a refrigerator or washing machine that integrates technology to perform specific tasks such as reducing energy demands during peak load times or performing inventory analysis of groceries.

Software as a service (SaaS)   Web-based software solution that users access through a web browser.

Software development kit (SDK)   Collection of APIs that developers can integrate into programs to use a specific device, platform, or operating system.

SQL-injection attack   Hacker attack that attempts to insert SQL queries into one or more fields of a web-based form. Depending upon how the server processes the form's data, the SQL commands may be inadvertently executed.

Storage area network (SAN)   Network that combines hardware and software to make storage devices, which may reside anywhere within a network, appear to be local.

Streaming media   Retrieval of media, such as audio or video, often within a web browser, that does not require a complete download of the media file before the playback can begin.

System requirements   Functional tasks and nonfunctional operations that a system must perform.

Thin operating system   System that performs only the minimal tasks needed for a user to run programs and save and retrieve information.

Total cost of ownership (TCO)   Total direct and indirect costs, including both capital and operating expenses, of owning a particular piece of equipment or other capital good. It is an important metric for organizations trying to decide whether to invest in their own data centers or move to the cloud.

Transcoder   Server that analyzes and possibly changes content destined to user devices.

Uninterruptible power supply (UPS)   Battery backup system that typically provides 10 to 15 minutes of power to devices in the event of a power failure, so that users can save files and shut down the systems in an orderly way.

Usability   Measure of a system's ease of use.

User-experience testing   Software test that attempts to simulate and evaluate user experience with the site, possibly including slower Internet bandwidth, an older browser, or a slower computer.

Vendor lock-in   Situation when it is difficult or impossible for a company to change a vendor because of the vendor's inability to export data or a unique service provided by the vendor, upon which the company relies.

Vertical scaling Process of scaling up; for example, moving a system to a faster disk drive, adding faster RAM, or using a faster disk drive to improve a system's performance.

Virtual desktop Desktop computer that runs two or more operating systems that users can quickly switch back and forth. A virtual desktop is well suited for developers, testers, and help-desk support staff who must service multiple operating systems.

Virtualization Hardware and/or software used to create a perception. For example, with virtual desktop software, a user running an Intel-based computer may be able to run multiple operating systems simultaneously. Similarly, using server virtualization, a single server may appear to be running multiple (different) server operating systems simultaneously, as if the server had multiple processors.

Virtual meeting Online meeting between two or more users. Using streaming video, users can achieve a face-to-face experience. Most virtual meeting platforms allow document sharing, whiteboard content presentation, and application sharing.

Virtual presentation Cloud-based presentation that users can retrieve and watch asynchronously at a time and from a place that best suits the users' needs. Virtual presentations often combine a PowerPoint presentation with video or audio.

Virtual private network (VPN) Hardware and/or software used to establish a secure connection to a local-area network across the Internet from a remote location. The remote user can, in turn, access network resources as if a physical connection to the local-area network existed.

Virtual server Server that runs two or more operating systems simultaneously. The operating systems may be the same, or they may be different, such as Windows and Linux. Many companies use server virtualization to consolidate servers and drive server CPU utilization.

Virus Program written by malicious programmers with the goal of damaging a target computer or disrupting the computer's normal operations.

Voice over Internet Protocol (VoIP) Technology that allows users to place phone calls over the Internet.

Web 2.0 Tools and websites that allow users to publish content (videos, blogs, tweets, and social media posts) without having to understand the web development process.

Web Service Description Language (WSDL) Language used to describe a web service, its methods, and their parameters.

Web services Web-based software modules that programs can call via the Internet to perform specific tasks.

Widget Application that, once downloaded and installed on a device, remains active (constantly runs), possibly updating its icon or display with context- or location-sensitive content.

Wiki Tool for online collaborative document editing. The largest and most popular Wiki is the Wikipedia online encyclopedia.

Windows Azure Microsoft platform that developers can use to move their applications to the cloud.

Yahoo! Pipes Tool that lets developers create mashups by joining (piping) the output of one data source into another data source, filter, or display tool without having to write program code.

Index

Figures and tables are indicated by *f* and *t* following page numbers.